HANDBOOK OF

ROCKS, MINERALS, AND GEMSTONES

HANDBOOK OF

ROCKS, MINERALS, AND GEMSTONES

Walter Schumann

Translated by Dr. R. Bradshaw
and Dr. K. A. G. Mills

HOUGHTON MIFFLIN COMPANY

Boston   New York

Originally published in German under the title:
Der Neue BLV Steine-und Mineralienfuhrer
Copyright © 1985 by BLV Verlagsgesellschaft mbH Munchen

Library of Congress Cataloging-in-Publication Data

Schumann, Walter.
[Neue BLV Steine- und Mineralienfuhrer. English]
Handbook of rocks, minerals, and gemstones / Walter Schumann ;
translated by R. Bradshaw.
p.   cm.
Includes bibliographical references and index.
ISBN 0-395-51138-0 (cloth).— ISBN 0-395-51137-2 (pbk.)
1. Rocks — Identification — Handbooks, manuals, etc.   2. Minerals —
Identification — Handbooks, manuals, etc. 3. Precious stones —
Identification — Handbooks, manuals, etc.   I. Title.
QE433.8.S3813 1993
552--dc20   92-28505
                                                          CIP

ISBN 0-395-51137-2 (pa.)   ISBN 0-395-51138-0 (cl.)

Photograph on p. 2:
Weathering structures in Bryce Canyon, Utah

Printed and bound in Italy
by Rotolito Lombarda S.p.A.

20 19 18 17 16 15

FOREWORD

Collecting stones has become a popular hobby that is gaining ever more friends among all sections of the population and all age groups. The increasing extent of leisure time wil! increase this trend still further. Nowadays, holidays and rock-collecting often go hand-in-hand; indeed, sometimes the intention to indulge in some rock-bashing determines where people spend their holidays and the ways in which the holidays develop.

My *Handbook to Rocks, Minerals, and Gemstones* seeks to be of help in this regard, and to bridge a gap. The text, based on the latest scientific insights, is composed in such a way that it can appeal both to the layman and to those who already have expert knowledge, namely, anyone who deals with rocks and gemstones professionally, as well as to students. More than 600 individual specimens, photographed in color and at natural size, have been carefully selected as being typical of the world of minerals and rocks. The text and illustrations are arranged opposite each other for ease of reference.

Many people have contributed to the success of this book. I thank them all. To Mr. Christian Weise, Dipl. Geophysics, I give my heartfelt thanks for providing so many valuable stones to be photographed. I am especially indebted to Mr. Hermann Eisenbeiss for his involvement and cooperation in the preparation of the color plates.

Walter Schumann

CONTENTS

GENERAL INTRODUCTION

DEFINITION OF TERMS

Stone Stone is the vernacular collective term for all solid constituents of the Earth's crust with the exception of ice. To a jeweller, on the other hand, the term stone means only precious stones and gemstones; to someone involved in the building trade it is the material with which buildings can be erected. However, in geology, the science of the Earth, we do not speak of stones but rather of rocks and minerals.

Rock A rock is a natural mixture of minerals. It forms an individual geological body of considerable extent. The science of rocks is called petrology or petrography.

Mineral A mineral is an entity which occurs naturally as part of the Earth's crust or the Moon's surface. Most minerals have a specific crystal form. The science of minerals is called mineralogy.

Micromounts Micromounts are very small mineral specimens up to approximately the size of a finger nail. The term micromount is only used in collector circles. A micromounter is a collector of very small specimens. This method of collecting has spread right across the world in recent years.

Crystal A crystal is a body of uniform material with a regular internal structure, a strict arrangement of the smallest particles (atoms, ions, molecules) in a crystal lattice. The science of crystals is called crystallography.

Precious Stone There is no universally valid definition of a precious stone. Most precious stones are minerals, rarely mineral aggregates, very occasionally organic materials and even synthetic products.
  Common to all precious stones is the fact that they are special and beautiful. It is not really possible, as popular belief would have it, to differentiate between genuine precious stones, semi-precious stones and ornamental stones because there are no suitable criteria. The term semi-precious stone is not very useful and should not be used. The science of precious stones is called gemmology.

Ore In the science of ore deposits the term ore is generally understood to be a mixture of minerals with a metal content which can be worked at a profit. Texturally it has the character of a rock. However, very occasionally, other raw materials which are needed in technology are also designated as ore even if they do not have a metallic character.

Meteorite Meteorites are solid fragments reaching Earth from outer space. They may be known as extra-terrestrial rocks.

Tektite Tektites are rounded, glassy stones. They originate by condensation of materials which are volatilised when giant meteorites strike the Earth. It is wrong to describe them as glassy meteorites.

THE LAYOUT OF THE BOOK

Organisation The material is divided into three sections which are concerned with minerals, rocks and meteorites. The presentation was chosen in such a way that each of the three parts can be understood on its own and also in conjunction with the other sections.

A comprehensive determinative key for minerals (pp.342-365) and an aid to the identification of rocks (pp.366-370) serve as guides for identifying individual specimens. Moon rocks are not dealt with as they do not represent a separate group in the generic system of rocks. Moon rocks are igneous rocks predominantly of basaltic and doleritic composition.

Illustrations The text is augmented by numerous large format illustrations. In this way the written descriptions are kept brief and sometimes reduced to a minimum. The originals for the photographs are not unique museum specimens nor micromounts but rather minerals and aggregates of the type which the collector can find himself or acquire from mineral dealers. With very few exceptions (which are indicated accordingly) the individual specimens are illustrated at approximately natural size. In this way the observer can get to know a mineral or rock in considerable detail with the naked eye, as he would in nature.

Text The text is kept brief in order to gain space for a large number of illustrations. Sometimes it is necessary to describe the specimens in abbreviated style. Diverse sub-divisions and many definitions are intended to make the information quick and easy to understand. Long accounts have been avoided as have abbreviations of special terms, which are more typical of the specialist literature in mineralogy.

The text of this book has been kept as simple and comprehensible as possible. No attempt has been made to include topics such as classes of symmetry, silicate structures or atomic arrangements of crystals which are important for the specialist, but would only confuse the layman. The author is quite aware of the problems which such simplification of scientific knowledge and insights can create, but it has been felt necessary to avoid over-complication.

Selection of individual objects Any selection of minerals and rocks is always subjective in some way or another. The criteria for the selection of individual objects in this book are their scientific aspects, but consideration has been given to those who collect simply as a hobby.

Chemical formulae Chemical formulae have been expressed in a simplified style.

Crystal sketches The crystal drawings of minerals in the text are only one example of the type of shape the mineral can occupy. Although there may be a number of other possible shapes, they are intended to give a general impression of mineral shapes. The examples were taken from various sources.

Localities Details about localities and regional locations are examples only and should not be taken as a comprehensive list of where the mineral can be found.

MINERALS

THE SCIENCE OF MINERALS

THE HISTORY OF THE MINERAL SCIENCES

A knowledge of how to use different minerals and mineral mixtures already existed in prehistoric times. Around 3500BC copper and tin, gold and silver, as well as numerous gemstones (malachite, turquoise, lapis lazuli, opal, agate) were in use in Mesopotamia for jewellery, weapons and implements.

The ability to find metallic elements in rock and to smelt them out of it was based in early antiquity on observation and experience. A scientific method of looking at the relations between minerals did not exist. The first scientific publication on what was then known of the mineral world was written by the Greek philosopher Aristotle (384-322BC). His mineral system was still regarded as valid into the nineteenth century.

During the whole of the Middle Ages no progress was made in mineralogy in Europe. The field of natural history was dominated by alchemy, astrology, speculation and the supposedly occult powers of stones. The lapidaria, books on stones published during this period, convey no new insights, but merely give an uncritical summary of the views prevailing in antiquity and the Middle Ages.

At the beginning of the sixteenth century, during the Renaissance, a rejuvenation of the natural sciences got underway. Georgius Agricola (1494-1555), a doctor born in Saxony, wrote the first scientific presentation of mining and minerals. He turned away from alchemy and described his own observations, thereby developing a systematic sub-division of minerals which remained valid until the beginning of the nineteenth century. Agricola provoked so much new thinking on the subject that he is described as "the father of mineralogy".

A new impulse to natural sciences was generated by the onset of the Industrial Revolution in the eighteenth century. The increased demand for mineral raw materials required the laying down of scientific foundations before the expansion of ore extraction and the development of new deposits could be pursued. The Saxon mineralogist A.G. Werner (1749-1817) devised a new classification of minerals which is basically still valid today.

In the past two hundred years the interaction of physics and chemistry with the study of minerals finally developed into the science which today is called mineralogy.

NAMING MINERALS

This multidisciplinary history of mineralogy has meant that the names of minerals have not been systematically derived, which can cause a great deal of confusion. Some were borrowed from the language of miners or from vernacular usage, others are purely artificial creations. They refer to place-names, to persons, to conspicuous properties or to supposedly occult-mystical powers. To further complicate matters, since mineral names have different linguistic origins (particularly Latin, Greek, Germanic, Oriental) the way they are spelt is not always uniform.

Crystal specimen with stalactitic quartz, dipyramidal apophyllite and globular gyrolite, Poona/India.

THE ORIGINS AND STRUCTURE OF MINERALS

THE ORIGINS OF MINERALS

Minerals are formed in various ways. The same kind of mineral can even form under quite different conditions. Most minerals require many thousands of years to develop, others need just a few years, and in some cases just a few hours. Mineral formation takes places either in the molten rock melt or magma; at or near the Earth's surface; or deep in the Earth's crust as a result of transforming, i.e. metamorphic, processes. The expert speaks accordingly of igneous, sedimentary and metamorphic origins.

Igneous origin Many minerals are formed directly from the magma. Feldspar, mica and quartz, for example, form as the magma cools down, deep in the Earth's crust, at temperatures from 1100°C to 550°C.

Other minerals form from exhalations, where gases escape from the magma. As these gases cool down, a reaction takes place with the adjacent rock forming chloride, fluoride and sulphate minerals, as well as gold and silver. As the magma continues to cool down to below 400°C substances separate out and this, together with the infiltration of materials from the adjacent rock, leads to the formation of minerals. This is how the minerals of the Alpine fissures have formed.

Sedimentary origin At or near the surface of the Earth minerals develop through the destruction (weathering) of rock and the subsequent formation of new rock. The principal agents are water, carbon dioxide and the oxygen in the air. In this process substances are dissolved in the upper layers, seep downwards and interact with the ground water to produce new minerals in specific areas which become rich in these minerals and are thus known as enrichment zones. Silver and copper deposits are formed in this way. In areas which have low rainfall and high temperatures saline minerals are formed: in salt lakes, salt swamps or cut off marine embayments. This occurs by a process of chemical precipitation as a result of the high level of evaporation.

There are also numerous organisms which directly or indirectly contribute to the formation of minerals, for example by supplying oxygen or removing carbonic acid, through processes of bacterial decay or growth of calcareous shells or siliceous skeletons from substances which are in solution.

Metamorphic origin When rocks are taken down into deeper parts of the Earth's crust, as a result of an increase in thickness of overlying sediments or by mountain-building processes, new minerals form through the reconstruction of minerals which are already present; this occurs because of the high temperature prevailing in these areas, combined with the great pressures being exerted. A similar metamorphic effect is achieved, though on a much smaller scale, where molten magma forces its way up in volcanic vents or along fissures and here makes contact with the adjacent rock.

Paragenesis Numerous minerals appear in regular associations because of the same or similar process of formation; this is known as paragenesis. Conversely, other minerals never occur together naturally as their formation processes are so different. Knowledge of paragenesis is an important aid both in searching for and in identifying minerals, and especially in the science of mineral deposits. Thus, for example, barite, fluorite and galena always occur together in certain rocks. On the other hand, feldspar and halite never appear in the same crystal specimen.

THE STRUCTURE OF MINERALS

Mineral A mineral is a naturally occurring part of the Earth's or the Moon's crust which has a specific or unique structure. Most minerals have characteristic crystal forms.

Chemical composition Minerals have a quite definite material composition, which is represented by a chemical formula (see the table of chemical elements, p.337). This is an idealised formula, that is to say, it only specifies the main components of the mineral. No account is taken of extremely small natural additions or impurities which can give rise to discoloration or even changes in colour.

Polymorphism There are some minerals which have the same chemical composition as others and are nonetheless minerals in their own right. This is caused by a difference in the type of crystal structure. This phenomenon (that the same chemical substance appears in varying crystal forms and thereby forms differing minerals) is called polymorphism, and the individual structures are known as structural modifications. Carbon, for instance, appears in the modifications graphite and diamond. Quartz, cristobalite, coesite, stishovite and tridymite, like opal, are polymorphs of silica.

Crystal lattice The decisive factor in determining the external appearance and the physical properties of a mineral is its internal structure, that is to say, the arrangement of the smallest structural parts, the atoms, ions or molecules. If the packaging of these parts is regularly ordered we speak of a space lattice or crystal lattice.

Crystalline, amorphous Minerals with a crystal lattice are called crystalline; those without a crystal structure, i.e. without a regular internal ordering of the smallest structural parts, are amorphous. A great majority of minerals are crystalline, but opal, for example, is amorphous.

Mixed crystals In some crystals individual elements can be replaced by related materials without the basic chemical and crystal structure changing. Since the exchange occurs in differing orders of magnitude a largish number of so-called mixed crystals results in a succession of mixtures. The plagioclases present such a series of mixtures (p.40).

Varieties Mineral varieties are variations within a type of mineral with typical characteristics. Colour varieties are used as gems and precious stones. Crystal inclusions, unusual forms of crystal and aggregate, can likewise lead to varieties if these unusual features do not just appear once but are present in a larger number of individual minerals. The basic chemical and crystalline structure is preserved to a large extent in accordance with the normal mineral formation.

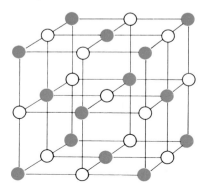

Schematic representation of the crystal lattice of halite; red: sodium ions, white: chlorine ions.

CRYSTAL SYSTEMS AND CRYSTAL FORMS

Cubic system

Cube

Octahedron

Rhombic dodecahedron

Tetragonal system

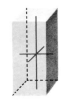

Tetragonal system

Dipyramid

Prism with dipyramid

Hexagonal system

Hexagonal prism

Hexagonal prism

Hexagonal dipyramid

CRYSTAL SYSTEMS AND CRYSTAL FORMS
Trigonal system

Dipyramid

Rhombohedron

Scalenohedron

Orthorhombic system

Prism

Dipyramid

Prism with pinacoid

Monoclinic system

3 pinacoids

2 pinacoids with 2 prisms

Clinopinacoid with 2 prisms

Triclinic system

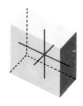

3 pinacoids

6 pinacoids

4 pinacoids

Crystal systems Most minerals are crystalline. They develop crystal forms, geometrical bodies which are specific to and typical of that mineral. All crystal forms can be assigned to seven crystal systems (cubic, tetragonal, hexagonal, trigonal, orthorhombic, monoclinic, triclinic). These systems are differentiated according to the axes of the crystals, the angles at which the axes intersect, and the symmetry. The crystal systems are shown with typical crystal forms on pp.14-15.

Cubic system (isometric system) All three axes are of equal length and are at right angles to each other. Typical crystal forms are cube, octahedron, dodecahedron, pentagonal dodecahedron, icositetrahedron, hexoctahedron.

Tetragonal system The three axes are perpendicular to one another; two are of equal length and lie in the horizontal plane, the third (the principal axis) is longer or shorter and is vertical. Typical crystal forms are four-sided prisms and pyramids, trapezohedra and eight-sided pyramids.

Hexagonal system Three of the four axes lie in one plane, are of equal length and intersect at angles of 120°, the fourth axis is not of the same length and is perpendicular to them. Typical crystal forms are six-sided prisms and pyramids, as well as twelve-sided pyramids and double pyramids.

Trigonal system (Rhombohedral system) Three of the four axes lie in the same plane, are of equal length and intersect at angles of 120°, the fourth axis is not of the same length and is perpendicular to them. Axes and angles correspond to the preceding system, and hence the two crystal systems are occasionally also combined with one another as hexagonal. The difference between them lies in the elements of symmetry. With the hexagonal system the cross-section of the prismatic base-form is six-sided, with the trigonal system it is three-sided. The six-sided hexagonal shape is formed when the corners of the triangle are bevelled off. Typical crystal forms of the trigonal system are three-sided prisms and pyramids, rhombohedra and scalenohedra.

Rhombic system (Orthorhombic system) Three axes of differing length are at right angles to one another. Typical crystal forms are basal pinacoids, rhombic prisms and pyramids as well as rhombic double pyramids.

Monoclinic system Two of the three axes of differing length are at right angles to one another, the third is inclined. Typical crystal forms are basal pinacoids and prisms with inclined terminal faces.

Triclinic system All three axes are of unequal lengths and are inclined to each other. Typical crystal forms are paired faces or pinacoids.

Distortions Every crystal – even of the same type of mineral – looks somewhat different. Crystals can be large and small, slender and thick, straight and crooked. The ideal form (ideal crystal), as it is always pictured in text-books and identification manuals, is almost never attained. In nature the fully grown crystal (as a real crystal) is usually rather deformed, that is to say, distorted. The faces and the relationship of the faces to each other are different in each crystal. But despite the differences in appearance the crystals still retain regular features which are clearly discernible. The interfacial angles (the angles which are formed between any two like faces) are always the same in the same kind of crystal.

Habit (German: *Tracht*) The totality of the forms which appear in a crystal is called a habit. There are simple forms (e.g. cube, rhombdodecahedron) and combinations of two or even several crystal forms.

Habit (German: *Habitus*) This is the term for the shape of a crystal, which can among other things be tabular, acicular, spiky, columnar or stumpy.

Pseudomorphism Mineral formations with crystal shapes which are not characteristic of the mineral are called pseudomorphs. They develop by virtue of the fact that under certain conditions crystals have been dissolved away and the space they have left has been filled up by another substance, during which process the crystal form has remained wholly or partially preserved. For example the external form of a mineral can represent a barite, whilst the mineral content is quartz. We speak then of a pseudomorph of quartz after barite. So-called petrified wood is also a pseudomorph (see p.38).

Massive Term for mineral or mineral aggregate without crystal faces, i.e. without regular boundaries.

Stufen (crystal stufen) Mineral aggregate with several separate individual crystals (e.g. rock crystal, p.37).

Druse A cavity in the rock (up to approximately 1 metre in diameter) with crystal accumulations or growths on the walls. See also geode.

Geode A former cavity in the rock (druse), which is wholly or almost wholly filled with minerals (No. 3, p.179). In many cases, however, the terms geode and druse are used as synonyms for a situation where a hollow space has been more or less completely filled up by a mineral.

Amethyst druse with a dense lining of crystals. Minas Gerais/Brazil.

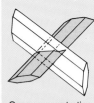

Gypsum penetration twin

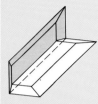

Gypsum swallowtail twin

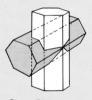

Staurolite interpenetration twin

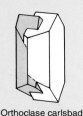

Orthoclase carlsbad twin

TWINS

Occasionally crystals of the same type and of the same form can grow regularly and symmetrically into one another. We then speak of twins, triplets, etc. depending on how many individuals are involved. According to the positioning of the crystals relative to one another we distinguish between contact twins and interpenetration twins. A variant of the latter are cruciform twins, which have crystals crossing one another at varying angles. Sometimes the terms interpenetration twin and cruciform twin are used as synonyms.

If the twinning within one group is repeated, then trillings, fourlings, eightlings etc. can also develop. Combinations of twins of several individuals are also called multiple twins.

Twins can often be recognised by the fact that they reveal re-entrant angles, i.e. angles whose apex points into the inside of the crystal. Such angles are never found in individual crystals.

The twin shapes often carry their own names: Brazil, Dauphine (Alpine or Swiss), and Japanese twins in quartz; swallowtail and Montmartre twins in gypsum; Carlsbad, Baveno and Manebach twins in orthoclase; Iron Cross twins in pyrite; Visiergraupen in cassiterite. Further illustrations of twins and multiple twins are Japanese twin/quartz [No. 3, p.37], Staurolite [No. 3, p.79] and Alexandrite [No. 9, p.165].

Twin formations in gypsum, staurolite and orthoclase-feldspar

MINERAL AGGREGATE

A mixture of minerals associated in the range of a centimetre up to a metre. Coarsely crystalline aggregates, so-called stufen (p.17), are rare, formations of small crystals are more usual.

Internal character

Sparry Many smooth, glistening little cleavage surfaces on the fracture surfaces of an aggregate which consists of minerals with perfect cleavage.

Granular Grains which are joined together and visible to the naked eye.

Compact Single individuals so small that they cannot be identified with the naked eye.

Oolitic Little spheres of pinhead to pea size. Similar terms: pisolitic, roe-like, shell-like.

Columnar Elongate arrangement of individuals in an aggregate. Similar terms: radiating, radially oriented, fibrous.

Lamellar Flat, leaf-like texture. Similar term: scaly.

External form

Globular Outer surface made up of hemispherical, smooth, often glistening units. Internal structure usually radial. Similar terms: bulbous, botryoidal, spherical, reniform, nodular, warty.

Stalactitic Longish bulbous, dripstone-type surface.

Rosette-like Lamellar individuals arranged in a rose-like form.

Tufted Longish individuals arranged in clusters. Similar term: sheaf-like.

Skeletal Flat formation similar to frost patterns. Similar terms: dendritic, moss-like, filiform, interwoven.

Crusted Thin overgrowth on another aggregate. Similar terms: encrusted, efflorescent, tarnished.

Earthy Usually crumbly mass which is shapeless and not very firm. Similar terms: powdery, floury.

1 Oolitic mineral aggregate (aragonite)
2 Radial mineral aggregate (pyrite)
3 Globular mineral aggregate (hematite)
4 Rosette-like mineral aggregate (gypsum)
5 Skeletal mineral aggregate (copper)

PROPERTIES OF MINERALS

It is often impossible to reach a positive identification of a mineral simply from the crystal form or other typical external characteristics. One usually has to examine further properties of the minerals. A beginner should start his identification of a mineral by considering streak, colour, Mohs' hardness, specific gravity (relative density), fracture and cleavage. To aid identification there are comprehensive mineral identification tables on pages 342-365.

COLOUR AND STREAK

Only very few minerals have a single, characteristic colour, like malachite (which is always green), cinnabar (red), azurite (blue) and sulphur (yellow). Many minerals appear in different colours, some even in all colours of the spectrum. The colour is therefore scarcely a determinative aid in recognising minerals. On the other hand, the streak colour, also called powder colour or streak for short, is an objective means of determining minerals.

Whereas the recognisable colouring in a mineral or a variety is generally caused by slight traces of impurities or by defects in the crystal lattice, and accordingly represents a "foreign" colour, the streak colour always reproduces the same unique, constant colour intrinsic to the whole mineral. With fluorite, for example, the streak colour is always white, regardless of whether the fluorite looks yellow, blue, green or black.

In order to obtain the streak colour a corner of the specimen is rubbed on a small, unglazed porcelain plate, the streak plate.

Streak colours. Upper (from left) orpiment, pyrite, cinnabar. Lower (from left) hematite, azurite, malachite.

Streak test on a streak plate. The pyrite, which is a brassy yellow colour, gives a greenish-black streak.

If necessary, the following may be used as a rubbing surface: the unglazed under-edge of a porcelain dish, a flower vase or the surface of an electric fuse, as well as the white reverse side of a tile. As one rubs a coloured, powdery streak may show up. These extremely finely powdered grains appear like thin, translucent little plates, so that the colouring of the mineral caused by the foreign material is nullified. If no streak colour is discernible when rubbing on the streak plate the streak is called colourless or white.

With minerals which are harder than the streak plate, that is to say above Mohs' hardness 6, a small piece of the mineral to be identified must be pulverised by grinding, and then rubbed on the streak plate.

For the streak test always use only fresh fracture surfaces and avoid oxidation coatings, weathered skins and tarnishing colours.

SURFACE SCHILLERIZATION AND LIGHT EFFECTS

With some minerals a schiller can be seen close to the surface; these strip-like light effects are dependent neither on the mineral's own colour, nor on impurities, nor indeed the chemical composition. The cause lies with properties involving reflection, interference and diffraction of light.

Adularescence The bluish-white schiller which appears on the surface in moonstone (No. 7, p171).

Aventurism Variegated play of colours: glistening reflections of leaf-like inclusions on an almost opaque background. (Aventurine Nos 1 and 4, p.177, sunstone No. 10, p.171).

Labradorescence Play of colours in metallic hues, especially in labradorite (No. 3, p.43).

Opalescence Milky blue or pearly appearance of the common opal (No. 5, p.39).

Opalisation Mottled play of colours of the precious opal (Nos 8 and 9, p.181).

Cat's eye (chatoyancy). Light effect which resembles the slit-eye of a cat. Arises through reflection of the light from parallel fibres, needles and cavities. Most effective when the cut is *en cabochon* (tiger's eye No. 2, p.177, moonstone No. 7, p.171).

Asterism Star-shaped rays of light which meet at a point. Formed like cat's eye, except that the reflecting fibres lie in different directions. (Synthetic sapphire No. 1, p.163, synthetic ruby No. 4, p.163).

MOHS' HARDNESS

When the mineral collector speaks of the hardness of a mineral he always means the scratch hardness; that is the resistance which a mineral exhibits when it is scratched with a sharp-edged material.

The concept of scratch hardness was introduced more than 150 years ago by the Viennese mineralogist Friedrich Mohs (1773-1839). Using ten minerals of differing hardness, he drew up a comparative scale (Mohs' hardness scale) which is valid throughout the whole world to the present day. Number 1 is the softest category, 10 the hardest. The minerals with the intermediate values scratch the mineral designated with lesser hardness and are scratched by the mineral with the next hardness on the scale. Minerals of equal hardness do not scratch one another. Categories of hardness are subdivided further into half categories. All minerals known to us today are assigned to this Mohs' hardness scale. In every mineralogy book the Mohs' hardness (hardness for short) is always given when describing minerals.

Minerals with a Mohs' hardness of 1 are considered as soft, those degrees 3-6 as medium hard, and those over 6 are designated as hard. In earlier times one also spoke of precious stone hardness when dealing with grades 8-10. Nowadays this practice is not accepted as there are valuable precious stones which do not possess a Mohs' hardness of 8.

The hardness of minerals is not equal on all crystal faces. In general, however, the differences are so slight that the collector does not need to take them into account. If there are great discrepancies one must take account of such surface-related differences in hardness. With kyanite, for example, the Mohs' hardness in the direction of the long bladed crystals is 4-4½; however, it is 6-7 at right angles to them.

Relative and absolute hardness scale

Mohs' hardness	Comparison mineral	Simple means of testing hardness	Absolute hardness
1	Talc	Can be scratched with fingernail	0.03
2	Gypsum	Can be scratched with fingernail	1.25
3	Calcite	Can be scratched with copper coin	4.5
4	Fluorite	Easily scratched with knife	5.0
5	Apatite	Can be scratched with knife	6.5
6	Orthoclase	Can be scratched with steel file	37
7	Quartz	Scratches window glass	120
8	Topaz		175
9	Corundum		1,000
10	Diamond		140,000

The fact that there are differences in hardness in the same crystal makes it possible to grind diamond with diamond, for materials of equal hardness normally do not scratch or grind one another. Diamond, well known to be the hardest material of all, can therefore only be ground with diamond powder, because it has considerable differences in hardness on the individual crystal surfaces and moreover in different directions (see sketch p.23). Statistically, diamond powder always contains quite hard splinters of a diamond crystal. The harder crystal surfaces are never ground down.

The Mohs' hardness scale is a relative hardness scale. With it one can only ascertain which mineral scratches which. No evidence is forthcoming about the **22** absolute measure of increase in hardness within the scale.

The Mohs' hardness scale cannot be used as a truly scientific basis for hardness testing since it is only relative and is also too inexact. Thus for such scientific purposes absolute hardness values are determined, which require the expenditure of great technical resources. In the table on page 22 the absolute hardness (grinding hardness according to Rosival) is listed against the Mohs' values. From this it is possible to see how unequal the span is within the individual Mohs' hardness categories. Nevertheless the Mohs' hardness scale is of great value to the collector as it is impossible for the collector to determine absolute hardness.

Methods of testing hardness Sets of professional scratching instruments are available (illustrated p.24) for testing hardness, but if these are not available, simple aids may be used to recognise some hardness grades. Thus a fingernail scratches up to a Mohs' hardness of 2, a copper coin up to hardness 3, a pocket-knife up to about 5, a knife made of very good quality steel even up to Mohs' hardness 5½. Steel files are even harder, they scratch up to hardness 6. With quartz, number 7 on the Mohs' hardness scale, window glass can be clearly scratched. Because of this simple application the Mohs' hardness scale is very popular with collectors. Without a great deal of fuss and trouble and without wasting any time one can undertake a rough determination of minerals on site, during walks or tours. In carrying out a scratch test one has to make sure that the examination takes place only with sharp-edged pieces on uncorroded, smooth surfaces. Grooved, flaky forms or weathered crystal surfaces in specimens to be determined give a mistaken impression of a lower degree of hardness.

After scratching a powdery streak remains on the unknown mineral. It can originate either from the testing material or from the object being tested. For this reason a finger needs subsequently to be wiped over the scratching surface. If the streak can be wiped off, then the testing material was softer than the unknown mineral. Otherwise it was harder and has produced a scratch in the test object. If the scratching is unclear a magnifying glass should be used.

The Mohs' hardness scale is of use only in determining minerals, not rocks. In the case of monomineralic rocks i.e. those which only consist of a single mineral like rock salt, limestone and marble, values may be approximated, which can be useful in determining types of rock and the minerals.

Hardness differences in diamond crystal (after E.M. and J. Wilks). The shorter the arrow, the greater the grinding hardness in that direction.

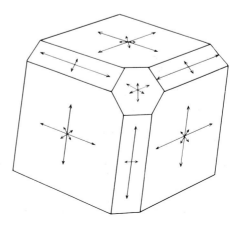

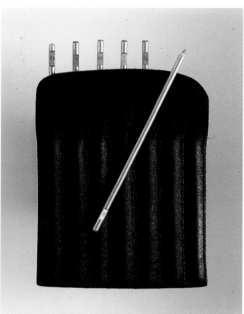

Set of scratching instruments with metal pins in which mineral splinters are set.

Test pieces in the Mohs' hardness scale, plus steel pin, knife and file as simple testing devices.

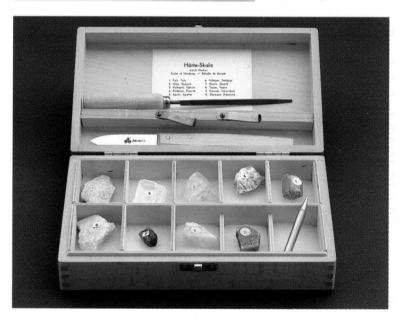

LUSTRE

Not only do cut precious stones show glistening surfaces, many minerals also have a characteristic lustre. It originates from the light reflected at the surface of the stone and is dependent on the refractive index of a mineral and the mineral's surface characteristics, but not on the colour. In describing minerals and in determinative tables in this book account is taken of vitreous and resinous lustre, silky and pearly lustre, adamantine lustre, greasy and waxy lustre as well as metallic lustre. Minerals without lustre are matt (or dull).

In the mineral world vitreous lustre is the most widespread, being found in about two thirds of all minerals. Metallic lustre is found only in opaque minerals, especially in native metals, sulphides and some oxides; silky lustre occurs in fibrous minerals or mineral aggregates. Pearly and greasy lustre appear especially on cleavage surfaces. Tarnishings, encrustation colours and surface weathering characteristics can have a prejudicial effect on the lustre of a mineral. Therefore lustre should be determined from an unaltered specimen. The determination should always be done in a clear, bright light. Lustre can vary with direction on crystal and cleavage surfaces.

TRANSPARENCY

Transparency is the degree to which a medium allows light to pass through it. There are minerals which are transparent, translucent (semi-transparent) and non-transparent (known in technical terminology as opaque).

In very thin slices many minerals which are otherwise opaque are transparent or translucent. In thin layers all metals are opaque. Granular, fibrous or columnar minerals as well as aggregates are always opaque, because the light is refracted again and again at the many boundary surfaces, until it finally becomes completely reflected or absorbed. For most precious stones transparency is a factor which influences their value.

DOUBLE REFRACTION

If a rhombohedral calcite crystal is laid onto a marked-out background, e.g. crossed lines, then the lines, viewed through the crystal, appear to be doubled. This is the result of so-called double refraction and is caused by the splitting of the light into two parts as it passes through the crystal. All non-cubic minerals which allow the passage of light show double refraction to a greater or lesser extent. In Iceland spar (clear-calcite) double refraction is particularly evident, and hence it is called reflecting spar. Double refraction is an exceptionally important determinative aid with gemstones.

Double refraction in Iceland spar calcite

SPECIFIC GRAVITY

Specific gravity (also called relative density) is the weight of a material in relation to the weight of the same volume of water. Density is mass per unit volume and is numerically equal to specific gravity. Thus quartz with a specific gravity of 2.65 is 2.65 times as heavy as the same volume of water. The specific gravity of minerals varies between 1 and 20. Values under 2 are regarded as light (amber about 1.0), those from 2 to 4 as normal (calcite about 2.7) and those above 4 as heavy (galena about 7.5). In mineralogy and mining practice all minerals with a specific gravity above 2.9 are considered as heavy minerals.

The more valuable precious stones and precious metals have a specific gravity clearly above that of sand (made from quartz and feldspar). They are therefore deposited by the flowing water of rivers and on the coast before the lighter sand minerals and are concentrated in so-called placer mineral deposits.

Density is calculated as follows:

Density = $\dfrac{\text{Weight of mineral}}{\text{Volume of mineral}}$

The weight of a mineral is measured with a balance. The more exact the weighing, the more certain is the identification of the unknown mineral. A beginner can start by using a set of letter scales. A weight determination to $\frac{1}{10}$ gram is quite good. The expert works to weight accuracies of $\frac{1}{100}$ gram, i.e. to two decimal places.

There are various ways of determining volume, by water displacement in a measuring cylinder or by the buoyancy process using a hydraulic balance. The latter method is more precise and is also suitable for small scale tests. It is based on the Archimedes principle: the buoyancy force equals the weight of the water displaced by the mineral. The unknown mineral is first of all weighed in air and then in water.

Schematic representation of the hydrostatic balance

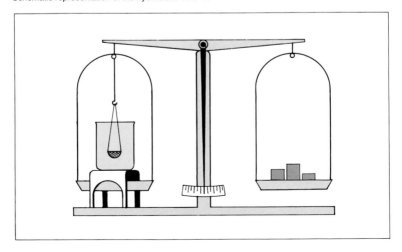

The weight difference corresponds to the weight of the displaced water and hence numerically to the volume of the mineral.

Example:
Weight in air   5.2 g.
Weight in water   3.3 g.
Difference = volume   1.9

Density = weight/volume = 5.2/1.9 = 2.7 g/cc or gcm^{-3}

The density in this test amounts to 2.7 g/cc and the specific gravity is thus 2.7; it could therefore be calcite.

It is important to make sure that when the mineral to be identified is being weighed in air it is dry and does not contain any foreign substance. However, some minerals naturally always have some small impurities or variations in their composition. In such cases the density values are similarly variable and can only be determined approximately. Anyone can set themselves up a hydrostatic balance by following the diagram in the illustration opposite. For the beginner a rebuilt set of letter scales is sufficient. The advanced collector should use precision scales so that measurements are possible to within $\frac{1}{100}$ gram. In gemmology the so-called flotation method is used alongside measurement with a hydrostatic balance in order to determine the density. It is founded on the basic idea that objects float in a liquid of equal density, that is to say, that they neither sink to the bottom nor float on the surface. The density of the unknown precious stones can be arrived at by using normalised liquids of known density, or for that matter by diluting heavy liquids until the stone being tested reaches the point where it floats.

The flotation method is recommended where precious stones are to be specifically sorted out from a collection of unknown stones or where the objective is to identify synthetic stones and imitations as opposed to genuine precious stones.

FRACTURE

If as the result of the use of force (a blow or pressure) minerals split up with irregular surfaces, we call it fracture; if on the other hand even surfaces are produced we call it cleavage (p.28). If twins are split this is known as parting. Whether a mineral can be cleaved or broken depends on the make-up of the lattice of the crystal. If the component parts of the lattice are distributed in such a way that no plane can be traced through the lattice, then the mineral splits up with irregular surfaces, and a fracture occurs. See the representations of crystal lattices on page 28. The fracture can be conchoidal (looking like the rounded impression of a shell), uneven, smooth, fibrous, hackly, splintery or earthy.

Conchoidal fracture in obsidian, volcanic glass

CLEAVAGE

Cleavage is the splitting of a mineral along smooth surfaces or planes. Whether a mineral can be cleaved or not depends on the lattice structure of the crystal. If the atoms, ions or molecules lie in such a relationship to one another that plane surfaces can be traced through the crystal lattice, then the mineral can be cleaved. If not, a fracture occurs, breaking off with irregular surfaces (p.27). The quality of the cleavage varies according to the strength of the cohesive forces between the component parts of the crystal. There is no uniform method of grading cleavage in mineralogy. When minerals are described in this book the following cleavage subdivisions are used:

very perfect – perfect – imperfect – none

Some minerals can only be split in one direction, others in two or more directions. In earlier times miners designated those minerals with very good cleavages in different directions as "spar" (from the German verb *spalten*, to cleave) e.g. feldspar, fluorspar, calc spar (calcite), heavy spar (barite). The cleavage planes are not related to the external form of the mineral. They are exclusively dependent on the lattice structure of the crystal. Even in minerals with different external forms the same cleavage configurations can occur. In galena and halite one always gets cubes, in calcite rhombohedra. For many minerals the angle of cleavage (the angle enclosed by two cleavage planes) is a typical determining feature. For example, the minerals hornblende and augite, which are very similar in appearance, can be differentiated by the cleavage angles if the bounding faces of the crystal are missing: hornblende has an angle of 124°, augite 87° (see sketch p.52).

Crystal faces are never as smooth nor are they usually as glistening as are cleavage surfaces. They are much more inclined to show small imperfections, indentations or other tiny unevennesses.

In the specialist literature of mineralogy the concept of cleavage is frequently represented by the symbol #.

For the precious stones expert, knowledge of cleavage and the direction of cleavage is of the greatest significance in the processes of grinding and setting.

Crystal lattice of halite

Crystal lattice of quartz

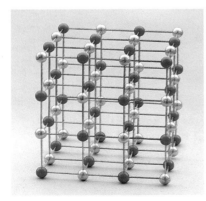
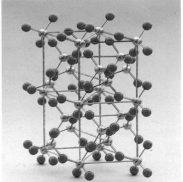

LUMINESCENCE

Luminescence is a collective term for the different ways in which a substance emits visible light under the influence of certain rays, with the exception of pure heat radiation. Of special interest to the mineral collector is luminescence in ultraviolet colours of the spectrum. The concept of fluorescence originated from the mineral fluorite, because it was in this mineral that this phenomenon of emitting light was recognised for the first time. If the substance carries on emitting light when the irradiation ceases we speak of phosphorescence, named after the well-known optical property of phosphorus.

The causes of fluorescence are certain disruptive factors (impurities or structure defects) in the crystal lattice. Most minerals respond to short-wave UV (254 nanometres). There are minerals which react exclusively to shortwave UV, others which react only to long-wave (366 nanometres) and others again which react to both short-wave and long-wave. The trade offers a rich assortment of the most varied ultraviolet apparatus. In determining minerals fluorescence is in general not suitable, for members of one mineral family can fluoresce in quite different colours, whilst others of the same mineral type do not light up at all under UV. Occasionally fluorescence is an aid in recognising a location, for sometimes it shows characteristics which are typical of a locality or deposit.

For the collector fluorescence has practical significance since by it he can recognise certain imitations. In minerals which have been glued together the cement alone sometimes shows fluorescence or fluoresces differently from the rest of the stone. Fluorescence has also proved itself a valuable aid in diagnosing gemstones, particularly in identifying synthetic stones.

The appearance of luminescence under X-rays makes it possible to distinguish genuine pearls from cultivated pearls. This is because the mother-of-pearl in salt-water pearls does not luminesce whereas that of fresh-water pearls lights up very brightly. Since the artificial nucleus of the cultivated pearl consists of fresh-water mother-of-pearl, cultivated pearls will accordingly show luminescence, in contrast to genuine pearls.

Fluorescing minerals in white light (left) and under UV-rays (right).

Sometimes an important aid in determining the identity of a mineral can be offered by simple tests of smell, taste, feel and solubility in water. The specialist has under certain circumstances to set up very special investigations, e.g. when it is a question of diagnosing gemstones and synthetics or of recognising ore minerals in a deposit. Often one only finally reaches absolute certainty about a mineral or a mineral aggregate by considering the optical effects of dispersion (breakdown of white light into the colours of the rainbow), absorption and absorption spectra (light extinction), microscopic studies using light incident onto polished specimens and of light transmitted through specimens which have been ground thin (slices of 0.03mm thickness), and many other methods of examination which are labour-intensive and require considerable resources in equipment.

In identifying a mineral the advanced collector should take into account further properties of some minerals which are briefly touched on in the following remarks.

Magnetism In minerals magnetic behaviour varies. There are minerals (e.g. magnetite) which themselves have a magnetic effect, and others (e.g. pyrrhotite) which are attracted by magnets; finally, there are those which do not react magnetically at all.

Both types of magnetic behaviour can be clearly determined with a compass needle. Suspended freely, the magnet needle reacts very sensitively to any magnetic influence. Place specimens next to the stationary magnet needle and observe how the needle is deflected. Because of the weaker magnetism involved, small pieces of mineral have to be moved to and fro as closely as possible above the magnet needle. With some minerals magnetism varies according to locality and iron content. This is why in mineralogical literature details given about magnetism are occasionally inaccurate.

Toughness Toughness (technically called tenacity) is a combination of a mineral's brittleness (brittle, malleable, sectile), ductility (sectile, ductile) and elasticity (elastically flexible, inelastically flexible or plastic).

The qualities of toughness can be a determinative aid for individual minerals. In general they are more the province of the specialist. In descriptions of minerals in this book toughness characteristics are mentioned individually under the heading "fracture".

Pleochroism In some transparent minerals colours and colour intensities are different in varying directions. The reason for this is an unequal absorption of light by double-refracting crystals in different directions. If two main colours appear one speaks of dichroism, with three colours of trichoism or pleochroism. Dichroism is only possible with tetragonal, hexagonal or trigonal crystal systems; trichroism is possible only with orthorhombic, monoclinic or triclinic crystal systems. The term pleochroism is also used as a collective term for both situations where more than one colour occurs. Amorphous minerals and those in the cubic crystal system have no pleochroism.

Pleochroism can appear in weak, clear or strong forms. It has to be taken into consideration when grinding precious stones in order to avoid false colourings, i.e. too light or too dark tones, and in order to achieve in the stones as great a colour intensity as possible.

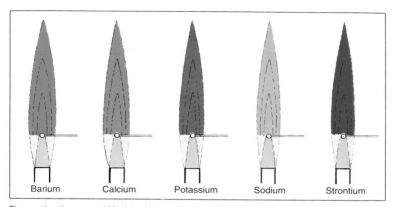

Flame coloration as an aid in determining minerals

| Barium | Calcium | Potassium | Sodium | Strontium |

Flame coloration Since a number of elements change the colour of a flame, a flame test may be used in order to ascertain the chemical composition of a mineral. Gas burners are preferable to candles as a source of flame, for they can be regulated in such a way that they burn without any flame colour of their own. Flame colouring is most easily visible in darkened rooms. Strontium has a purple-red effect, lithium carmine red, calcium brick red, sodium yellow, barium yellowish green, boron green, copper blue and green, potassium violet. A small splinter of a mineral is sufficient as a test specimen. Hold the specimen in the flame with a pair of tweezers or with a loop in a platinum wire until it glows.

Behaviour under the blowpipe Melting reactions and flame coloration using a blowpipe aid the determination of minerals. This is known in specialist circles as blowpipe analysis. Such a blowpipe is made of brass, has a wooden mouth-piece and a hair-thin opening at the other end. By blowing through the blowpipe, the flame of a Bunsen burner, candle or spirit burner can be heated up considerably and aimed at a mineral specimen as a tongue of flame. The resulting reduction and oxidation processes have melting, corrosive and sublimation effects as well as causing the formation of gases and the coloration of the flame. All of this allows conclusions to be drawn about the chemical composition of the mineral specimen.

Radioactivity The property of emitting rays without energy input is known as radioactivity. There are three types of rays: alpha, beta and gamma rays. Alpha radiation is rarely seen as it diminishes very quickly. Beta radiation is somewhat stronger, but it has a short range and poor powers of penetration. Gamma radiation is the most intensive. It can penetrate iron and thick walls.

Radiation is measured by use of a so-called Geiger counter. A mineral collector would be recommended to use an instrument with an optical-accoustic gauge. As the source of the rays is approached, individual crackling sounds merge to give a clicking tone which becomes louder the more radiation is present. Care should be taken when dealing with radioactive minerals, as radiation can pose a danger to health. Never store radioactive substances in living or sleeping areas, pack larger pieces in lead containers, wash your hands carefully after contact and keep away from children.

CLASSIFICATION OF MINERALS

There are about 3000 known minerals, and each year new minerals are being discovered. Over and beyond that there are several thousand variations called varieties. It is scarcely possible to keep overall track of such a large number. Therefore it is necessary to group minerals according to the same or similar properties.

There are various possible ways of achieving this. Minerals can, for instance, be sorted out according to the way in which they are formed, their distribution within rocks or according to external characteristics, e.g. crystal shape, hardness, lustre or density. One or other grouping can be useful, depending on the object of the exercise. In the scientific sphere of mineralogy it is in the main the practice to classify minerals according to their chemical composition and then according to their structure. In modern mineralogy the 'mineral system' always means this system of chemical classification. There are models with differing groupings, but within mineralogy an ordering into nine classes of minerals has been generally established. Someone interested in minerals who collects them according to this system is known quite simply as a systematist.

For someone with no prior scientific education in mineralogy, and for those who have a professional interest in stones (like stonemasons, sculptors and building experts) the chemical system of mineral classification is in general not acceptable. For this reason minerals are presented in this book in the way in which they are most easily comprehensible to the non-expert, that is to say, as rock-formers, as constituents of ores, and as precious stones. Of course, if this system of ordering minerals is used cases of overlap in assigning minerals to one or other part of the system cannot be avoided. Generous compromises have been necessary but they have been taken on board quite consciously.

The list tabulated below is the one which is valid for someone interested in rocks who is collecting them according to the scientific system.

The choice of minerals for the presentations that follow was determined by their significance for petrology and as ore, by their use as precious stones as well as their popularity with those who pursue mineralogy as a hobby. Such a selection process is inevitably subjective to some extent.

THE SCIENTIFIC MINERAL SYSTEM

Minerals can be grouped into nine classes. The last class comprises organic compounds, which are similar to the other minerals.

Class I	Elements
Class II	Sulphides and related compounds
Class III	Haloids
Class IV	Oxides and hydroxides
Class V	Nitrates, carbonates, borates
Class VI	Sulphates, chromates, molybdates, tungstates
Class VII	Phosphates, arsenates, vanadates
Class VIII	Silicates (neso or island-silicates, soro or group silicates, cyclo- or ring-silicates, Ino- or chain- and band-silicates, phyllo- or sheet silicates, tecto- or framework-silicates)
Class IX	Organic compounds

MINERALS IN A SCIENTIFIC CLASSIFICATION SCHEME (SELECTION)

Class I: Elements
Amalgam, antimony, arsenic, diamond, gold, graphite, copper, platinum, mercury, sulphur, silver, tellurium, bismuth.

Class II: Sulphides and related compounds
Acanthite, antimonite, argentite, arsenopyrite, berthierite, bismuth glance, bornite, boulangerite, bournonite, chalcocite, chalcopyrite, cinnabar, cobaltite, covellite, cubanite, enargite, freibergite, galena, gersdorffite, jamesonite, jordanite, linnaeite, lollingite, marcasite, millerite, molybdenite, niccolite, orpiment, patronite, pentlandite, petzite, polybasite, proustite, pyrargyrite, pyrrhotite, pyrite, realgar, safflorite, schapbachite, schwazite, sphalerite, sperrylite, skutterudite, stannite, stephanite, stibiopalladinite, sylvanite, tennantite, tetrahedrite, wurtzite.

Class III: Haloids
Atacamite, carnallite, calomel, chlorargyrite, fluorite, halite, salmiak, sylvite.

Class IV: Oxides and hydroxides
Alumogel, anatase, arsenolite, asbolan, bismite, bixbyite, boehmite, brannerite, braunite, brookite, cassiterite, chromite, chrysoberyl, coesite, columbite, coronadite, corundum, cristobalite, cryptomelane, cuprite, diaspore, franklinite, gahnite, gibbsite, goethite, ice, hematite, hausmannite, heterogenite, hollandite, ilmenite, lepidocrocite, magnetite, manganite, molybdite, niobite, opal, perovskite, pitchblende, psilomelane, pyrochlore, pyrolusite, quartz, rutile, sassolite, senarmontite, spinel, stishovite, tantalite, tenorite, thorianite, tridymite, uraninite,wolframite, zincite.

Class V: Nitrates, carbonates, borates
Ankerite, aragonite, aurichalcite, azurite, bismutite, boracite, borax, calcite, cerussite, colemanite, dolomite, gaylussite, hambergite, hydrozincite, kernite, kurnakovite, leadhillite, magnesite, malachite, phosgenite, rhodochrosite, saltpetre, siderite, sinhalite, smithsonite, soda, soda nitre, strontianite, ulexite, witherite.

Class VI: Sulphates, chromates, molybdates, tungstates.
Alumite, anglesite, anhydrite, barite, brochantite, celestite, chalcanthite, crocoite, epsomite, gypsum, halotrichite, hanksite, jarosite, kainite, kieserite, linarite, polyhalite, powellite, scheelite, schoenite, thenardite, wulfenite.

Class VII: Phosphates, arsenates, vanadates
Adamite, amblygonite, annabergite, apatite, autunite, beryllonite, brazilianite, cacoxenite, carnotite, descloizite, erythrite, lazulite, mimetesite, monazite, mottramite, olivenite, pharmacolite, purpurite, pyromorphite, scholzite, stolzite, strengite, torbernite, turquoise, uranocircite, vanadinite, variscite, vivianite, wardite, wavellite.

Class VIII: Silicates
Aegirine, actinolite, allanite, analcite, andalusite, anthophyllite, apophyllite, arfvedsonite, augite, axinite, benitoite, bertrandite, beryl, bronzite, cancrinite, chabazite, chamosite, chlorite, chrysocolla, clinochlore, cordierite, danburite, daphnite, datolite, delessite, diopside, dioptase, dumortierite, enstatite, epidote, euclase, fassaite, fayalite, feldspars, forsterite, garnierite, glaucophane, garnets, gyrolite, harmotome, hauyne, hedenbergite, hemimorphite, heulandite, hornblende, hypersthene, illite, ilvaite, jadeite, kaliophilite, kaolinite, kornerupine, kyanite, lapislazuli, laumontite, leucite, melilite, mesolite, mica, milarite, montmorillonite, natrolite, nepheline, neptunite, nosean, okenite, olivine, omphacite, pectolite, penninite, petalite, phenacite, phillipsite, piemontite, prehnite, pyrophyllite, rhipidolite, rhodonite, riebeckite, sepiolite, serpentine, sillimanite, scapolite, scolecite, sodalite, sphene, spodumene, staurolite, stilbite, talc, thomsonite, thorite, thuringite, topaz, tremolite, tourmaline, uranophane, vesuvianite, willemite, wollastonite, zoisite, zircon.

Class IX: Organic
Amber, mellite, ozokerite, whewellite.

ROCK-FORMING MINERALS

Of the 3000 known minerals only a few dozen are essential constituents of rocks. We distinguish between major, medium and minor constituents according to their proportions by volume.

Major constituents Minerals which occur in large amounts in the rock.

Medium constituents Minerals which are present in the rock but are less common. They are also called accessories.

Minor constituents Minerals which normally occur in the rock in subordinate amounts, but which occasionally occur locally in a high percentage and because of this can be characteristic of the rock.

There is no commonly accepted demarcation of constituents in terms of percentages, but major constituents ought not to be below 10%.

In the following the minerals are presented according to the way in which they tend to appear in the three rock groups, igneous, sedimentary and metamorphic. In this treatment it is not possible to avoid certain compromises, for minerals certainly do develop in igneous, sedimentary or metamorphic form (p.12), but this does not mean that such minerals are restricted to each particular group. There is a whole series of minerals which occur in two or even in all three of the above mentioned rock groups. In order to avoid repetition in the presentation the minerals are described and illustrated only in one of the rock groups.

Minerals of ores and gemstones, which themselves are also constituents of rocks, are dealt with according to their economic significance as an independent group in each case.

MINERALS OF IGNEOUS ROCKS

Major constituents of igneous rocks are quartz, feldspars, foids, mica, augite, hornblende and olivine. Medium constituents are apatite, hematite, ilmenite, magnetite, natrolite, nepheline, sphene, zircon and several others.

In volcanic eruptions ashes and lava blobs can be hurled hundreds of metres into the air. Stromboli volcano, Lipari Islands, July 1977.

35

QUARTZ GROUP

Quartz and opal as well as the rare minerals tridymite, cristobalite, coesite and stishovite are members of the quartz group. They are all made of silica.

Quartz [1-6]

Composition SiO2	*Colour* colourless, white
Hardness 7	*Streak* white
Specific Gravity 2.65	*Lustre* vitreous, greasy
Cleavage none	*Transparency* transparent to opaque
Fracture conchoidal	*Crystal system* trigonal

Generally the crystals exhibit a six-sided prism with pyramidal terminations. Horizontal striations on the vertical faces are the essential determinative feature. Occasionally there are inclusions of other minerals and frequently of gases and fluids. Large man-sized crystals are known. Quartz may pseudomorph many other minerals.

Interpenetration twins (Dauphiné and Brazil) are for the most part so intimately intergrown that the individual crystals are difficult to decipher. Juxtaposition twins (Japan [3]) have prominent re-entrant angles. In general, quartz crystals occur in groups [4]. Aggregates may be compactly granular [6], columnar or fibrous. Since quartz is mechanically resistant and only weakly chemically attacked (only soluble in hydrofluoric acid) it is very widespread and, after feldspar, is the most abundant mineral in the upper crust of the Earth. It is a major constituent of silica-rich igneous and metamorphic rocks as well as in most sands. Generally quartz appears colourless or milky and turbid.

LOCALITIES: Fichtelgebirge, Pfalz/Germany, Alps, Brazil, Herkimer, Arkansas/USA, Cumberland/England.

Quartz is the raw material for the glass and ceramic industries. In technology (because of the piezoelectric effect) it serves as regulator in radio transmitters and clocks. Pretty coloured quartzes are popular semi-precious and gemstones (pp. 174/176).

The name quartz comes from German miners' language of the Middle Ages. It is not possible to be certain of the original meaning.

Doubly-terminated quartz [2] Quartz crystal with terminating pyramids at both ends. "Floater" (for example in carbonate rock).
Sceptre quartz [1] A bigger crystal capping a slender stem, a crystal oddity.
Ferruginous quartz [5] Quartz aggregate coloured yellow, brown or red by iron oxide.
Macrocrystalline colour varieties Amethyst [1], aventurine, rock crystal [4], blue quartz, citrine, ferruginous quartz, vein quartz (p.198), common quartz [6], milky quartz [2], morion, prase, smoky quartz, rose quartz. See also page 174.
Macrocrystalline form varieties Fibrous quartz, phantom quartz, prismatic quartz [4], skeletal quartz, star quartz, sceptre quartz [1].
Microcrystalline varieties Chalcedony in the wider sense (p.38)
Pseudomorph varieties Falcon's eye, fossil wood, quartz-cat's eye, tiger's eye.

---

1 Sceptre quartz (amethyst), Mexico
2 Doubly terminated quartz,
  Warstein/Westphalia/Germany
3 Japan twin, Arizona/USA
4 Rock crystal with pyrite, Trepca/Yugoslavia

5 Ferruginous quartz,
  Warstein/Westphalia/Germany
6 Common quartz, pebble specimen,
  Rhineland/Germany

1

2

3

4

5

6

Chalcedony

In its wider sense chalcedony includes microcrystalline quartz (agate, true chalcedony, chrysoprase, dendritic agate, heliotrope, hornstone, jasper, carnelian, moss agate, onyx, sard), in a narrower sense only the grey-blue variety.

True chalcedony [1]

Composition SiO_2	Colour bluish, white-grey
Hardness 6½-7	Streak white
Specific Gravity 2.58-2.64	Lustre waxy, dull
Cleavage none	Transparency translucent
Fracture uneven, conchoidal	Crystal system trigonal

Chalcedony is made-up of very small, parallel-oriented fibres. Aggregates radiating, stalactitic, botryoidal or reniform. Always porous and therefore able to be dyed. Occurs as crusts and cavity fillings. LOCALITIES: Brazil, India, Madagascar, Namibia. Used in jewellery (p.178)

Polyhedral quartz [2] Pseudo-agate

These geometrical forms are druses of chalcedony, sometimes the layers alternate with coarsely crystalline quartz. Many fanciful names. Originates as the filling of interstices between tabular crystals which are later dissolved away. LOCALITY: Brazil.

Moss agate [3]

Moss agate is colourless, translucent chalcedony (not agate!) with green moss-like hornblende. Occurs as fissure fillings or secondarily as pebbles. LOCALITIES: India, China, USA. Used in jewellery.

Silicified wood [4] Hornstone, Petrified wood

Silicified wood (hornstone) is formed when circulating water dissolves the organic constituents, which were covered by sediment, and replaces them with mineral matter (especially chalcedony). Hornstone is therefore a pseudomorph of chalcedony after wood. LOCALITIES: Arizona/USA. Egypt, Patagonia/Argentina

Opal [5]

Composition $SiO_2 \cdot nH_2O$	Colour white, all colours, in parts opalescent
Hardness 5½-6½	Streak white
Specific Gravity 1.98-2.50	Lustre vitreous, greasy
Cleavage none	Transparency transparent to opaque
Fracture conchoidal, brittle, splintery	Crystal system trigonal

Opal is amorphous and has small amounts of finely crystalline cristobalite and tridymite which cause the rainbow iridescence, the opalescence. Water content 1-30%. Occurs as crusts and nodules. LOCALITIES: worldwide but particularly Australia. Three groups of opal varieties; opaque common opal [5] (hyalite, honey-, liver-, milk-, prase-, wax-, water-opal), the opalescent precious opal and the orange-red fire opal. Jewellery and gemstones (p.180).

---

1 Chalcedony in natural colour, unpolished, Minas Gerais/Brazil
2 Polyhedral quartz, Brazil
3 Moss agate, sliced, Kathiavar/India
4 Silicified wood, polished cut surface, Oregon/USA
5 Common opal (liver opal), Hungary

FELDSPAR GROUP

The Feldspar group contains silicate minerals with a lot of similar properties. They make up more than 60% of the upper crust of the Earth. The name derives either from their wide distribution (in every field – "feld") or from "fels" (rock).

Potash feldspar = orthoclase in a wider sense

Common orthoclase
(*sensu stricto*)
Adularia
Moonstone
Sanidine
Microcline
Amazonite

Calcium-sodium feldspar = plagioclase

	%Na	%albite = Ab	% anorthite = An
Albite, pericline	100	100–90	0– 10
Oligoclase (sunstone)	80	90–70	10– 30
Andesine	60	70–50	30– 50
Labradorite	40	50–30	50– 70
Bytownite	20	30–10	70– 90
Anorthite	0	10– 0	90–100

Alkali feldspar Mixed crystal between potash feldspar and soda feldspar, eg anorthoclase, perthite, also sodium bearing orthoclase and microcline.

Orthoclase [5]

Composition K[AlSi$_3$O$_8$]	*Colour* white, yellow, flesh pink, also others
Hardness 6	*Streak* white
Specific Gravity 2.53-2.56	*Lustre* vitreous, pearly
Cleavage perfect	*Transparency* transparent to opaque
Fracture conchoidal, uneven, brittle	*Crystal system* monoclinic

Crystal form tabular, prismatic. Cleavage angle 90°. Interpenetration twins (Carlsbad [2], Baveno, Manebach). Compact, sparry masses. Occurs in pegmatites [No 3, p257] and other silica-rich rocks. Used as raw material in the ceramic and glass industries. LOCALITIES: Fichtelgebirge/Germany, Tauern/Austria, Tessin/Switzerland, Sweden, Cornwall/England, Scotland, New England/USA.
Adularia [6] Transparent variety of orthoclase in Alpine tension veins.
Sanidine [1] Transparent to opaque, frequently cracked variety of orthoclase in young acid volcanic rocks.

Microcline [4]

Composition K[AlSi$_3$O$_8$]	*Colour* white, yellow, pinkish, also others
Hardness 6	*Streak* white
Specific Gravity 2.53-2.56	*Lustre* vitreous, pearly
Cleavage perfect	*Transparency* cloudy to opaque
Fracture conchoidal, uneven, brittle	*Crystal system* triclinic

Crystals tabular, frequently twinned. Massive, sparry, coarsely crystalline masses. Occurs in acid rocks. LOCALITIES: Oberpfalz/Germany, Scandinavia, Colorado, Virginia/USA, Brazil. Used as raw material in the ceramic industry, the green variety amazonite [3] is used in jewellery (see also p.170).

---

1 Sanidine, Vetralia/Latium/Central Italy
2 Carlsbad twin, Colorado/USA
3 Amazonite, Pikes Peak/Colorado/USA
4 Microcline, Seterdalen/Norway
5 Orthoclase, Arendal/Norway
6 Adularia, Wallis/Switzerland

Plagioclase [1, 3, 4]

Plagioclase exhibits a mixed crystal series between albite ($Na[AlSi_3O_8]$) and anorthite ($Ca[Al_2Si_2O_8]$); see table p.40. The intermediate members, each with its own name (oligoclase, andesine, labradorite, bytownite), have recently been distinguished by their % content of albite (Ab) and anorthite (An) eg $Ab_{32}An_{68}$ = Labradorite.

Composition $nNa[AlSi3O_8]+nCa[Al_2Si_2O_8]$	Colour colourless, white, grey-greenish,
Hardness 6-6½	bluish, reddish, sometimes schillerization
Specific Gravity 2.61-2.77	Streak white
Cleavage perfect	Lustre vitreous, pearly
Fracture conchoidal uneven, brittle	Transparency cloudy to opaque

Single crystals (triclinic system) rare, tabular, prismatic, generally lamellar twinned. Aggregates compact granular. Occurs mainly in igneous and metamorphic rocks. LOCALITIES: worldwide. Of no use in technology. Labradorite (Labradorstone) [3] used for decorative stone, the sunstone variety sometimes used in jewellery [No. 10, p.171].

FOIDS FELDSPATHOIDS

Silica-deficient minerals which take the place of feldspars in rather silica poor rocks. Leucite, analcite, nepheline, sodalite, nosean, hauyne, melilite among others belong to this group. Quartz can never occur in association with them.

Leucite [2]

Composition $K[AlSi_2O_6]$	Colour whitish, grey
Hardness 5½-6	Streak white
Specific Gravity 2.45-2.50	Lustre dull, vitreous, greasy
Cleavage none	Transparency translucent to opaque
Fracture conchoidal, brittle	Crystal system tetragonal

Crystals usually icositetrahedra (known as leucitohedra), mostly embedded. Granular aggregates. Occurs in young volcanic rocks. LOCALITIES: Kaiserstuhl/Baden/Germany, Vesuvius and Alban Hills/Italy, Arkansas/USA. Used locally for potash fertilizer.

Analcite [5]

Composition $Na[AlSi_2O_6]\cdot H_2O$	Colour white, yellow, pinkish, also others
Hardness 5-5½	Streak white
Specific Gravity 2.24-2.31	Lustre vitreous
Cleavage none	Transparency transparent to cloudy
Fracture conchoidal, uneven, brittle	Crystal system cubic

Single crystals growing on surfaces form icositetrahedra. Granular and crusty aggregates. Occurs in basaltic and phonolitic rocks, in ore veins. LOCALITIES: Fassatal/Dolomites/Italy, Sicily, Bohemia, Ireland, Lake Superior/USA.

---

1 Albite, Habachtal/Tyrol
2 Leucite, Rocca Monfina/Italy
3 Labradorite, Labrador/Canada

4 Pericline with chlorite coating, Tauern/Austria
5 Analcite, Farmsen/L. Saxony/Germany

Hauyne [1]

Composition $(Na,Ca)_{8-4}[(SO_4)_{2-1}|(AlSiO_4)_6]$	*Colour* blue, rarely yellow or red
Hardness 5½	*Streak* white
Specific Gravity 2.44-2.50	*Lustre* vitreous, greasy, pearly
Cleavage perfect	*Transparency* transparent to opaque
Fracture conchoidal	*Crystal system* cubic

Crystals, aggregates and occurrence as nosean and sodalite.

Nosean [2]

Composition $Na_8[SO_4|(AlSiO_4)_6]$	*Colour* grey, yellowish, green, bluish, white
Hardness 5½	*Streak* white
Specific Gravity 2.28-2.40	*Lustre* vitreous, greasy
Cleavage perfect	*Transparency* transparent to opaque
Fracture conchoidal	*Crystal system* cubic

Crystals and aggregates as sodalite. Occurs in volcanic rocks.

Nepheline [3]

Composition $KNa_3[AlSiO_4]_4$	*Colour* white-grey, light, rarely colourless
Hardness 5½-6	*Streak* white
Specific Gravity 2.60-2.65	*Lustre* vitreous, greasy
Cleavage imperfect	*Transparency* transparent to opaque
Fracture conchoidal, uneven, brittle	*Crystal system* hexagonal

Crystals short columnar. Massive, compact aggregates. Occurs in igneous rocks.
Elaeolite Cloudy variety of nepheline.

Melilite [4]

Composition $(Ca,Na)_2 (Al,Mg)[(Si,Al)_2O_7]$	*Colour* yellow to brown, grey, white, colourless
Hardness 5-5½	*Streak* white, grey
Specific Gravity 2.95-3.05	*Lustre* vitreous, waxy
Cleavage imperfect	*Transparency* transparent to translucent
Fracture uneven, conchoidal, brittle	*Crystal system* tetragonal

Short columnar crystals. Granular aggregates. Occurs in basic volcanic rocks.

Sodalite [5]

Composition $Na_8[Cl_2|(AlSiO_4)_6]$	*Colour* blue, grey, white, yellowish
Hardness 5-6	*Streak* white
Specific Gravity 2.13-2.29	*Lustre* vitreous, greasy,
Cleavage perfect	*Transparency* transparent to opaque
Fracture uneven, conchoidal	*Crystal system* cubic

Embedded rhombdodecahedra. Granular aggregates. In igneous rocks.

Kaliophilite [6] ($K[AlSiO_4]$)
Similar to nepheline; thin white needles. Occurs in volcanic rocks.

MICA GROUP

Because of their excellent cleavage all micas have a glistening appearance (hence the name in German – glimmer) on flat faces. Muscovite, biotite and phlogopite are important rock-forming minerals particularly in igneous and metamorphic rocks. Sericite, paragonite and margarite occur especially in metamorphic rocks (p.92), glauconite exclusively in sedimentary rocks, zinnwaldite and lepidolite usually in pegmatites.

Biotite [1]

Composition K(Mg,Fe)$_3$[(OH,F)$_2$|AlSi$_3$O$_{10}$]	*Colour* dark brown, dark green, black
Hardness 2½-3	*Streak* white
Specific Gravity 2.70-3.30	*Lustre* pearly, vitreous, metallic
Cleavage very perfect	*Transparency* transparent to opaque
Fracture laminar, elastically flexible	*Crystal system* monoclinic

Tabular crystals embedded and surface growing, hexagonal outline. Aggregates leaf-like, scaly, compact granular. Constituent of igneous and metamorphic rocks. Known popularly in Germany as Katzengold (cat's gold) if a pale bronze-colour.

Muscovite [2] Muscovy glass

Composition KAl$_2$[(OH,F)$_2$|AlSi$_3$O$_{10}$]	*Colour* colourless, lightly tinted
Hardness 2-3	*Streak* white
Specific Gravity 2.78-2.88	*Lustre* vitreous, pearly, metallic
Cleavage very perfect	*Transparency* transparent to translucent
Fracture laminar, flexible	*Crystal system* monoclinic

Tabular plate-like crystals with hexagonal outline, embedded and surface growing, rarely well-formed. Aggregates leaf-like, compact. Occurs in plutonic rocks, pegmatites and metamorphic rocks; since it is also acid – and weathering-resistant it occurs in sands. LOCALITIES: Urals/Russia, Norway, Ontario/Canada, Tanzania, Zimbabwe, India, New Hampshire, South Dakota, North Carolina/USA. Used for electrical and heat insulation.
Silver mica Known popularly in Germany as Katzensilber (cat's silver) if it has a silvery lustre.
Fuchsite (Chrome mica) [3] Green coloured, chrome-bearing variety of muscovite.
Sericite [No 2, p13] finely scaly, silky lustred variety of muscovite in metamorphic rocks.

Phlogopite [4]

Composition KMg$_3$[(F,OH)$_2$|AlSi$_3$O$_{10}$]	*Colour* grey, yellow, green-brown, colourless
Hardness 2-2½	*Streak* white
Specific Gravity 2.75-2.97	*Lustre* pearly, metallic
Cleavage very perfect	*Transparency* transparent to translucent
Fracture laminar, flexible	*Crystal system* monoclinic

Tabular crystals. Scaly, compact leaf-like aggregates. Occurs in pegmatites and metamorphic rocks. Localities: Baikal area /Russia, Ontario/Canada, Madagascar, Sweden, Finland, Colorado/USA. Used for electrical insulation.

---

1 Biotite, Miask/Urals/Russia
2 Muscovite, Moss/Norway

3 Fuchsite, Tyrol/Austria
4 Phlogopite, Templeton/Ontario/Canada

Zinnwaldite [1] Lithium-iron mica

Composition KLiFe^{2+}Al[(F,OH)$_2$|AlSi$_3$O$_{10}$]	Colour grey, brown, rarely violet, green, black
Hardness 2-3	Streak white
Specific Gravity 2.90-3.20	Lustre pearly, vitreous, metallic
Cleavage very perfect	Transparency opaque to translucent
Fracture laminar, elastically flexible	Crystal system monoclinic

Lamellar crystals, surface-growing or intergrown. Aggregates leaf-like, scaly. Occurs in granites, pegmatites, greisen.

Lepidolite [2]

Composition KLi$_2$Al[(F,OH)$_2$|Si$_4$O$_{10}$]	Colour pink, violet, white, grey, greenish
Hardness 2-3	Streak white
Specific Gravity 2.80-2.90	Lustre pearly, vitreous
Cleavage very perfect	Transparency transparent to translucent
Fracture laminar, elastically flexible	Crystal system monoclinic

Crystals with six-sided outline. Scaly or fine grained aggregates. Occurs in granites and granite pegmatites. Raw material for lithium salts.

PYROXENE GROUP

In this group belong augite, aegirine, bronzite, diopside with diallage and chrome-diopside, enstatite, fassaite, hedenbergite, hypersthene, omphacite and spodumene.

Augite [3,4]

Composition (Ca,Mg,Fe)[(Si,Al)$_2$O$_6$]	Colour black, greenish, brownish
Hardness 5-6	Streak white, grey-green
Specific Gravity 3.2-3.6	Lustre vitreous
Cleavage imperfect	Transparency opaque
Fracture conchoidal, uneven, brittle	Crystal system monoclinic

Crystals embedded and surface growing, short prismatic, eight-sided outline (see p.52). Granular aggregates. Dominantly in basic volcanic rocks but also in many other igneous and metamorphic rocks. LOCALITIES: Eifel/Germany, Bohemia/Czechoslovakia, France, Montana and Colorado/USA
Common augite Dark iron-bearing augite.
Basaltic augite Titanium-bearing augite.

Aegirine [5] Acmite

Composition Na Fe [Si$_2$O$_6$]	Colour dark green, green-black, brownish
Hardness 6-6½	Streak yellowish to brownish, green
Specific Gravity 3.43-3.60	Lustre vitreous, resinous
Cleavage perfect	Transparency opaque
Fracture uneven	Crystal system monoclinic

Crystals embedded, long prismatic. Aggregates fibrous. Occurs in light coloured igneous rocks and also in metamorphic rocks. LOCALITIES: Norway, Kola/Russia, Rumania, Magnet Cove/Arkansas/USA, Libby/Montana/USA.

---

1 Zinnwaldite, Zinnwald/Erzgebirge/Saxony/ Germany
2 Lepidolite, Minas Gerais/Brazil
3 Augite, Lochkov/Bohemia/Czechoslovakia

4 Augite crystals disseminated in volcanic tuff, Vesuvius/Italy
5 Aegirine, Eker/Norway

Enstatite [1]

Composition Mg₂[Si₂O₆]	*Colour* grey, green, brownish, colourless
Hardness 5½	*Streak* white
Specific Gravity 3.26-3.28	*Lustre* vitreous
Cleavage imperfect	*Transparency* transparent to opaque
Fracture uneven, brittle	*Crystal system* orthorhombic

Crystals mostly small and rare, short prismatic, tabular, often laminated. Aggregates compactly granular, sparry. Occurs predominantly in intermediate and basic igneous rocks, as well as in metamorphic rocks. LOCALITIES: Harz/Germany, Norway, Caucasus, Urals/Russia, Sierra Nevada/California, Texas, Maryland, N Carolina/USA.

Hypersthene [2]

Composition (Fe,Mg)₂[Si₂O₆]	*Colour* green-black, black-brown, reddish
Hardness 5-6	*Streak* white
Specific Gravity 3.35-3.84	*Lustre* vitreous, metallic
Cleavage imperfect	*Transparency* opaque
Fracture uneven, brittle	*Crystal system* orthorhombic

Richly-faceted crystals, columnar, tabular. Mostly massive, granular-laminated aggregates. Occurs in basic igneous rocks and gneisses. LOCALITIES: Massif Central/France, Baikal area/Russia, Labrador/Canada, New York, Adirondack, Colorado/USA.

Bronzite [3]

Composition (Mg,Fe)₂[Si₂O₆]	*Colour* brown, green, bronzy
Hardness 5-6	*Streak* white
Specific Gravity 3.25-3.35	*Lustre* silky, metallic, vitreous
Cleavage imperfect	*Transparency* opaque
Fracture uneven,	*Crystal system* orthorhombic

Rarely well-formed, short-prismatic crystals. Aggregates granular, sparry. Occurs in basic to intermediate igneous and metamorphic rocks. LOCALITIES: Harzburg/ Harz/Germany, S Tyrol/Italy, South Africa, Urals/Russia, Greenland, Montana/USA.

Diopside [4]

Composition CaMg[Si₂O₆]	*Colour* green, grey, yellow, colourless
Hardness 5-6	*Streak* white
Specific Gravity 3.27-3.31	*Lustre* vitreous
Cleavage imperfect	*Transparency* translucent
Fracture rough, brittle	*Crystal system* monoclinic

Embedded and surface-growing crystals, short columnar, tabular. Aggregates granular, long columnar. Occurs in igneous and metamorphic rocks. LOCALITIES: Zillertal/Austria, Erzgebirge/Germany, Vesuvius/Italy, Urals/Russia, New York/USA.
Diallage [4] Bronzy, metallic-looking variety with perfect cleavage.
Violan Blue variety from Piemont/Italy.
Chrome diopside [No 3, p.91] Bright emerald green variety. Gemstone.

AMPHIBOLE GROUP

To this group belong arfvedsonite and hornblende which mainly occur in igneous rocks and actinolite, tremolite, riebeckite, glaucophane and anthophyllite which appear in metamorphic rocks.

Arfvedsonite [1]

Composition	*Fracture* uneven, brittle
$Na_3(Mg,Fe)_4(Fe,Al)[Si_4O_{11}]_2[OH,F]_2$	*Colour* dark blue, black
Hardness 5½-6	*Streak* blue-grey, colourless
Specific Gravity 3.44-3.46	*Lustre* vitreous
Cleavage perfect	*Transparency* translucent to opaque

Crystals (monoclinic system) prismatic, tabular, rare. Embedded grains, long columnar aggregates. Occurs in light coloured alkaline igneous rocks, rarely in metamorphic rocks. LOCALITIES: Ukraine, Langesundfjord/Norway, Greenland, New Hampshire, Colorado/USA.

Hornblende [4, 6] Common hornblende

Composition	*Fracture* uneven, brittle
$Ca_2Na(Mg,Fe^2)_4(Al,Fe^3)[(Si,Al)_4O_{11}]_2[OH]_2$??	*Colour* green to black
Hardness 5-6	*Streak* grey-green, grey brown
Specific Gravity 3.02-3.27	*Lustre* vitreous occasionally milky
Cleavage perfect	*Transparency* translucent to opaque

Short columnar crystals (monoclinic system) with six-sided outline, embedded and surface-growing. Augite which is similar has eight-sided cross section (see below). Aggregates massive, long columnar, fibrous, rarely granular. Occurs in intermediate and basic igneous rocks, more rarely in metamorphic rocks especially amphibolites.

Hornblende crystal:
Cross section 6 sided
Cleavages intersect at 124°

Augite crystal:
Cross section 8 sided
Cleavages intersect at 87°

Olivine [5] Peridot, Chrysolite

Composition $(Mg,Fe)_2[SiO_4]$	*Colour* green, yellow, brown, grey, colourless
Hardness 6½-7	*Streak* white
Specific Gravity 3.27-4.20	*Lustre* vitreous, greasy
Cleavage imperfect	*Transparency* transparent to translucent
Fracture conchoidal, brittle	*Crystal system* orthorhombic

Olivine is a mixed crystal (solid solution series) of the minerals forsterite [2, 3] and fayalite. Generally embedded prismatic or thick-tabular crystals. Aggregates granular. Occurs in basic igneous and metamorphic rocks. LOCALITIES: Eifel/Germany, Urals/Russia, Transvaal/South Africa, Arizona/USA. Gemstone olivine p.170.

---

1 Arfvedsonite in Syenite,
   Berkum/Rhineland/Germany
2 Forsterite, yellow-green encrustation, USA
3 Forsterite, Washington/USA

4 Hornblende, Schima/Bohemia/Czechoslovakia
5 Olivine, Dreiser Weiher/Eifel/Germany
6 Hornblende, Kragerö/Norway

1

2

3

4

5

6

Apophyllite [1]

Composition KCa₄[Fl(Si₄O₁₀)₂]·8H₂O	*Colour* colourless, different colours
Hardness 4½-5	*Streak* white
Specific Gravity 2.3-2.4	*Lustre* pearly, vitreous
Cleavage perfect	*Transparency* transparent to translucent
Fracture uneven, brittle	*Crystal system* tetragonal

Composition $KCa_4[Fl(Si_4O_{10})_2] \cdot 8H_2O$

Crystals always surface-growing, prismatic, dipyramidal, cube-like, tabular. Aggregates granular, laminated. Occurs in basalts and ore veins. LOCALITIES: St Andreasburg/Harz/Germany, Bohemia/Czechoslovakia, Kongsberg/Norway, Poona/India, Nova Scotia/Canada, New Jersey/USA.

Datolite [2]

Composition CaB[OHISiO₄]	*Colour* colourless, yellow, green, red
Hardness 5-5½	*Streak* white
Specific Gravity 2.9-3.0	*Lustre* vitreous, greasy
Cleavage none	*Transparency* transparent to translucent
Fracture conchoidal, uneven, brittle	*Crystal system* monoclinic

Composition $CaB[OHISiO_4]$

Surface-growing, short prismatic or thick- tabular crystals. Aggregates massive granular, dense, fibrous. Occurs in basic igneous rocks, in metamorphic rocks and occasionally in ore veins. LOCALITIES: Schwarzwald, Harz/Germany, Norway, Massachusetts, New Jersey/USA.

Apatite [3, 4]

Composition Ca₅[Fl(PO₄)₃]	*Colour* colourless, white, also all other colours
Hardness 5	*Streak* white
Specific Gravity 3.16-3.22	*Lustre* greasy, vitreous
Cleavage imperfect	*Transparency* transparent to opaque
Fracture conchoidal, uneven, brittle	*Crystal system* hexagonal

Composition $Ca_5[Fl(PO_4)_3]$

Richly facetted, columnar or tabular crystals, embedded or surface growing. Aggregates massive granular, dense, fibrous, or radiating. Occurs in igneous and metamorphic rocks, in phosphorite (p294), also sedimentary. LOCALITIES: Kola/Russia, Alnö/Sweden, Mexico, South Africa, Maine/USA, Ontario/Canada. The most important phosphate fertiliser.
Asparagus stone Yellowish green variety of apatite
Moroxite Bluish green variety of apatite

Fluorite [5] Fluorspar

Composition CaF₂	*Colour* rarely colourless, all colour tones
Hardness 4	*Streak* white
Specific Gravity 3.18	*Lustre* vitreous
Cleavage perfect	*Transparency* transparent to translucent
Fracture conchoidal, splintery, brittle	*Crystal system* cubic

Composition CaF_2

Crystals usually cubes, mostly surface-growing. Interpenetration twins common. Aggregates granular, sparry, dense. Frequently fluorescent. Occurs in igneous rocks, in ore deposits, in sedimentary rocks. LOCALITIES: Wölsendorf/Oberpfalz and Harz/Germany, Mexico, Illinois/USA, Derbyshire/England. Used as a flux (hence the name) in the metal industry and in the production of hydrofluoric acid.

1 Apophyllite, Poona/India
2 Datolite with a small white crystal of danburite, Charcas/Mexico
3 Massive apatite, Kragerö/Norway
4 Apatite with rock-crystal, Mexico
5 Fluorite, Pöhla, Erzgebirge/Germany.

1

2

3

4

5

Scapolite [1]

Composition	Fracture conchoidal, brittle
$Na_8[(Cl_2,SO_4,CO_3)I(AlSi_3O_8)_6]$ = marialite	Colour colourless, white, grey, green, red
$Ca_8[(Cl_2,SO_4,CO_3)_2I(AlSi_3O_8)_6]$ = meionite	Streak white
Hardness 5-6½	Lustre vitreous, greasy
Specific Gravity 2.54-2.77	Transparency transparent to opaque

Scapolite is the term for a mixed crystal series. Prismatic crystals (tetragonal system) mostly surface-growing, cleavage perfect. Aggregates massive granular, long columnar, dense. Occurs in igneous and metamorphic rocks, also in the vicinity of iron ore-bodies. LOCALITIES: Bodenmais/Bayerischer Wald and Saualpe/Karnten/Germany, Kiruna/Sweden, LakeSuperior/USA.

Rutile [2, 3]

Composition TiO_2	Colour colourless, yellow, red, brown, black
Hardness 6-6½	Streak yellowish brown
Specific Gravity 4.2-4.3	Lustre adamantine, metallic
Cleavage perfect	Transparency transparent to opaque
Fracture conchoidal, uneven, brittle	Crystal system tetragonal

Mostly elongated prismatic to acicular crystals, embedded and surface growing, twins and repeated twins common. Aggregates massive granular. Occurs in many rock types and in placer deposits. LOCALITIES: Kragerö/Norway, Virginia/USA, Oaxaca/Mexico, Australia, South Africa. Important raw material of titanium.
Sagenite Reticulate growth of rutile twins.
Nigrine Black variety of rutile.

Cryolite [4] Ice stone

Composition Na_3AlF_6	Colour white, grey, brown, black, red
Hardness 2½-3	Streak white
Specific Gravity 2.95	Lustre vitreous, pearly
Cleavage none	Transparency translucent
Fracture uneven, brittle	Crystal system monoclinic

Crystals pseudo-cubic frequently twinned. Mostly massive, sparry aggregates. Occurs in pegmatites. LOCALITIES: Ivigtut/W Greenland, Miask/Urals/Russia, Colorado/USA. Used in the production of aluminium and in enamel manufacture.

Witherite [5]

Composition $BaCO_3$	Colour colourless, white, grey, yellowish
Hardness 3-3½	Streak white
Specific Gravity 4.28	Lustre vitreous, greasy, dull
Cleavage imperfect	Transparency transparent to translucent
Fracture uneven, brittle	Crystal system orthorhombic

Crystals columnar, dipyramidal, interpenetration twins. Aggregates massive, botryoidal, crusty, fibrous. Poisonous! Occurs in veins. LOCALITIES: Harz/Germany, Alston Moor/England, California/USA. Used in the glass and ceramic industries.

---

1 Scapolite, Lake Baikal area/Russia
2 Golden rutile in rock crystal, Brazil
3 Surface-growing rutile crystals, Namibia
4 White cryolite with black-grey galena and brown siderite, Ivigtut/W.Greenland
5 Witherite, Alston Moor/N England

ZEOLITE GROUP

Representatives: chabazite, harmotome, heulandite, laumontite, mesolite, natrolite, phillipsite, scolecite, stilbite, thomsonite. Of great importance in technology because the crystalline water can be substituted by other liquids and gases.

Chabazite [1]

Composition (Ca,Na₂)[Al₂Si₄O₁₂].6H₂0	*Colour* colourless, white, reddish, brownish
Hardness 4-5	*Streak* white
Specific Gravity 2.08-2.16	*Lustre* vitreous
Cleavage imperfect	*Transparency* transparent to translucent
Fracture uneven, brittle	*Crystal system* trigonal

Crystals pseudo-cubic mostly surface-growing. Aggregates massive, crusty. Occurs in volcanic rocks, also as precipitates from hot springs. LOCALITIES: Vogelsberg/Hessen/Germany, Westerwald/Rhineland/Germany, Czechoslovakia, Ireland, New Zealand, Yellowstone Park/USA.

Mesolite [2]

Composition Na₂Ca₂[Al₂Si₂O₁₀]₃·8H₂O	*Colour* colourless, white
Hardness 5-5½	*Streak* white
Specific Gravity 2.2-2.4	*Lustre* vitreous, silky
Cleavage perfect	*Transparency* transparent to translucent
Fracture conchoidal, brittle	*Crystal system* monoclinic

Crystals long prismatic, acicular. Aggregates fibrous, dense, also earthy. Occurs in gas cavities in volcanic rocks. LOCALITIES: Giants Causeway/Ireland, Faeroes, Iceland, Skye/Scotland, Jefferson/Colorado/USA.

Laumontite [3]

Composition Ca[AlSi₂O₆]₂·4H₂O	*Colour* colourless, white, yellowish, reddish
Hardness 3-3½	*Streak* white
Specific Gravity 2.25-2.35	*Lustre* vitreous, pearly, dull
Cleavage perfect	*Transparency* transparent to opaque
Fracture uneven, brittle	*Crystal system* monoclinic

Long columnar crystals. Aggregates finely fibrous, columnar, earthy. Laumontite breaks down in air to become turbid and dull. Occurs in gas cavities and joints of igneous and metamorphic rocks, also in ore veins. LOCALITIES: Sarntal/S Tyrol, Harzburg/Harz/Germany, New Jersey/USA.

Natrolite [4]

Composition Na₂[Al₂Si₂O₁₀]·2H₂O	*Colour* colourless, white, yellowish, brownish
Hardness 5-5½	*Streak* white
Specific Gravity 2.20-2.26	*Lustre* vitreous, silky, pearly
Cleavage perfect	*Transparency* transparent to translucent
Fracture conchoidal, brittle	*Crystal system* orthorhombic

Crystals long prismatic, acicular. Aggregates radiating, fibrous, also floury, dense. Occurs in cavities in volcanic rocks, also in ore veins. LOCALITIES: Hohentwiel/Hegan/Germany, Auvergne/France, Iceland, New Jersey/USA, San Benito/California/ USA, Asbestos/Canada, N Ireland.

---

1 Chabazite, Nova Scotia/Canada
2 Mesolite with water clear scolecite, India
3 Laumontite with dusting of chlorite, Austria
4 Natrolite, Westerwald/Hessen/Germany

Harmotome [1]

Composition Ba[Al$_2$Si$_6$O$_{16}$]·6H$_2$O	*Colour* white, grey, lightly coloured.
Hardness 4½	*Streak* white
Specific Gravity 2.44-2.50	*Lustre* vitreous
Cleavage imperfect	*Transparency* translucent, milkily cloudy
Fracture uneven, brittle	*Crystal system* monoclinic

Crystals columnar, mostly interpenetration twins. No aggregates. Occurs particularly in ore veins, more rarely in cavities of volcanic rocks. LOCALITIES: Idar-Oberstein/Pfalz/Germany, St Andreasberg/Harz/Germany, Bodenmeis/Bayerischer Wald/Germany, Kongsberg/Norway, Strontian/Scotland, Manhattan/USA.

Stilbite [2] Desmine

Composition Ca[Al$_2$Si$_7$O$_{18}$]·7H$_2$O	*Colour* colourless, white, yellow-, reddish,grey
Hardness 3½-4	*Streak* white
Specific Gravity 2.09-2.20	*Lustre* vitreous, pearly
Cleavage perfect	*Transparency* transparent to translucent
Fracture uneven, brittle	*Crystal system* monoclinic

Rarely as columnar or tabular single crystals. Usually as sheaf-like bundles of coalescing interpenetration twins. Aggregates long-columnar, radiating, laminated. Occurs in cavities in igneous rocks, in ore veins, in metamorphic rocks and also in Alpine clefts. LOCALITIES: St Andreasberg/Harz/Germany, Fassatal/Dolomites, Kongsberg/Norway, Faeroes, Iceland, New Jersey/USA, Skye/Scotland, Nova Scotia/Canada.

Phillipsite [3]

Composition KCa[Al$_3$Si$_5$O$_{16}$]·6H$_2$O	*Colour* colourless, white, yellow-, reddish,grey
Hardness 4-4½	*Streak* white
Specific Gravity 2.2	*Lustre* vitreous
Cleavage imperfect	*Transparency* transparent to translucent
Fracture uneven, brittle	*Crystal system* monoclinic

Single crystals tabular, columnar, rare. Usually interpenetration twins, small, surface-growing. Occurs in cavities in volcanic rocks, particularly basalts; at times in saline lakes. LOCALITIES: Kaiserstuhl/Baden/Germany, Vogelsberg/Hessen/Germany, Vesuvius/Italy, N Ireland, Iceland.

Heulandite [4]

Composition Ca[Al$_2$Si$_7$O$_{18}$]·6H$_2$0	*Colour* colourless, white, yellow, red.
Hardness 3½-4	*Streak* white
Specific Gravity 2.18-2.22	*Lustre* vitreous, pearly
Cleavage perfect	*Transparency* transparent to translucent
Fracture uneven, brittle	*Crystal system* monoclinic

Thin and thick-tabular crystals, frequently individually growing on surfaces. Aggregates lamellar, radiating, sparry. Occurs in cavities in volcanic rocks, particularly basalts, also in metamorphic rocks, in Alpine clefts and in ore veins. LOCALITIES: Idar-Oberstein/Pfalz/Germany, St Andreasberg/Harz/Germany, Kongsberg/Norway, Faeroes, Iceland, India, Hawaii and New Jersey/USA, Nova Scotia/Canada.

---

1 Harmotome, Strontian/Scotland
2 Stilbite, St Andreasberg/Harz/Germany
3 Phillipsite, Tuscany/Italy
4 Heulandite, Poona/India

MINERALS OF SEDIMENTARY ROCKS

A series of minerals occurs exclusively or predominantly in sedimentary rocks. Saline minerals, many carbonate minerals, some sulphate and phosphate minerals, as well as most clay minerals are members of this series. Ice, which also counts as a mineral of sedimentary rocks, is, however, only of interest to the scientist. Other minerals such as quartz, chalcedony, opal, feldspar and mica are also to be found in sedimentary rocks but in general they occur predominantly in igneous rocks. They are therefore described in that section.

CLAY MINERAL GROUP

Clay minerals are the main constituents of argillaceous rocks and important constituents of rocks. They include chlorite, illite, kaolinite and montmorillonite. Since most clay minerals can only be determined under the microscope or sometimes even only with X-rays, they are rarely collected. Only chlorite forms large crystals (p.84).

SALINE MINERAL GROUP

The term salt is defined differently in chemistry and geology. Salts in geology are understood to be products of precipitation from solutions following evaporation of fluids, generally of water.
The minerals of these salts are:
Chlorides (carnallite, halite, sylvite)
Sulphates (anhydrite, gypsum, kainite, kieserite, polyhalite, scholenite, thenardite)
Borates (boracite, borax, colemanite, ulexite)
Nitrates (saltpetre, soda nitre)

Gypsum [1-4] Selenite

Composition CaSO$_4$·2H$_2$O	*Colour* colourless, white, many other colours
Hardness 1½-2	*Streak* white
Specific Gravity 2.2-2.4	*Lustre* vitreous, pearly, silky
Cleavage perfect	*Transparency* transparent to opaque
Fracture conchoidal, fibrous, brittle	*Crystal system* monoclinic

Prismatic and tabular crystals, embedded or surface growing. Frequently twinned (swallow-tail, montmartre). Aggregates massive granular, parallel fibrous, rosette-like, compact. Occurs in salt deposits, in ore mineral deposits, as concretions in argillaceous rocks. LOCALITIES: worldwide. Used as building materials and raw material in the ceramic industry. Transparent cleavage pieces were formerly used as protective glass for pictures of the Virgin Mary hence the name Marienglas (Mary glass) or Fraueneis (Woman ice) in German.

Desert rose [4] (gypsum rose, sandrose) Popular name for rosette- like gypsum aggregates, formed in desert areas by the evaporation of rising groundwater. If many sand grains are included, coarsely crystalline forms known as sand crystals are produced.

---

1 Gypsum aggregate, Eisleben/Thüringia/ Germany
2 Gypsum crystal, Cartagena/Spain

3 Gypsum crystal, Valencia/Spain
4 Sand rose, Sahara/Tunisia

Thenardite [1]

Composition Na₂SO₄	*Colour* colourless, white grey
Hardness 2½-3	*Streak* white
Specific Gravity 2.66-2.67	*Lustre* vitreous, resinous
Cleavage perfect	*Transparency* transparent to translucent
Fracture uneven, brittle	*Crystal system* orthorhombic

Crystals dipyramidal, tabular. Aggregates granular, crusty, efflorescences. Salty taste. Occurs in salt deposits of terrestrial origin. LOCALITIES: Kazakhstan, Arizona/USA, Canada. Used in the production of soda.

Schoenite [2] Picromerite

Composition K₂Mg[SO₄]₂·6H₂O	*Colour* colourless, white, weakly coloured
Hardness 2½	*Streak* white
Specific Gravity 2.03	*Lustre* vitreous
Cleavage perfect	*Transparency* transparent to opaque
Fracture conchoidal	*Crystal system* monoclinic

Crystals short prismatic, rare. Aggregates massive, crusty, earthy, compact. Bitter taste. In dry air it becomes turbid and alters to langbeinite. Occurs in marine salt deposits. LOCALITIES: Stassfurt/Germany, Galicia/Poland.

Anhydrite [3]

Composition CaSO₄	*Colour* colourless, white, grey, bluish, violet
Hardness 3½	*Streak* white
Specific Gravity 2.9-3.0	*Lustre* vitreous, pearly
Cleavage perfect	*Transparency* transparent
Fracture conchoidal, brittle, splintery	*Crystal system* orthorhombic

Crystals prismatic, tabular, cubic-looking, mostly disseminated. Aggregates massive granular, sparry, fibrous, compact. Changes slowly to gypsum by addition of water. Occurs in salt deposits, commonly in veins, in pegmatites and Alpine clefts, in individual cases in metamorphic rocks and lavas. LOCALITIES: Nordheim/Lower Saxony/Germany, E Harzvorland/Germany.

Halite [4] Rock salt

Composition NaCl	*Colour* colourless, white, grey, brown, red
Hardness 2	*Streak* white
Specific Gravity 2.1-2.2	*Lustre* vitreous
Cleavage perfect	*Transparency* transparent to translucent
Fracture conchoidal, brittle	*Crystal system* cubic

Crystals predominantly cubic, growing into cavities, rarely embedded. Aggregates coarse and fine grained, fibrous. Salty taste. Mixed with CaCl₂ and MgCl₂ makes halite hygroscopic. Occurs in salt deposits. LOCALITIES: near Hannover/Germany, Stassfurt/Germany, Salzkammergut/Austria, Galicia/Poland, Alsace/France, southern States/USA, Cheshire/England. Used as culinary salt. Important raw material for the chemical industry, for the winning (extraction) or the production of caustic soda, chlorine, sodium, and hydrochloric acid, amongst others.

---

1 Thenardite, San Luis, California/USA
2 Schoenite (white) on halite (watery), Hessen/Germany

3 Anhydrite (bluish) with halite, Mexico
4 Halite Heringen/Hessen/Germany

Sylvite [1]

Composition KCl	*Colour* colourless, many colour tones
Hardness 1½-2	*Streak* white
Specific Gravity 1.99	*Lustre* vitreous, greasy
Cleavage perfect	*Transparency* transparent, turbid
Fracture uneven, brittle	*Crystal system* cubic

Crystals cubic. Aggregates granular and sparry. Bitter salty tasting. Hygroscopic if impurities present. Occurs in potash salt deposits. Potash fertiliser.

Kieserite [2]

Composition MgSO₄·H₂O	*Colour* white, yellowish, colourless
Hardness 3½	*Streak* white
Specific Gravity 2.57	*Lustre* vitreous
Cleavage perfect	*Transparency* translucent, turbid
Fracture uneven, brittle	*Crystal system* monoclinic

Crystals rare. Granular aggregates. Transforms in air to epsomite (bitter salt, Epsom salt). Occurs in potash salt deposits. Extracted for magnesium salts.

Carnallite [3]

Composition KMgCl₃·6H₂O	*Colour* colourless, white, red, yellow, brown
Hardness 1-2	*Streak* white
Specific Gravity 1.6	*Lustre* vitreous, resinous, metallic
Cleavage none	*Transparency* transparent to translucent
Fracture conchoidal, brittle	*Crystal system* orthorhombic

Crystals tabular, rare. Granular aggregates. Bitter taste, strongly hygroscopic. Occurs in potash-salt deposits. Potash fertiliser.

Kainite [4]

Composition KMg[Cl‖SO₄·3H₂O	*Colour* colourless, white, grey, yellow, brown.
Hardness 2½-3	*Streak* white
Specific Gravity 2.1-2.2	*Lustre* vitreous
Cleavage perfect	*Transparency* translucent
Fracture splintery	*Crystal system* monoclinic

Crystals tabular, prismatic, rare. Saccharoidal aggregates. Salty bitter tasting. Occurs in potash-salt deposits. Potash fertiliser.

Polyhalite [5]

Composition K₂Ca₂Mg[SO₄]₄·2H₂O	*Colour* colourless, white, grey, red, yellow
Hardness 3-3½	*Streak* white
Specific Gravity 2.77-2.78	*Lustre* greasy, vitreous, resinous
Cleavage perfect	*Transparency* translucent
Fracture fibrous, brittle	*Crystal system* triclinic

Crystals prismatic, rare. Fibrous, scaly, granular aggregates.

---

1 Whitish turbid sylvite with yellowish halite, Kern County/California/USA
2 Kieserite, Hattorf/Philippsthal/Hessen/Germany
3 Carnallite, Hattorf/Philippsthal/Hessen/Germany
4 Kainite, Hattorf/Philippsthal/Hessen/German
5 Polyhalite, Hallein/Austria

1

2

3

4

5

Boracite [1]

Composition Mg[Cl|B$_7$O$_{13}$]	*Colour* colourless, pale tints
Hardness 7-7½	*Streak* white, light grey
Specific Gravity 2.9-3.0	*Lustre* vitreous, adamantine
Cleavage none	*Transparency* transparent to translucent
Fracture conchoidal, brittle	*Crystal system* cubic

Cubic, octahedral or combination crystals, always embedded. Aggregates compact, granular, nodular. Occurs in marine salt-deposits. LOCALITIES: Stassfurt/Germany, Luneberg, Hildesheim/L Saxony/Germany, Yorkshire/England, Lousiana/USA, Bolivia. Used in the production of boric acid and borates.

Stassfurtite Fibrous variety of boracite.

Colemanite [2]

Composition Ca[B$_3$O$_4$(OH)$_3$]·H$_2$0	*Colour* colourless, white, grey, yellowish
Hardness 4-4½	*Streak* white
Specific Gravity 2.44	*Lustre* vitreous, adamantine
Cleavage perfect	*Transparency* transparent to translucent
Fracture uneven, conchoidal	*Crystal system* monoclinic

Crystals short columnar, richly faceted. Aggregates granular, compact. Occurs in dried-out saline lakes. LOCALITIES: Death Valley/California/USA, Panderma/Turkey, Chile. Important raw material for the extraction of boron.

Ulexite [3] Boronatrocalcite

Composition NaCa[B$_5$O$_6$(OH)$_6$]·5H$_2$O	*Colour* colourless, white
Hardness 2	*Streak* white
Specific Gravity 1.96	*Lustre* vitreous, silky
Cleavage perfect	*Transparency* transparent to translucent
Fracture fibrous	*Crystal system* triclinic

Crystals very rare and very small. Nodular aggregates with very fine fibres, also earthy masses. Parallel- fibre-aggregates exhibit a fibre optics effect (hence the term television stone). Occurs in borax lakes of N. and S. America, Caspian Sea area. Important raw material for the extraction of boron.

Borax [4] Tincal

Composition Na$_2$[B$_4$O$_5$(OH)$_4$]·8H$_2$O	*Colour* colourless, white, grey, yellow
Hardness 2-2½	*Streak* white to grey
Specific Gravity 1.7-1.8	*Lustre* vitreous, waxy, greasy
Cleavage perfect	*Transparency* translucent, turbid
Fracture conchoidal, brittle	*Crystal system* monoclinic

Stumpy tabular crystals. Aggregates granular, fibrous, earthy. Sweetish-salty tasting. Becomes turbid in air. Occurs in, and on the shores of, terrestrial salt lakes, the so-called borax lakes. LOCALITIES: California, Nevada/USA, Kazakhstan, Tarapaca/Chile. The most important boron mineral. Used in the chemical, glass and steel industries, in pharmacy and for rocket-propellants.

68

1 Boracite, Luneburg/L.Saxony/Germany
2 Colemanite, Boron/California/USA
3 Ulexite, Boron/California/USA
4 Borax with hanksite crystals, California/USA

1

2

3

4

CARBONATE MINERAL GROUP

The best-known carbonate minerals, more or less important as rock-formers, are ankerite, aragonite, calcite, dolomite and strontianite. To these can be added those which are important ore minerals: azurite, cerussite, hydrozincite, magnesite, rhodochrosite, siderite, smithsonite.

Aragonite [1,2]

Composition $CaCO_3$	Colour colourless,white,variously coloured
Hardness 3½-4	Streak white
Specific Gravity 2.95	Lustre vitreous, greasy
Cleavage imperfect	Transparency transparent to translucent
Fracture conchoidal	Crystal system orthorhombic

Crystals embedded and surface growing, prismatic, acicular, tabular. Frequently twinned. Aggregates massive, crusty, radiating, fibrous, stalactitic. Recognition characteristic: vigorous effervescence with drops of cold, concentrated hydrochloric acid. Occurs as sinter formation at hot springs, occasionally in mineral veins, in clefts and cavities in younger volcanic rocks. The shells of many molluscs (mussels, snails among others) and pearls consist, for the most part, of aragonite. LOCALITIES: Kaiserstuhl/Baden, Erzberg/Steiermark, Hüttenberg/Karnten, Leogang/Salzburg/Austria, Carlsbad/ Czechoslovakia, Sicily/Italy, Aragon/Spain, Colorado/USA, Alston Moor/England.
Flosferri [1] Entwining, nodular or stalactitic aragonite aggregate formed as a result of leaching of iron mineral deposits.

Calcite [3,4] Calcspar

Composition $CaCO_3$	Colour colourless, white, different colours
Hardness 3	Streak white
Specific Gravity 2.6-2.8	Lustre vitreous
Cleavage perfect	Transparency transparent to opaque
Fracture conchoidal, uneven	Crystal system trigonal

Crystals almost always grow on surfaces; more than a hundred different forms and more than 1000 combinations. Of all minerals calcite is by far the richest in forms. The basic forms are rhombohedra, prisms and scalenohedra. Frequently twinned. Well-formed crystals in druses and other cavities.

Aggregates granular, columnar, fibrous, compact, powdery, earthy, oolitic, stalactitic. In concretions and as a petrifying material. Major rock-forming constituent in limestones, sinters and marbles, medium constituent (cementing agent) in many sedimentary rocks, also in igneous and metamorphic rocks. Recognition characteristic: vigorous effervescence with drops of cold, dilute hydrochloric acid. LOCALITIES: N & S Calcareous Alps, Jura mountains/France/Switzerland/S.Germany, Champagne/France, N England, Colorado, Oklahoma/USA. Used in the building industry, as raw material in the chemical, glass and cellulose industry, in the smelting of iron ores.

Iceland spar Clear, colourless, rhombohedral variety of calcite with marked double-refraction. Used in optical instruments.

1 Flosferri, Arizona/USA
2 Aragonite twins, Morocco
3 Calcite, Chihuahua/Mexico
4 Calcite, Namibia

Ankerite [1] Brown spar, iron dolomite

Composition CaFe[CO₃]₂	*Colour* white, yellowish, grey, brown
Hardness 3½-4	*Streak* white, pale grey
Specific Gravity 2.9-3.8	*Lustre* vitreous, pearly, waxy
Cleavage perfect	*Transparency* transparent to opaque
Fracture conchoidal, brittle	*Crystal system* trigonal

Crystals mostly rhombohedral. Aggregates saddle-shaped, curved, compact granular, columnar, sparry, massive. Occurs in ore veins, particularly in siderite deposits. LOCALITIES: Huttenberg/Karnten, Eisenerz/Steiermark, Freiberg/Saxony, Muzo/Colombia, Jefferson County/New York/USA, Nova Scotia/Canada.
Brown spar A synonym for ankerite or a variety of ankerite which becomes brown as a result of oxidation of iron and manganese.

Dolomite [2] Bitter spar

Composition CaMg[CO₃]₂	*Colour* colourless, white, grey, various
Hardness 3½-4	*Streak* white, pale grey
Specific Gravity 2.85-2.95	*Lustre* vitreous
Cleavage perfect	*Transparency* transparent to translucent
Fracture conchoidal, brittle	*Crystal system* trigonal

Richly faceted crystals, embedded and surface growing, frequently curved, mostly composed of rhombohedral forms, occasionally contact twinned. Aggregates granular, columnar, sparry, porous.

Occurs in ore and mineral veins. Rock forming mineral in dolomites, dolomitic marbles, together with calcite in limestone.

Recognition characteristic: vigorous effervescence on addition of warm hydrochloric acid, with cold dilute hydrochloric acid only if the specimen is previously powdered. LOCALITIES: Pfitsch/Tyrol, Leogang/Salzburg, Trieben/Steiermark/Austria, Wölsendorf/Oberpfalz, Wallis/Switzerland, Cornwall/England, Missouri, Iowa, Vermont, Michigan/USA. Used in the building industry, as fire resistant stone, particularly for furnace linings.

Named after the French mineralogist, D. de Dolomieu, who first described the mineral in 1791. The Dolomites in the S.Calcareous Alps were then named after the mineral. The synonym bitter spar which is nowadays rarely used was coined in reference to other Mg-minerals (eg epsomite) which do indeed taste bitter. Dolomite itself does not taste bitter.

Strontianite [3]

Composition SrCO₃	*Colour* colourless, grey, white, lightly tinted
Hardness 3½	*Streak* white
Specific Gravity 3.76	*Lustre* vitreous, greasy
Cleavage imperfect	*Transparency* transparent to opaque
Fracture conchoidal, brittle	*Crystal system* orthorhombic

Crystals prismatic, acicular, spiky, dipyramidal, tabular. Aggregates tufted, radiating, fibrous, massively granular, reniform. Occurs in ore veins, in limestone and marls, occasionally as concretions in limestone. Localities: Munsterland/Westphalia, Clausthal-Zellerfeld/Harz/Germany, E Africa, San Bernardino/California/USA, Strontian/Scotland. Raw material for the extraction of strontium.

1 Ankerite, Sunk/Steiermark/Austria
2 Dolomite, Arkansas/USA

3 Strontianite on barite, spiky and tufted, Konitz near Saalfeld/ Thüringia/Germany

Celestite [1] Celestine

Composition SrSO$_4$	*Colour* colourless, white, bluish, lightly tinted.
Hardness 3-3½	*Streak* white
Specific Gravity 3.9-4.0	*Lustre* vitreous, pearly, greasy
Cleavage perfect	*Transparency* transparent to translucent
Fracture conchoidal, uneven, brittle	*Crystal system* orthorhombic

Crystals tabular, surface growing. Aggregates granular, fibrous, compact, nodular. Occurs in beds, as cleft fillings, as concretions in limestone and gypsum rock. Occasionally in cavities in volcanic rocks. LOCALITIES: Giershagen/Westphalia/ Germany, Bristol/England, Agrigento/Sicily, Lake Erie and Ohio/USA. Raw material for the extraction of strontium.

Vivianite [2]

Composition Fe$_3$[PO$_4$]$_n$·8H$_2$O	*Colour* colourless to white, sky blue
Hardness 1½-2	*Streak* white or blue, also brown
Specific Gravity 2.6-2.7	*Lustre* vitreous, pearly, metallic
Cleavage perfect	*Transparency* translucent
Fracture fibrous, brittle, thin flexible	*Crystal system* monoclinic

Crystals acicular, columnar, tabular, surface growing. Aggregates rosette-like, globular, reniform. When earthy known as blue iron-earth or blue earth. Occurs in argillaceous rocks, in bogs, in limonite deposits and brown-coal deposits. Also (blue coloured) in fossil bones and teeth (odontolite or tooth turquoise). LOCALITIES: Waldsassen/Oberpfalz/Germany, Thüringia/Germany, Cornwall/ England, Colorado/USA.

Wavellite [3] Fischerite

Composition Al$_3$[(OH)$_3$l(PO$_4$)$_2$]·5H$_2$O	*Colour* colourless, greenish yellowish
Hardness 3½-4	*Streak* white
Specific Gravity 2.34-2.4	*Lustre* vitreous
Cleavage imperfect	*Transparency* translucent
Fracture conchoidal, uneven, brittle	*Crystal system* orthorhombic

Crystals prismatic, finely acicular, rare. Radiating, globular, aggregates, also reniform, nodular. Occurs in clefts, sandstone, phosphorite deposits. LOCALITIES: Amberg/Oberpfalz, Lake Dill area/Hessen, Langenstriegis/Saxony/Germany, Montgomery/Arkansas/USA, Cornwall/England. In certain cases exploited for extraction of phosphorus.

Barite [4] Heavy spar

Composition BaSO$_4$	*Colour* colourless, white, often also coloured
Hardness 3-3½	*Streak* white
Specific Gravity 4.48	*Lustre* vitreous, pearly
Cleavage perfect	*Transparency* transparent to translucent
Fracture conchoidal, uneven, brittle	*Crystal system* orthorhombic

Crystals tabular, surface growing. Aggregates scaly, granular, sparry, reniform. Occurs in limestone and argillaceous rock, as concretions in sandstones, as fissure fillings. LOCALITIES: Meggen/Westphalia, Wölsendorf/Oberpfalz, Lauterberg/Harz/ Germany, Alston Moor and Cumberland/England, Ardèche/France, Connecticut, Colorado, S.Dakota, Oklahoma/USA. Raw material for white paint, material for increasing the specific gravity of drilling fluids, for pyrotechnics and for protection against X-rays.

1 Celestite, Madagascar
2 Vivianite, Leadville/Colorado/USA
3 Wavellite, Arkansas/USA
4 Barite with chalcopyrite, Alston Moor/England

MINERALS OF METAMORPHIC ROCKS

Numerous minerals occur exclusively or predominantly in metamorphic rocks.
They include actinolite, andalusite, axinite, chlorite, cordierite, epidote, fassaite,
garnet group, graphite, hedenbergite, kyanite, margarite, omphacite, prehnite,
pyrophyllite, riebeckite, sepiolite, serpentine, sillimanite, staurolite, talc, tremolite,
vesuvianite, wollastonite, zoisite; kernite and okenite are here as contact minerals.
Other minerals such as quartz, feldspars, mica, hornblende, augite, olivine as well
as calcite and dolomite can certainly be found in metamorphic rocks but occur
predominantly in igneous and/or sedimentary rocks. They are therefore described
in those specific sections.

Andalusite [2]

Composition Al$_2$[O|SiO$_4$]	Colour colourless, variously coloured
Hardness 7½	Streak white
Specific Gravity 3.11-3.22	Lustre vitreous, dull
Cleavage imperfect	Transparency transparent to opaque
Fracture uneven, splintery, brittle	Crystal system orthorhombic

Embedded crystals, thick columnar. Aggregates radiating columnar granular.
Occurs in gneiss and schist. LOCALITIES: Lisenzalpe/Kärnten/Austria, Mursinsk/
Urals/Russia, White Mountain, California, Pennsylvania, Massachusetts/USA.
Used for high-temperature resistant ceramics.

Chiastolite [1] Andalusite crystals with cruciform carbonaceous-clayey inclusions.
Occurs embedded in pelitic schists.

Sillimanite [3]

Composition Al$_2$[O|SiO$_4$]	Colour grey, brownish, greenish
Hardness 6-7	Streak white
Specific Gravity 3.22-3.25	Lustre vitreous, greasy, silky
Cleavage perfect	Transparency transparent to translucent
Fracture uneven	Crystal system orthorhombic

Single crystals very rare, acicular, without terminations. Usually radiatingly
fibrous, felted aggregates. Occurs in gneiss, micaschist, granulite, eclogite.
LOCALITIES: Bodenmais/Oberpfalz, Freiberg/Saxony/Germany, Sellrain/Tyrol,
Assam/India, Zimbabwe, South Carolina/USA. Used for high temperature-
resistant ceramics.

Axinite [4]

Composition	Fracture conchoidal, brittle
Ca$_2$(Fe,Mg,Mn)Al$_2$B[OH|O|(Si$_2$O$_7$)$_2$]	Colour brown, grey, violet, green
Hardness 6½-7	Streak white
Specific Gravity 3.26-3.36	Lustre vitreous
Cleavage perfect	Transparency transparent to translucent

Crystals (triclinic system) richly faceted, wedge-shaped to tabular, embedded and
surface growing. Aggregates columnar, sparry, compact. Occurs in Alpine clefts,
in calc silicate rocks, in druses of granites. LOCALITIES: Harz, Fichtelgebirge,
Schwarzenberg/Erzgebirge/Germany, Cornwall/England, Dauphiné/France,
Franklin/New Jersey and California/USA.

---

1 Chiastolite, Chile
2 Andalusite in quartz, Czechoslovakia

3 Sillimanite, Benson Mines/New York/USA
4 Axinite with chlorite, Dauphiné/France

Vesuvianite [1] Idocrase

Composition $Ca_{10}(Mg,Fe)_2Al_4[(OH)_4|(SiO_4)_5 | (Si_2O_7)_2]$	*Fracture* uneven, splintery, brittle
Hardness 6½	*Colour* brownish, grey, many other shades
Specific Gravity 3.27-3.45	*Streak* white
Cleavage imperfect	*Lustre* vitreous, greasy
	Transparency transparent to opaque

Crystals (tetragonal system) embedded and growing on surface, frequently well-formed, usually short and thick columnar but also long columnar and acicular. Aggregates compact, massively granular, radiating. Occurs in metamorphic rocks such as marble, calc silicate rocks, serpentinite; very rarely also in igneous rocks. LOCALITIES: Pfitschtal/Tyrol/Austria, Zermatt/Wallis/ Switzerland, Vesuvius, Monzoni/Dolomites/Italy, New Jersey, Arkansas, California/USA, Quebec/Canada.
Egeran Local name for a radiating vesuvianite aggregate from Eger/ Czechoslovakia and Göpfersgrün/Fichtelgebirge/Germany.
Wiluite Vesuvianite variety with characteristic lineations on the crystal faces. Localities: R Wilui/E Siberia.

Staurolite [2,3,4]

Composition $Fe[OH]_2 \cdot 2Al_2SiO_5$	*Colour* reddish brown, brownish black
Hardness 7-7½	*Streak* white
Specific Gravity 3.65-3.77	*Lustre* vitreous, greasy
Cleavage imperfect	*Transparency* translucent to opaque
Fracture conchoidal, uneven	*Crystal system* monoclinic

Crystals embedded, short or long columnar. Interpenetration twins characteristic with right angled cross (90°) or oblique-angled cross (60°). Frequently grows oriented with kyanite. Occurs in metamorphosed pelitic rocks, in gneiss and mica schists, occasionally as residual minerals, after weathering, in sands. LOCALITIES: Steiermark/Austria, Sterzing/S Tyrol, Fannin County/ Georgia/USA, Ducktown/ Tennessee/USA, Scotland, Namibia.

Kyanite [4,5] Disthene

Composition $Al_2[O|SiO_4]$	*Colour* blue, other colours possible
Hardness 4-4½ and 6-7	*Streak* white
Specific Gravity 3.53-3.65	*Lustre* vitreous, pearly
Cleavage perfect	*Transparency* transparent to translucent
Fracture fibrous, brittle	*Crystal system* triclinic

Crystals in ruler-like columns, embedded, often with stripes across. Contact twins. Big difference in hardness along the length (4-4½) and across (6-7). Aggregates radiating, grows in oriented intergrowth with staurolite. Occurs in metamorphic rocks – gneiss, micaschists, eclogite, occasionally also as residual minerals, after weathering, in sands. LOCALITIES: Tessin/Switzerland, Serbia/Yugoslavia, Machakos/Kenya, Calcutta/India; Virginia, Hampshire County/Massachusetts, Gaston/North Carolina/USA, Scotland. A raw material for the manufacture of high-temperature-resistant materials.

GARNET GROUP

Silicate minerals with similar crystal structure. Pyralspite series – pyrope, almandine, spessartite. Ugrandite series – uvarovite, grossular, andradite.

Composition silicate	*Colour* colourless, all colours except blue
Hardness 6½-7½	*Streak* white
Specific Gravity 3.4-4.6	*Lustre* vitreous, greasy, resinous
Cleavage imperfect	*Transparency* transparent to opaque
Fracture conchoidal, splintery, brittle	*Crystal system* cubic

Crystals embedded and growing on surface, rhombdodecahedra (garnetohedra) icositetrahedra. Large crystals weighing several hundred kilograms are known. Aggregates massive granular to compact. Occurs in gneiss, micaschists, eclogite, in calcareous and dolomitic metamorphic rocks, frequently in sands. Rare in igneous rocks. Worldwide occurrence. Used as grinding and polishing agent as well as for gemstones (p.166).

Almandine [5] Common garnet $Fe_3Al_2[SiO_4]_3$
Colour: brown, red to violet, almost black. Popularly almandine and also pyrope are known as carbuncle. LOCALITIES: Ötztal and Zillertal/Tyrol, Falun/Sweden, Sverdlovsk/Urals, Sri Lanka, India, Scotland, Norway; Adirondacks, California, S Dakota Michigan/USA.

Andradite [2] $Ca_3Fe_2[SiO_4]_3$
Colour: brown, black, also colourless, green, yellow. Demantoid [3] green variety. Melanite: grey black variety. Topazolite [4]: greenish, yellow variety. LOCALITIES: Wurlitz/Fichtelgebirge, Kaiserstuhl/Baden, Zermatt/Switzerland, Pinzgau/Austria.

Grossularite $Ca_3Al_2[SiO_4]_3$
Colour: colourless, green, yellowish, brown, red. Hessonite (cinnamon stone) [1]: brown-orange variety. Hydrogrossularite: opaque, greenish variety. Leucogarnet: colourless variety. Tsavorite (Tsavolite): green variety. LOCALITIES: Auerbach/ Bergstrasse/Hessen, Piemont/Italy, Sri Lanka, Asbestos/Canada, Concepcion del Oro/Mexico, South Africa, Minot/Maine/USA, Warren/New Hampshire/USA, California and Colorado/USA.

Pyrope Bohemian garnet, Cape ruby $Mg_3Al_2[SiO_4]_3$
Colour: red, brown red, rose red. Popularly called carbuncle, as is almandine. Rhodolite: rose red variety. LOCALITIES: Zöblitz/Saxony, Bohemia/Czechoslovakia, Transvaal/ South Africa, Australia, N Carolina, Arizona, New Mexico/USA.

Spessartite $Mn_3Al_2[SiO_4]_3$
Colour: yellow, orange, red brown. LOCALITIES: Spessart/Unterfranken/Germany, Sweden, Madagascar, Sri Lanka, Minas Gerais/Brazil.

Uvarorite $Ca_3Cr_2[SiO_4]_3$
Colour: emerald green. LOCALITIES: Outukumpu/Finland, Urals/Russia, Transvaal/South Africa, India.

---

1 Hessonite, Italy
2 Andradite, Stanley Butte/Arizona/USA
3 Demantoid, Val Malenco/Bernina/Italy

4 Topazolite, California/USA
5 Almandine embedded in micaschist,
  Zillertal/Tyrol/Austria

Prehnite [1]

Composition $Ca_2Al_2[(OH)_2|Si_3O_{10}]$	*Colour* colourless, white, grey, greenish,
Hardness 6-6½	yellowish. *Streak* white
Specific Gravity 2.8-3.0	*Lustre* vitreous, pearly
Cleavage imperfect	*Transparency* transparent to translucent
Fracture uneven	*Crystal system* orthorhombic

Single crystals rare, tabular, characteristically curved. Aggregates reniform, globular, radiating. Occurs in cavities in schists and calc silicate rocks as well as in basic igneous rocks, rarely also in granite. LOCALITIES: Idar-Oberstein/Pfalz and Harzburg/Harz/Germany, Fassatal/S Tyrol, Dauphiné/France, Bergen Hill/New Jersey/USA, Kilpatrick Hills and Campsie Hills/Scotland.

Zoisite [2]

Composition $Ca_2Al_3(O|OH|SiO_4|Si_2O_7)$	*Colour* grey, green, yellowish, pink, blue
Hardness 6-6½	*Streak* white
Specific Gravity 3.15-3.36	*Lustre* vitreous, pearly
Cleavage perfect	*Transparency* opaque, turbid
Fracture uneven	*Crystal system* orthorhombic

Crystals mostly embedded, prismatic, vertically striated, terminal faces rarely well-developed. Aggregates massive, sparry, long columnar with coarse striations. Occurs in metamorphic rocks. LOCALITIES: Saualpe/Karnten/Austria, Rauris/ Salzburg, Zermatt/Wallis/Switzerland, Tanzania, Ducktown/Tennessee, Wyoming and S Carolina/USA. Pretty coloured varieties are used as stones in jewellery.
Thulite rose-red variety of zoisite (photo, p.171)
Tanzanite blue variety of zoisite (photo, p.171)
Anyolite green zoisite variety or zoisite amphibolite from Tanzania, a green rock with black hornblende inclusions and large rubies. Ornamental stone.

Epidote [3]

Composition $Ca_2(Fe,Al)Al_2[O|OH|SiO_4|Si_2O_7]$	*Colour* green, yellow, black, grey
Hardness 6-7	*Streak* grey
Specific Gravity 3.35-3.38	*Lustre* vitreous
Cleavage perfect	*Transparency* transparent to opaque
Fracture conchoidal, uneven, splintery	*Crystal system* monoclinic

Crystals prismatic, richly faceted, striated, twinned. Aggregates massive, radiating, sparry, compact. Occurs in metamorphic and igneous rocks. Well-formed crystals in cavities in these rocks. LOCALITIES: Knappenwand/Untersulzbachtal/Salzburg, near Bourg d'Oisons/ Dauphiné/France, Riverside/California and Haddam/Connecticut/USA. Occasionally used in jewellery.
Piemontite [4] Red to dark red variety of epidote. Rare crystals, streak is cherry-red. Usually radiating aggregates in manganese deposits.
Pistacite Pistachio green, iron-rich epidote variety. Occasionally also used as a synonym for epidote.
Clinozoisite Iron-poor or iron-free variety of epidote.
Tawmawite Chromium-bearing variety of epidote. Tawmaw/Burma, Finland.

---

1 Prehnite, Radautal near Bad
  Harzburg/Harz/Germany
2 Zoisite, Jaurez/Baja California/Mexico

3 Epidote, Baja California/Mexico
4 Piemontite, Aostatal/Italy

1
2
3
4

Pyrophyllite [1]

Composition Al₂[(OH)₂|Si₄O₁₀]	*Colour* white, grey, yellowish, greenish
Hardness 1-1½	*Streak* white
Specific Gravity 2.66-2.90	*Lustre* vitreous, pearly
Cleavage perfect	*Transparency* translucent to opaque
Fracture uneven, flexible	*Crystal system* monoclinic

Tabular crystals always intergrown. Finely scaly or radiating aggregates, also compact masses. Feels greasy. Occurs in beds or on joints in schists, also in ore mineral veins. LOCALITIES: Eifel/Germany, Belgium, Luxembourg, Hirvivaara/ Finland, Deep River/N Carolina, Lincoln County/Georgia, Mariposa County/ California/USA. Used for electroceramics and as a filler in the paper and rubber industries. For Agalmatolite see under talc.

Chlorite [2,3]

Collective name for a mixed crystal series of similarly composite minerals. Most important members: chamosite [No. 5, p.107], daphnite, delessite, clinochlore [2], penninite, rhipidolite (prochlorite), thuringite.

Composition (Fe,Mg,Al)₆[(OH)₂|(SiAl)₄O₁₀]	*Colour* green, black, brown, white, colourless
Hardness 2-3	*Streak* grey-green, brown
Specific Gravity 2.6-3.4	*Lustre* vitreous, pearly, dull
Cleavage perfect	*Transparency* transparent to opaque
Fracture lamellar, inelastically flexible	*Crystal system* monoclinic

Single crystals tabular, barrel-shaped, disseminated and grow on surfaces. Aggregates scaly, platy, fine grained, compact. Occurs in metamorphic rocks (particularly chlorite schists) and in Alpine clefts, often overlays other minerals. **Kammererite** [3] Chromium-bearing variety of penninite with peach-blossom-red crystals or pink-red tarnish. Occurs in chromite deposits.

Talc [4]

Composition Mg₃[(OH)₂|Si₄O₁₀]	*Colour* colourless, white, greenish, yellowish
Hardness 1	*Streak* white
Specific Gravity 2.7-2.8	*Lustre* pearly, greasy
Cleavage perfect	*Transparency* transparent to opaque
Fracture uneven, splintery, flexible	*Crystal system* monoclinic

Well-developed larger crystals are unknown. Aggregates scaly, laminated, compact, shell-like, reniform. Feels greasy. Occurs bedded as well as joint fillings in crystalline schists, also in limestone and dolomite. LOCALITIES: Göpfersgrün/ Fichtelgegirge/Germany, Kärnten, Zillertal/Tyrol/Austria, Barberton/Transvaal/ South Africa, Vermont, New Hampshire Pennsylvania, N Carolina/USA, Quebec/Canada, Shetlands/Scotland. Used for light-fast colours, finely ground (known as talcum) as base for ointments and powder, for high- voltage insulations, for fire-resistant construction materials.
Soapstone Synonym for talc generally or only for compact talc aggregate.
Steatite Synonym for soapstone as well as for talc. In technology soapstone which is heated.
Potstone Synonym for soapstone or term for a chlorite-bearing soapstone.
Agalmatolite (bildstein, pagodite) Compact talc variety, also compact pyrophyllite variety or mixture of talc and pyrophyllite. For carved figures.

1 Pyrophyllite, Indian Gulch/California/USA
2 Clinochlore, Bayerischer Wald/Germany
3 Kammererite, Guleman/Turkey
4 Talc, Futa Pass/Florence/Italy

Actinolite [1] Byssolite
Mineral of the amphibole group (p.52)

Composition Ca$_2$(Mg,Fe)$_5$[(OH,F)|Si$_4$O$_{11}$]$_2$	Colour green, white, grey, colourless
Hardness 5½-6	Streak white
Specific Gravity 2.9-3.3	Lustre vitreous, silky
Cleavage perfect	Transparency translucent to opaque
Fracture splintery, uneven, brittle/flexible	Crystal system monoclinic

Crystals prismatic, long columnar. Aggregates long columnar, irregularly radiating, as well as massive and coarse grained. Occurs in metamorphic rocks. Used as asbestos.
Amianthus [4] (Byssolite, actinolite asbestos) Fibrous actinolite. Asbestos.
Mountain leather (Mountain cork, mountain wood) Acicular, felted actinolite or chrysotile (p.88).
Nephrite (Beilstein) Microcrystalline, felted actinolite aggregate. Very tough. Occurs as pebbles and in actinolite schists. LOCALITIES: Jordansmühl/Silesia/ Germany, L Baikal region/Russia, China, New Zealand, Wyoming/USA, British Columbia/Canada. Used in prehistoric times for tools, weapons and utensils; cut as jade (p.168)

Tremolite [2] Grammatite
Mineral of the amphibole group (p.52)

Composition Ca$_2$Mg$_5$[OH|Si$_4$O$_{11}$]$_2$	Colour white, grey, greenish
Hardness 5½-6	Streak white
Specific Gravity 2.9-3.1	Lustre vitreous, silky
Cleavage perfect	Transparency translucent
Fracture fibrous, brittle	Crystal system monoclinic

Crystals long prismatic, acicular, long columnar, mostly embedded. Aggregates radiating, fibrous, felted. Occurs in metamorphic rocks. LOCALITIES: Tessin/ Switzerland, Paakila/Finland, near Turia/Italy, Namibia, Edwards/New York, Berkshire County/Connecticut, Orange County/New York/USA. Used as asbestos.

Riebeckite
Mineral of the amphibole group (p.52)

Composition Na$_2$Fe$_4$[OH|Si$_4$O$_{11}$]$_2$	Colour blue, blue-black
Hardness 5-6	Streak blue-grey
Specific Gravity 3.0-3.4	Lustre vitreous, silky
Cleavage perfect	Transparency translucent
Fracture uneven, brittle	Crystal system monoclinic

Crystals long prismatic, very rare. Usually granular or fibrous aggregates. Occurs in quartzites and other metamorphic rocks, frequently in acid igneous rocks. Localities: Schirmeck/Vosges/Germany, Langesund/Norway, Krivoi Rog/Ukraine, Transvaal/South Africa, Rhode Island, Quincy, Massachusetts/USA.
Crocidolite [3] Blue asbestos, riebeckite asbestos. Finely fibrous variety of riebeckite. Elastically flexible, can be easily spun. Silicified crocidolite (falcon's eye, tiger's eye) used in jewellery (p.176).

Asbestos Term for the most finely fibrous minerals of the amphibole group (amianthus, anthophyllite, crocidolite, tremolite) and of the serpentine group. More important economically is the serpentine asbestos, chrysotile (p.88). Asbestos is fire resistant and acid resistant. More recently asbestos dust has been recognised as being cancer-inducing.

1 Actinolite in talc schist, Stubachtal/Austria
2 Tremolite, Campolungo/Ticino/Switzerland
3 Crocidolite, Transvaal/S.Africa
4 Amianthus, Piemont/Italy

Serpentine [1,2]

Composition $Mg_6[OH]_8|Si_4O_{10}]$	*Colour* green, grey, white, yellow
Hardness 2½-4	*Streak* white
Specific Gravity 2.0-2.6	*Lustre* resinous, greasy, silky, dull
Cleavage perfect, separable fibres	*Transparency* translucent to opaque
Fracture conchoidal, splintery	*Crystal system* monoclinic

No crystals known. Aggregates fine grained to compact. Occurs in layers, in veins and joints in serpentinite and marble.

Two structural varieties can be recognised: antigorite and chrysotile.
Antigorite [1] (Scaly serpentine) Compact, finely scaly variety of serpentine.
Chrysotile [2] (Fibrous serpentine) Finely-to coarsely-fibrous variety. Irregularly fibrous to felted aggregates are called (just as is felted actinolite p.86) mountain leather, mountain cork, mountain wood; aggregates with parallel fibres are called chrysotile asbestos.

More varieties are distinguished according to their economic usefulness.
Common serpentine [1] Compact, turbid, speckled. Of no economic value.
Precious serpentine (p.323) Compact green to yellowish. Ornamental stone.
Chrysotile asbestos [2] (Serpentine asbestos, asbestos). Silky lustred, parallel-fibred chrysotile. Used for heat-resistant equipment and clothing, for brake linings, for asbestos cement. LOCALITIES: Russia, Canada, South Africa, Zimbabwe.

Sepiolite [3] Meerschaum

Composition $Mg_4[(OH)_2|Si_6O_{15}]\cdot2H_2O+4H_2O$	*Colour* white, yellow, grey
Hardness 2-2½	*Streak* white
Specific Gravity 2.0	*Lustre* white
Cleavage not determinable	*Transparency* opaque
Fracture conchoidal	*Crystal system* orthorhombic

No crystals. Aggregates earthy, nodular, porous. In the fresh state soapy and soft, hard when dried. Sticks to the tongue. Occurs as concretions in serpentine rocks. Unique economically important deposits in Eskishehir/Turkey. Used for heat and sound insulation, for smoking wares.

Graphite [4]

Composition C	*Colour* dark to pale grey, black
Hardness 1	*Streak* grey to black
Specific Gravity 2.1-2.3	*Lustre* metallic, dull
Cleavage perfect	*Transparency* opaque
Fracture uneven, flexible	*Crystal system* hexagonal

Well-formed crystals rare, hexagonal plates. Aggregates granular, scaly also columnar, earthy to compact. Graphite feels greasy; colour rubs off in the hand. Fire-proof when air is excluded. Occurs in gneisses, schists, marbles. LOCALITIES: Kropfmühl and Pfaffenreuth/Bayerischer Wald/Germany, Bohemia/ Czechoslovakia; Pargas/Finland, New Jersey/USA, Quebec/Canada, Sonora/ Mexico, Madagascar. Used for electrodes, crucibles, lubricants, pencils, as a retarding substance in atomic reactors.

1 Antigorite-serpentine, Snarum/Norway
2 Chrysotile-serpentine, Quebec/Canada
3 Sepiolite, Eskishehir/Turkey
4 Graphite, Trieben/Steiermark/Austria

1
2
3
4

Hedenbergite [1]

Mineral of the pyrocene group (p.48)

Composition CaFe[Si$_2$O$_6$]	*Colour* black, green-black, brown-black
Hardness 5½-6	*Streak* grey-green
Specific Gravity 3.4-3.6	*Lustre* vitreous
Cleavage imperfect	*Transparency* translucent to opaque
Fracture uneven,conchoidal,brittle	*Crystal system* monoclinic

Good crystals rare, prismatic, acicular. Aggregates compactly granular, columnar, radiating. Occurs in calc silicate rock, particularly in skarns and in magnetite deposits. LOCALITIES: Nordmark/Sweden, Elba and Tuscany/Italy, Kazakhstan, Franklin/New Jersey/USA.

Chromediopside [3]

Light emerald-green variety of diopside (p.50). Occurs in calcium-rich metamorphic rocks. LOCALITIES: Outukumpu/Finland, Upper Burma, Madagascar, Namibia. If transparent used as a stone in jewellery.

Fassaite [4]

Mineral of the pyroxene group (p.48). Scientifically considered an aluminium-rich or iron-poor variety of augite.

Composition Ca(Mg,Fe,Al)[(Si,Al)$_2$O$_6$]	*Colour* green
Hardness 6	*Streak* white
Specific Gravity 2.96-3.34	*Lustre* vitreous
Cleavage imperfect	*Transparency* translucent to opaque
Fracture uneven, conchoidal, brittle	*Crystal system* monoclinic

Richly faceted, short prismatic crystals, embedded and growing on surfaces. Aggregates granular and compact. Occurs in calcite- and dolomite-marble. LOCALITIES: Fassatal/S Tyrol/Austria, Vesuvius and Adamello/Italy, Helena/Montana/USA.

Omphacite Ca(Mg,Fe,Al)[(SiAl)$_2$O$_6$]

Mineral of the pyroxene group. Mixed crystals with diopside, jadeite, hedenbergite and aegirine. Chemically, and in its green colour, the same as fassaite, in optical properties similar to diopside. Crystals very rare. Disseminated grains in eclogite. LOCALITIES: Saualpe/Karnten/Austria, Val d'Aosta/Italy, California/USA.

Cordierite [2] Dichroite, iolite

Composition Mg$_2$Al$_3$[AlSi$_5$O$_{18}$]	*Colour* blue, violet, grey, brownish,colourless
Hardness 7-7½	*Streak* white
Specific Gravity 2.50-2.75	*Lustre* vitreous, greasy
Cleavage imperfect	*Transparency* transparent to translucent
Fracture conchoidal, uneven, brittle	*Crystal system* orthorhombic

Crystals rare, embedded or growing on surfaces, usually prismatic. Aggregates massive, disseminated grains, compact. Strong dichroism. Occurs mainly in metamorphic rocks, occasionally in igneous rocks, sporadically in sedimentary rocks. LOCALITIES: Bodenmeis/Bayerischer Wald/Germany, Kragerö/Norway, Falun/Sweden, Orijarvi/Finland, Haddam/Connecticut/USA. Used as a raw material for ceramics.

---

1 Hedenbergite, New South Wales/Australia	3 Chromediopside, Outukumpu/Finland
2 Cordierite Kisko/Finland	4 Fassaite, etched out of calcite, Fassatal/S.Tyrol.

Margarite [1] Calcium mica, pearl mica
Mineral of the mica group (clintonite)

Composition CaAl$_2$[(OH)$_2$|Al$_2$Si$_2$O$_{10}$]	*Colour* white, grey, pink, yellowish
Hardness 4-4½	*Streak* white
Specific Gravity 2.99-3.08	*Lustre* pearly
Cleavage perfect	*Transparency* translucent
Fracture lamellar, brittle	*Crystal system* monoclinic

Well-formed crystals rare. Aggregates granular, lamellar, scaly. Occurs in chlorite- and mica-schists. LOCALITIES: Zillertal/Tyrol/Austria, Pfitschtal/S Tyrol/Italy, St Gotthard/Switzerland, Naxos/Greece, Izmir/Turkey, Hampden County/ Massachusetts and Chester County/Pennsylvania/USA.

Paragonite Sodium mica
Mineral of the mica group similar to margarite. White to greenish aggregates. Occurs in schists.

Kernite [2]

Composition Na$_2$[B$_4$O$_6$(OH)$_2$]·3H$_2$O	*Colour* colourless, white
Hardness 2½	*Streak* white
Specific Gravity 1.91	*Lustre* vitreous
Cleavage perfect	*Transparency* transparent to opaque
Fracture fibrous, splintery, brittle	*Crystal system* monoclinic

Crystals pyramidal, wedge shaped. Aggregates massive, sparry, fibrous. Occurs in veins as contact metamorphic alteration products. LOCALITIES: Kern County/California/USA, Tincalayu/ Argentina, Turkey. Important boron mineral.

Wollastonite [3]

Composition Ca$_3$[Si$_3$O$_9$]	*Colour* colourless, white, grey, lightly coloured
Hardness 4½-5	*Streak* white
Specific Gravity 2.78-2.91	*Lustre* vitreous, pearly, silky
Cleavage perfect	*Transparency* transparent to translucent
Fracture splintery	*Crystal system* triclinic and monoclinic

Good crystals rare, mostly thick tabular, embedded. Aggregates radiating, laminated, tabular. Occurs in calcareous and calcsilicate rocks. LOCALITIES: Auerbach/Hessen/Germany, Pargas/Finland, Santa Fé/Mexico, California/USA. Used for welding rods, heat-resistant ceramics, mineral fibres (rock wool).

Okenite [4]

Composition CaH$_2$[Si$_2$O$_6$]·H$_2$O	*Colour* white, yellowish, bluish
Hardness 5	*Streak* white
Specific Gravity 2.28-2.33	*Lustre* pearly
Cleavage perfect	*Transparency* transparent to translucent
Fracture uneven	*Crystal system* triclinic

Crystals rare, flat-leaf-shaped. Usually massive, very finely fibrous aggregates. Occurs (as a contact mineral) in basalts. LOCALITIES: Antrim/Ireland, Faeroes, Disko Island/Greenland, Poona/India, Montana/USA.

1 Margarite, Chester/Massachusetts/USA
2 Kernite, Kern County/California/USA
3 Wollastonite, Bergstrasse/Hessen/Germany
4 Acicular okenite on gyrolite, Poona/India

1
2
3
4

ORE-FORMING MINERALS

Ore-forming minerals are minerals from which metals can be obtained by a smelting process. They are only of use economically if they appear in large quantities as ore in deposits.

Ore In economic geology the term "ore" is used for a mineral assemblage with useful metal content. Structurally it has the character of a rock. In some cases other raw materials needed in technology are designated as ore even when they lack a metallic character.

In petrology, on the other hand, all metallic constituents of a rock are called ore. In the science of ore deposits there is a strict distinction made between ore minerals (i.e. ore-forming minerals) and the actual ores, which are always composed of several minerals.

Many old German mineral names coined by miners end in - *erz* (ore), e.g. chromeisenerz (chromite), federerz (jamesonite feather ore), rotbleierz (crocoite), zinnerz (cassiterite). This nomenclature, which is in no way consistent, often leads to quite false assumptions because according to modern definitions not all such minerals are in fact constituents of ores and hence of economic value.

Mineral deposit Natural accumulation of minerals or mineral aggregates which are usable and worth extracting.

Names of ore minerals The names of ore minerals relate to metal content, colour, striking characteristics and other factors. Many terms were coined by miners centuries ago. Old mining practice also explains the sub-division of sulphide minerals into blendes (German Silberblende, Zinkblende – silver blende, sphalerite), fahle (Antimonfahlerz – tetrahedrite), glanze (Bleiglanz, Kupferglanz – galena, chalcocite) and kiese, (Maignetkies, Schwefelkies – pyrrhotite, pyrite).

Spelling of the names of ores The way in which the names of ores, ore minerals and other metallic minerals are spelt is often misleading. In order to avoid confusing ores with German mineral names which end with *-erz* (ore) eg. Zinnerz (tin ore) in the descriptions which follow, the actual ores i.e. the mineral accumulations are identified by the use of a hyphen eg. zinn-erz. Consequently, if written without a hyphen, zinnerz is the ore mineral which is also called zinnstein or cassiterite. Zinn-erz on the other hand is a tin-bearing rock, or ore in the sense used in economic geology.

Classification of ore minerals Ore minerals are usually classified according to the metal content. If a mineral includes several metals in its chemical composition it can accordingly be allocated to different types of metal. Classifying metals and metal compounds into groups is treated in very different ways in the technological, industrial or economic sphere.

In this book the ore minerals are allocated to the following metal groups: precious metals, ferrous metals (as an umbrella term for iron and for elements for improving the quality of steel) and non-ferrous metals (including both non-ferrous metals and light metals). Sulphur-bearing minerals are included as a further group.

Terrace-like ore extraction on the Erzberg in Eisenerz/Steiermark/Austria.

ORE DEPOSITS

Many elements, including therefore metals, are not workable when evenly distributed in the Earth's crust. They are only worth extracting when they accumulate in certain zones or complexes. Such an accumulation of metal-bearing minerals or mineral aggregates is called ore, its appearance in the Earth's crust is called an ore deposit.

According to the way in which they originate we distinguish between magmatic, sedimentary and metamorphic deposits.

MAGMATIC DEPOSITS

Magmatic deposits have developed from molten rock in the depths of the earth. As this molten rock cools down the originally homogeneous material separates and crystallises dependent upon the prevailing temperature. We distinguish between liquid-magmatic, pegmatitic, pneumatolytic and hydrothermal deposits.

Liquid-magmatic deposits Liquid-magmatic deposits occur in the initial phase of cooling at temperatures between 1200 and 600°C, mainly in basic melts. Both the minerals which crystallised out first and the immiscible partial melts sink through the remaining melt to the bottom of the magma body as a result of gravity.

The ore minerals which form are native metals (platinum), sulphides (pyrrhotite, chalcopyrite, pentlandite), and oxides (magnetite, chromite, ilmenite). Significant liquid-magmatic deposits are to be found in Kiruna/Sweden, near Nižnij Tagil/Urals/Russia, Sudbury/Ontario/Canada, and the Bushveld/Transvaal/South Africa.

Pegmatitic deposits At temperatures of 600-500°C, coarsely crystalline rock bodies, known as pegmatites, form from silica-rich residual magma combining with enriched, gaseous, easily volatile constituents. They are found on the margins of or in cavities in plutons and as fissure fillings in veins.
Typical ore minerals include beryl, lepidolite and zinnwaldite, zircon and sphene, cassiterite, wolframite and molybdenite.

The pegmatite body in Hagendorf/Oberpfalz/Germany is one of the largest formations of its kind in the whole of Europe.

Pneumatolytic deposits Residual gas mixtures from a magma body (most usually a granite pluton) which has already crystallised out to a large extent, penetrate at temperatures of 500-400°C into fissures in the adjacent rock and into joints in the already much cooled-down pluton, crystallise out and form veins and also impregnations if the adjacent rock is very porous.

Characteristic representative ores are cassiterite, zinnwaldite and wolframite, also molybdenite and pyrite.

The tin deposits of the Erzgebirge of Saxony/Germany and Bohemia/Czechoslovakia, of Malaysia and Bolivia, the tungsten deposits of Korea, Burma and Indonesia and finally the molybdenum deposit of Climax/Colorado/USA belong to this type of formation.
Contact-pneumatolytic replacement deposits, a variety of pneumatolytic deposits, develop from a reaction of the hot gases with the adjacent rock, during which the pre-existing minerals are replaced by others (e.g. wolframite and scheelite).

Hydrothermal deposits At temperatures of 400-0°C, as a result of a lowering of temperature and pressure, dissolved substances precipitate in warm waters and form metal concentrations known as hydrothermal deposits.

According to the way in which they develop we distinguish between hydrothermalore veins, hydrothermal replacement deposits (caused by the exchange of minerals, so-called metasomatism) and hydrothermal impregnations. The number of hydrothermally formed deposits of ore minerals and of their parageneses is very large. Characteristic of these are metal accumulations of antimony, lead, gold, cobalt, copper, mercury, silver and zinc.

Among hydrothermally-formed deposits are the siderite ores of Siegerland/North Rhine Westphalia/Germany, the Erzberg in Steiermark/Austria and Bingham/Utah/USA as well as Tsumeb/Namibia and Trepca/Yugoslavia.

Volcanic deposits The deposits known as magmatic are for the most part plutonic, that is to say they are related to a magma body formed in the depths of the Earth. The converse of these are the formations formed in association with volcanic rocks. However, these may also occasionally be transitional both to plutonic and to sedimentary deposits.

To the volcanic deposits belong sub-volcanic ones, i.e. formations deep in volcanoes, volcanic exhalations both submarine and on the surface of the Earth, as well as post-volcanic thermals, the hot springs. Characteristic ore minerals are gold and silver, hematite and pyrite, as well as sulphur. One of the most important deposits in the world, the Comstock-Lode in Nevada/USA is of sub-volcanic origin, the iron deposit of the Lahn-Dill-Revier in Hessen/Germany is of submarine-volcanic origin.

SEDIMENTARY DEPOSITS

Sedimentary deposits originate from the weathering of rocks, through the agency of water or through chemical processes under certain climatic conditions. The temperature range within which sedimentary ore formation takes place extends from a few degrees below freezing point up to about 70°C.

Placer and clastic deposits Under the effects of water and wind metallic minerals become enriched in sands and gravels to form metal concentrations, known as placer or alluvial deposits; this occurs because of their resistance to weathering and their high density. According to the mineral present we distinguish between chromite, gold, ilmenite, cassiterite, magnetite, monazite and platinum placer deposits.

There are significant gold alluvial deposits in the upper Lena/Russia. The gold deposits of the Witwatersrand near Johannesburg/South Africa are lithified alluvial deposits. Beach placer deposits, caused by currents and the pounding of the waves are to be found in India, Brazil and Carolina/USA. The clastic deposit at Peine-Ilsede/Lower Saxony/Germany was formed (over a hundred million years ago) in a beach or littoral zone. Up to a hundred years ago gold alluvial deposits were also worked in rivers in Europe.

Deposits in oxidation and reducing zones The uppermost parts of ore bodies which crop out on the surface are subjected to weathering. Here an oxidation zone forms which is strongly enriched with iron but is poor in precious metals: miners call this "iron hat" or "gossan". Gossan ores are porous, corroded on the surface and of a brown to black colour. Sometimes green malachite and deep-blue azurite indicate an oxidation zone. Because they were easily accessible these deposits were much worked in earlier times, and as a result they have almost entirely disappeared.

The compounds which are released in the oxidation zone are carried down by percolating water into the ground water and precipitated there. This area of mineral enrichment, known as a reducing zone, contains in particular sulphide ores of copper (chalcocite, covellite, chalcopyrite, bornite), of silver (acanthite) and also native copper, silver and gold.

Weathering deposits

Although all sedimentary deposits have some sort of connection with weathering processes, weathering deposits (in the narrower sense of the term) are only those mineral accumulations which reveal a clear dependency on certain climates. In dry zones (with an arid climate) heavy metal combinations of copper, cobalt, lead, vanadium and uranium are precipitated. In damp, humid climatic areas bauxites and limonites develop, the latter occasionally appearing in the form of pisolitic limonite and as bog iron ore.

Marine deposits

By this term we do not mean deposits which are nowadays present in the oceans but rather the metal accumulations which are actually formed in the sea. Oolitic iron-ores develop in shallow sea areas from iron-bearing solutions emanating from the mainland. The iron compounds which are precipitated in an electrolytic process by sea-water settle in shell-like layers around some kind of core and build up little spheres ranging from half a millimetre to pea size, which then finally collect on the sea floor. The minette-ores of Lorraine/Luxembourg are examples of this type of oolite-formation [No. 4, p.295]. There are significant deposits in Newfoundland/Canada, in Alabama/USA, and on the Kertsch peninsula/Russia. Oolitic manganese ores are to be found in the Ukraine and in the Caucasus. The mineral-rich Mansfeld Kupferschiefer deposits in the foothills of the Harz mountains in Germany have developed by a similar process of precipitation of heavy metal compounds in the sea.

METAMORPHIC DEPOSITS

No new deposits develop through metamorphism (p.304). All that can happen is that accumulations of igneous or sedimentary ores which are already present are altered by the formation of new minerals, through dissolution and coarsening of the constituent minerals as well as the structure of the ores themselves.

This kind of metamorphic reconstruction has taken place in the copper deposits of Outukumpu/Finland, the skarn-ores in Central Sweden, the ore deposits of Krivoi Rog/Ukraine, the itabirite ores of Brazil, and the taconite ores of the Lake Superior region/USA.

FORMS OF ORE BODIES

Ore bodies have extremely varied shapes, depending on the manner in which they have evolved, the way they have been built up and their structure.

Seam Platy ore accumulation of no great thickness, but of considerable extent in length and breadth. They are always of sedimentary origin and usually oriented parallel to the strata of the Earth's crust. The originally horizontal layering can be disturbed by mountain building processes.

Bed An ore body which has a relatively large thickness in relation to its surface extent.

Vein (German: "Gang") Fissure which is tectonically broken open and filled up with ores. The content of the vein is always younger than the adjacent rock. In

German vernacular mining language the term "Ader" (literally: vein in a body) is used only for very small veins. An array of veins is known as a vein system.

Lens Ore body which tapers towards the outer edge in the manner of a lens.

Streak Not very large ore body which is elongated and has a recognisable banded structure.

Pocket Small, irregularly shaped ore body in exotic foreign surroundings.

Stock Short, thick ore vein with irregular boundaries.

Stock work Massive ore body with small ore veins running through it in net-like fashion, without any clear delimitation from the adjacent rock.

Impregnation Diffusely distributed ore in the pores of a rock.

Placer Accumulation of heavy and resistant minerals in sands and gravels. A distinction is made between fluvial, marine and beach placers according to location or mode of origin.

CUT-OFF GRADE OF ORE DEPOSITS

The cut-off grade of an ore deposit is dependent on many factors, such as the composition of the ore, the total quantity available, mining possibilities, efficiency of processing the ore, transport situation, investment costs and market situation. It can change in the course of time. Thus old slag heaps are nowadays in some cases being worked because of new processing methods and because the selling prices of raw materials have risen.

  The object in modern working is to extract at a profit as many as possible of the various minerals contained in an ore. Usually the raw ore mined is used to prepare ore concentrates which can then be transported for smelting.

The following table (after G. Wagner, 1960) shows how the cut-off grade of a deposit is dependent on the amount of enriched metal. By its very nature such a summary can only be a rough schematic synopsis.

Cut-off grade of ore deposits

Metal	Average abundance in Earth's crust		Minimum exploitable grade		Concentration factor
	g/t	%			
Aluminium	81,300	8.13	30	%	3.7
Iron	50,000	5.00	25	%	5
Manganese	1,000	0.10	35	%	350
Chromium	200	0.02	30	%	1500
Nickel	80	0.008	1.5	%	188
Zinc	80	0.008	4	%	500
Copper	70	0.007	1	%	140
Tin	40	0.004	1	%	250
Lead	16	0.0016	4	%	2500
Silver	0.1	0.00001	500	g/t	5000
Gold	0.005	0.0000005	5	g/t	1000

MINERALS OF PRECIOUS METAL ORES

Silver, gold, and platinum ore minerals belong to this group

Native silver [2]

Composition Ag	*Colour* white, grey, brownish, tending to black
Hardness 2½-3	*Streak* white
Specific Gravity 9.6-12	*Lustre* metallic
Cleavage none	*Transparency* translucent to opaque
Fracture hackly, ductile	*Crystal system* cubic

Crystals cubic, rare. Mostly compact masses, lumps, dendritic, filiform. Occurs on joints and in druses, occasionally in placer deposits. LOCALITIES: Kongsberg/ Norway, Joachimstal/Czechoslovakia, Colorado/USA, Cobalt/Canada, Huanchaca/ Bolivia, Broken Hill/Australia. Silver is used in metallurgy, electronics, the photographic industry, for coins and for jewellery.

Proustite [1] Light-red silver ore

Composition Ag$_3$AsS$_3$	*Colour* cinnabar red
Hardness 2½	*Streak* cinnabar red
Specific Gravity 5.57	*Lustre* adamantine
Cleavage perfect	*Transparency* translucent to opaque
Fracture conchoidal, brittle	*Crystal system* trigonal

Crystals prismatic, pyramidal. Aggregates dendritic, massive, as encrustations. Darkens very quickly if exposed to strong light. Occurs in ore deposits. LOCALITIES: Wittichen/Schwarzwald/Germany, St Marie aux Mines/Alsace/France, Cobalt/Canada, Chanarcillo/Chile, Colorado and Arizona/USA. Important silver ore.

Pyrargyrite [3,5] Dark-red silver ore Ag$_3$SbS$_3$

Similar to proustite. Differences; pyrargyrite harder (2½-3), specific gravity higher (5.85). Cleavage imperfect, colour dark-red, streak cherry-red.

Argentite [4,6] Silver glance

Composition AgS	*Colour* lead grey to black
Hardness 2-2½	*Streak* grey
Specific Gravity 7.2-7.4	*Lustre* metallic tending to dull
Cleavage imperfect	*Transparency* opaque
Fracture conchoidal, uneven	*Crystal system* cubic and monoclinic

Two modifications: cubic argentite *sensu stricto* and monoclinic acanthite. Argentite crystals are cubic. Acanthite crystals prismatic, tabular. Aggregates of both modifications are massive, filiform and platy. Occur in vein deposits. LOCALITIES: Norway, Mexico, Utah/USA. Important silver ore.

Silver glance Comprehensive term for argentite and acanthite or synonym for argentite.
Black silver Sooty encrustation on argentite

---

1 Proustite, Erzgebirge/Saxony/Germany
2 Native silver, Batopilas/Mexico
3 Pyrargyrite, Quiruvilca/Peru
4 Argentite, Oberschlema/Erzgebirge/ Saxony/
Germany
5 Dark red silver ore, Sonora/Mexico
6 Argentite and calcite,
Pfibram/Bohemia/Czechoslovakia

The photographs show a magnification of up to about 50% compared with the originals.

Sperrylite [1]

Composition PtAs$_2$	*Colour* tin white
Hardness 6-7	*Streak* grey-black
Specific Gravity 10.58	*Lustre* metallic
Cleavage imperfect	*Transparency* opaque
Fracture conchoidal, brittle	*Crystal system* cubic

Only small crystals, embedded. Very important platinum mineral.

Native platinum [2] Pt
Crystals very rare, mostly irregular grains. Colour and streak steel grey to silver-white. Specific gravity 14-19. Hardness 4-4½. Metallic lustre.

Sylvanite [3] Graphic ore AuAgTe$_4$
Crystals small, disseminated, flat, reticulated, skeletal. Colour and streak dark grey with yellowish tinge. Specific gravity 8.0-8.3, hardness 1½-2, metallic lustre. Important gold-silver-telluride.

Native gold [4,5] Au
Crystals rare, mostly compact masses, grains, nuggets, sheet-like. Colour and streak golden to brassy yellow. Specific gravity 15.5-19.3. Hardness 2½-3. Most important ore of gold. Important producers: South Africa, Russia, Canada.

Nugget [4,2] Gold or platinum lumps in placer deposits.
Mountain gold Gold from primary deposits, usually with a silver content.
Placer gold Gold from placer deposits i.e. in secondary deposits.
Electrum Gold with a silver content of 15-50%.

Petzite [6] Ag$_3$AuTe$_2$
No crystals, always massive. Colour steel-grey to iron black. Streak grey. Specific gravity 8.7-9.2. Hardness 2½-3. Rare silver and gold ore.

Stephanite [7] 5Ag$_2$S·Sb$_2$S$_3$
Short prismatic or thick tabular crystals, rarely massive. Colour lead grey to black. Streak black. Specific gravity 6.2-6.4. Hardness 2-2½. Metallic lustre; dull if tarnished. Locally important silver ore.

Chlorargyrite [8] Cerargyrite, silver chloride, horn silver AgCl
Crystals small, rare. Usually hornlike masses; colourless, when held against the light almost brownish to black. Streak white. When fresh adamantine lustre but later waxy and dull. Specific gravity 5.5-5.6. Hardness 1½-2. Locally important ore of silver.

Polybasite [9] (AgCu)$_{16}$·Sb$_2$S$_{11}$
Short prismatic, tabular crystals, also compact masses. Colour grey black, deep red in thin slivers, streak black to deep red. Specific gravity 6.0-6.2. Hardness 1½-2. Metallic lustre. Locally important ore of silver.

---

1 Sperrylite, tin white disseminated grains, Sudbury/Ontario/Canada
2 Platinum nugget, Urals
3 Sylvanite, tarnished grey and yellow, USA
4 Gold nugget, Tipuani/Bolivia
5 Gold on quartz, Zimbabwe

6 Petzite (grey) with gold, Colorado/USA
7 Stephanite with native silver, Aue/Saxony/Germany
8 Chlorargyrite (brown) with malachite, USA
9 Polybasite with pyrite, Sonora/Mexico

The illustrations are enlarged about 50% compared with the originals.

MINERALS OF IRON ORES

To this group belong the ore minerals of iron. We also include in the group those minerals whose alloying metals improve the quality of iron – the so called iron-improvers.

IRON ORE MINERALS

Chief representatives are chamosite, goethite, hematite, lepidocrocite, magnetite, siderite, thuringite. The uses of iron are well known.

Magnetite [1] Magnetic iron ore

Composition Fe_3O_4	Colour iron black
Hardness 5½	Streak black
Specific Gravity 5.2	Lustre metallic, dull
Cleavage imperfect	Transparency opaque
Fracture conchoidal, brittle	Crystal system cubic

Crystals embedded and surface growing, octahedron, rhombdodecahedron. Compact, disseminated, granular to dense aggregates. Occurs as accessory constituent in many rocks. Discrete intra-magmatic and sedimentary deposits. LOCALITIES: Lahn- Dill area/Hessen/Germany, Lothringen/France, Kirunavaare, Gellivaara, Grangesberg, Taberg/Sweden, Otanmäki/Finland, Transvaal/South Africa, Minnesota, Wyoming/USA, Urals/Russia. Important and most widespread iron ore.

Hematite [2-4]

Composition Fe_2O_3	Colour grey-black, red-brown, tarnishes
Hardness 6-6½	Streak red to red-brown
Specific Gravity 5.2-5.3	Lustre metallic, dull
Cleavage none	Transparency opaque
Fracture conchoidal, brittle	Crystal system trigonal

Crystals embedded and surface growing, dipyramidal, cuboid, rhombohedral, tabular. Aggregates granular, densely scaly, radiating, earthy. Occurs as an accessory constituent in many rocks. Individual deposits may be intramagmatic, sedimentary, metamorphic. Oolites [No. 4, p.295], itabirites and micaceous hematite are "ferrolites". LOCALITIES: Lahn-Dill area/Germany, Kirunavaare, Grängesberg/Sweden, Elba/Italy, Krivoi Rog, Urals/Russia, Minas Gerais/Brazil, Minnesota/USA, Cumbria/England. Very important ore of iron.

Iron glance [2] (Specularite) Coarsely crystalline hematite, grey black, metallic lustre.
Hematite rose [3] Specularite variety with rosette-like crystal plates.
Micaceous iron Specularite variety in thin lamellar aggregates.
Red iron ore Dense hematite variety, red to red brown, usually without lustre.
Kidney ore [4] Red iron ore with smooth, globular, upper surface.
Bloodstone Dense red iron ore variety. Occasionally used in jewellery.
Reddle Earthy, powdery, red iron ore variety. A colouring material.

1 Magnetite in chlorite schist, Tyrol/Austria
2 Hematite, Rio Marina/Elbe/Italy
3 Hematite rose, Fibbia/Ticcino/Switzerland
4 Kidney ore, Cumberland, England

Limonite [1,2] Brown iron ore

A mixture of different minerals, predominantly goethite. Occurs in almost all soils, in the oxidation zones of ore deposits. LOCALITIES: Salzgitter/L. Saxony/ Germany, Lothringen/France, Luxembourg, Lincolnshire/England, Canada. Important iron ore.

Brown iron ore Synonym for limonite or for formless, powdery, formation.

Brown hematite [1] Reniform variety of limonite; smooth, black upper surface.

Brown oolitic iron Fish-roe-like little spheres of limonite.

Pisolitic iron ore Bean sized limonite concretions in cavities in limestone.

Bog iron ore Structureless, often cellular, limonite masses with encrusted plant remains.

Lake ore Limonite segregations in shallow lakes, similar to bog iron ore.

Ochre Yellow-brown limonite masses with different mixtures.

Goethite [4] Needle iron ore

Composition FeO(OH)	*Colour* black, brown, yellowish
Hardness 5-5½	*Streak* brown
Specific Gravity 3.8-4.3	*Lustre* adamantine, silky, dull
Cleavage perfect	*Transparency* translucent to opaque
Fracture uneven, brittle	*Crystal system* orthorhombic

Crystals small, prismatic, acicular. Radiating aggregates, compact, dense, powdery. Occurs in limonite. For localities and uses see limonite.

Needle iron ore Synonym for goethite or the name for surface-growing goethite.

Przibramite [4] Brown globular aggregates with short goethite needles.

Lepidocrocite Rubinglimmer (ruby mica)

Properties similar to goethite. Occurs also in common with limonite.

Siderite [3] Iron spar, sparry ironstone

Composition FeCO₃	*Colour* yellowish, brown, black, tarnishes
Hardness 4-4½	*Streak* white, brown, black
Specific Gravity 3.7-3.9	*Lustre* vitreous, pearly
Cleavage perfect	*Transparency* translucent to opaque
Fracture conchoidal, brittle	*Crystal system* trigonal

Rhombohedral crystals. Aggregates compact, sparry, fine grained, oolitic. Occurs in veins and beds. LOCALITIES: Siegerland/Germany, Erzberg/Steiermark, Hüttenberg/Karnten/Austria, Lothringen/France, Bilbao/Spain, Cornwall/England, Connecticut/USA. Important iron ore.

Chamosite [5]

Composition (Fe,Mg,Al)₆[(OH)₂|(Si,Al)₄O₁₀]	*Colour* green-grey to black
Hardness 2-3	*Streak* green-grey
Specific Gravity 3.0-3.4	*Lustre* vitreous, dull
Cleavage very perfect	*Transparency* opaque
Fracture uneven	*Crystal system* monoclinic

Granular, dense, oolitic masses. Occurs in iron ores. LOCALITIES: Uri/Switzerland, Czechoslovakia, Lothringen, Brittany/France, Northampton/England. Important iron ore.

---

1 Brown hematite, Waldsassen, Oberpfalz/Germany
2 Limonite, Auerbach/Oberpfalz/Germany
3 Siderite, Eisenerz/Steiermark/Austria

4 Przibramite-goethite, San Antonio/Chihuahua/Mexico
5 Chamosite, Nucic/Bohemia/Czechoslovakia

MANGANESE ORE MINERALS

Principal members of the group are hausmannite, manganite, psilomelane, pyrolusite, rhodochrosite, rhodonite. Manganese is used for ferromanganese and spiegeleisen (manganese alloy with iron).

Pyrolusite [1]

Composition MnO_2	*Colour* iron grey to dark grey
Hardness crystals 6½, massive 2-6	*Streak* black
Specific Gravity 4.5-5.0	*Lustre* metallic, dull
Cleavage perfect	*Transparency* opaque
Fracture uneven, brittle	*Crystal system* tetragonal

Crystals prismatic, rare and small. Usually botryoidal, globular, radiating aggregates, also earthy and oolitic masses. Usually causes slight discoloration when handled. Occurs in sedimentary deposits on its own or as an accessory in other manganese deposits. LOCALITIES: Siegerland, Hunsruck/Germany, Ukraine, Minas Gerais/Brazil, Arkansas/USA, Cornwall/England. Important manganese ore.

Weichmangenerz (soft manganese ore) German synonym for pyrolusite or term for earthy deposit of pyrolusite. Also the name for ore minerals similar to pyrolusite.
Polianite Obsolete name for the crystalline form of pyrolusite.
Wad [2] Earthy to powdery variety of pyrolusite.

Manganese nodules [3]
Nodules of 2-5cm diameter grown concentrically around a core and distributed over the ocean floor at depths of 4000-6000m. They are ore nodules with a manganese content of up to 40% (hence the name). Copper, nickel, cobalt, and zinc are present in amounts from 0.2-1.0%.

Psilomelane [4] Hard manganese ore

Composition $(Ba,H_2O)_2Mn_5O_{10}$	*Colour* black, black-brown
Hardness 4-6	*Streak* black, brown
Specific Gravity 4.7	*Lustre* metallic, dull
Cleavage none	*Transparency* opaque
Fracture uneven, brittle	*Crystal system* monoclinic

Crystals unknown. Fine grained, dense masses, radiating, also earthy. Occurs in the oxidation zone of manganese-bearing ore deposits. LOCALITIES: Black Forest, Saxony/Germany, Caucasus, Ukraine, Cornwall/England, Michigan/USA. Important manganese ore. The so-called dendrites [No. 3, p.281] are very-finely-crystalline psilomelane. Psilomelane is rarer than hitherto supposed. Other manganese minerals such as coronadite, hollandite and cryptomelane have, of late, become more important than psilomelane.

Black globular ore [4] Knobbly, botryoidal, reniform and radiating aggregates of psilomelane. Smooth surfaces which appear polished.
Hard manganese ore Synonym for psilomelane or collective term for manganese minerals with a similar composition to psilomelane.
Manganomelane Group name for microcrystalline manganese minerals which so far in mining have been called hard manganese ore. Occasionally also used as a synonym for psilomelane.

---

1 Pyrolusite, California/USA
2 Wad, Bieber near Giessen/Hessen/Germany
3 Manganese nodules, Pacific at 4000m depth
4 Psilomelane, Raubach/Westerwald/Germany

Rhodochrosite [1,2] Manganese spar, Himbeerspat (raspberry spar)

Composition MnCO₃	*Colour* rose red, brown, black
Hardness 3½-4	*Streak* white
Specific Gravity 3.3-3.6	*Lustre* vitreous
Cleavage perfect	*Transparency* translucent
Fracture uneven, brittle	*Crystal system* trigonal

Rhombohedral crystals, rare and mostly small, frequently saddle shaped, curved, growing into druses. Aggregates compactly granular, sparry, dense, radiating, globular, also as coatings and crusts. Occurs in vein deposits in stocks and layered sedimentary rocks. LOCALITIES: Elbingerode/Harz/Germany, Siebenbürgen/ Romania, Las Cabesses/Pyrenees/France, Huelva/Spain, Cripple Creek/Colorado/ USA, Cornwall/England. Locally important manganese ore. Fine coloured rose-red forms [1] with light and dark wavy layers are used as jewellery and ornamental stones. Most important occurrence is in Argentina near San Luis, east of Mendoza where since the 13th Century stalagmitic rhodochrosite has developed in the abandoned silver mines of the Incas.

Manganite [3]

Composition MnOOH	*Colour* brown black, grey
Hardness 4	*Streak* dark brown, black
Specific Gravity 4.3-4.4	*Lustre* metallic
Cleavage perfect	*Transparency* translucent to opaque
Fracture uneven, brittle	*Crystal system* monoclinic

Long prismatic crystals with vertical parallel striations, frequently cruciform twinned. Aggregates radially- and chaotically-radiating, also oolitic, rarely granular. When fresh the crystals and aggregates are brown/black and show a dark brown streak; when weathered (that is when altered to pyrolusite) the colour is steel grey and the streak black. Occurs in manganese ore veins in igneous rocks and also in other deposits. LOCALITIES: Ilfeld/Harz/Germany, Cornwall/England, Nickopol/Ukraine, Negauree/Michigan/USA. Because of its high manganese content of more than 60% manganite is an important ore of manganese. Since the occurrences, however, are quantitatively restricted, manganite is only of subordinate importance nowadays.

Hausmannite [4]

Composition Mn₃O₄	*Colour* iron black, brownish tinge
Hardness 5½	*Streak* reddish brown
Specific Gravity 4.7-4.8	*Lustre* metallic
Cleavage perfect	*Transparency* opaque
Fracture uneven, brittle	*Crystal system* tetragonal

Crystals dipyramidal, often horizontally striated, frequently twinned, usually encrusting. Aggregates compactly granular to fine grained dense, sparry. Occurs in manganese ore deposits as medium constituent; does not occur in an ore body on its own. LOCALITIES: Ilfeld/Harz/Germany, Langban/Sweden, Urals/Russia, Batesville/Arkansas/USA. Since not very widespread of no importance economically.

MOLYBDENUM ORE MINERALS

Molybdenite, molybdite, ferrimolybdite, powellite and wulfenite belong to the molybdenum ore minerals group. Molybdenum is used for special steels in order to improve their properties (in particular resistance to corrosion, toughness and strength when heated). It is further used in the chemical industry, in electronics and as a lubricant at high temperatures.

Molybdenite [1,3] Molybdenum glance

Composition MoS_2	*Colour* lead grey with violet tinge
Hardness 1-1½	*Streak* dark grey, leek-green when rubbed
Specific Gravity 4.7-4.8	*Lustre* metallic
Cleavage very perfect	*Transparency* opaque
Fracture inelastically flexible	*Crystal system* hexagonal

Six-sided, flat crystals are rare and generally not well-formed. Aggregates curved lamellar to scaly, occasionally dense. Feels greasy, rubs off on the fingers. Occurs disseminated and in veins, particularly in granitic rocks. Accessory constituent in many ore deposits. Rarely in very large quantities. LOCALITIES: Moss/Norway, Cornwall/England, British Columbia/Canada, Climax/Colorado/USA, Queensland/Australia. Most important molybdenum ore.

Molybdenum ochre [2]

Molybdenum ochre is in part used as a synonym for molybdite, but in part as the collective term for a series of weathering products of molybdenum minerals, particularly of molybdite and ferrimolybdite.

Molybdite

Composition MoO_3	*Colour* greenish yellow, orange, brown
Hardness 2	*Streak* yellowish, brownish
Specific Gravity 4.0-4.5	*Lustre* silky, dull
Cleavage imperfect	*Transparency* opaque
Fracture uneven	*Crystal system* orthorhombic

Microcrystalline aggregates, disseminated, fibrous, crusts. Occurs in quartz with molybdenite. LOCALITIES: Buena Vista, Climax/Colorado/USA.

Wulfenite [4] Yellow lead ore

Composition $PbMoO_4$	*Colour* yellow-orange, grey, colourless
Hardness 3	*Streak* white
Specific Gravity 6.7-6.9	*Lustre* resinous, adamantine
Cleavage imperfect	*Transparency* transparent to translucent
Fracture uneven, conchoidal, brittle	*Crystal system* tetragonal

Crystals usually tabular but also pyramidal and short columnar, mostly encrusting lead ore. Aggregates compact, dense, rare, forms crystalline crusts, cellular-cavernous masses. Occurs in oxidation zones of lead ore deposits. LOCALITIES: Bleiberg/Kärnten/Austria, Mežica/Yugoslavia, Pribram/Czechoslovakia, Tsumeb/Namibia, Utah, Arizona/USA. Locally important molybdenum ore.

1 Molybdenite in quartz Nevada/USA
2 Molybdenum ochre on quartz, Norway

3 Molybdenite on quartz, Australia
4 Wulfenite, Mežica/Yugoslavia

NICKEL ORE MINERALS

The most important minerals are chloanthite, garnierite, niccolite and pentlandite. Nickel is used in the manufacture of stainless steel, for alloying with iron and non-ferrous metals, for nickel plating and as a catalyst.

Chloanthite [1]

Composition $(Ni,Co)As_3$	*Colour* tin white, steel grey, dark grey
Hardness 5½	*Streak* grey-black
Specific Gravity 6.4-6.6	*Lustre* metallic
Cleavage none	*Transparency* opaque
Fracture uneven, brittle	*Crystal system* cubic

Cubic crystals. Aggregates compact, dense, disseminated, reniform, green tarnish. Occurs in copper-nickel deposits. LOCALITIES: Erzgebirge, Wittichen/Schwarzwald/ Germany, Dauphiné/France, Morocco, Cobalt/Canada, Connecticut/USA, Cornwall/England. Important nickel ore.

Pentlandite [2] Iron nickel sulphide

Composition $(Ni,Fe)_9S_8$	*Colour* bronze yellow, tobacco brown
Hardness 3½-4	*Streak* black
Specific Gravity 4.6-5.0	*Lustre* metallic
Cleavage perfect	*Transparency* opaque
Fracture conchoidal, brittle	*Crystal system* cubic

Crystals unknown. Small bodies in magnetite deposits, as accessory constituents in basic plutonic rocks. LOCALITIES: Sudbury/Ontario/Canada, Norilsk/Siberia, Transvaal/South Africa. Most important nickel ore.

Niccolite [3] red nickel sulphide, kupfernickel, nickeline

Composition NiAs	*Colour* copper red
Hardness 5-5½	*Streak* brown black
Specific Gravity 7.5-7.8	*Lustre* metallic, tarnishing dull
Cleavage imperfect	*Transparency* opaque
Fracture conchoidal, brittle	*Crystal system* hexagonal

Crystals tabular, pyramidal. Compact masses, reniform-botryoidal. Frequently encrusted with greenish annabergite. Occurs in vein mineral deposits. LOCALITIES: Schwarzwald, Ergebirge/Germany, Ontario/Canada, Colorado/USA. Important nickel ore.

Garnierite [4]

Composition $(Ni,Mg)_6[(OH)_8|Si_4O_{10}]$	*Colour* yellow-green, blue-green
Hardness 2-4	*Streak* light green
Specific Gravity 2.2-2.7	*Lustre* greasy
Cleavage none	*Transparency* opaque
Fracture conchoidal, sharp-edged	*Crystal system* monoclinic

Crystals unknown. Dense, amorphous aggregates. Product of tropical weathering of ultrabasic igneous rocks and serpentinites. LOCALITIES: Cuba, Brazil, SE Asia, Oregon/USA. Important nickel ore.

---

1 Chloanthite, Schneeberg/Saxony/Germany
2 Pentlandite, Sudbury/Ontario/Canada

3 Niccolite, St. Joachimsthal/Erzgebize/ Czechoslovakia
4 Garnierite, Riddle/Oregon/USA

TUNGSTEN ORE MINERALS

Wolframite and scheelite belong here. Important metal for improving the quality of steel.

Wolframite [1]

Composition (Fe,Mn)WO$_4$	*Colour* dark brown to black
Hardness 5-5-1/2	*Streak* dark brown, black
Specific Gravity 7.12-7.60	*Lustre* metallic, greasy
Cleavage perfect	*Transparency* opaque
Fracture uneven, brittle	*Crystal system* monoclinic

Crystals tabular prismatic, acicular, with vertical striations. Aggregates compact, lamellar leaf-like, radiating. Occurs in veins. LOCALITIES: Coruna/Spain, Panasqueira/Portugal, Colorado/USA, Canada, Cumbria/England. The most important tungsten ore.

Scheelite [2]

Composition CaWO$_4$	*Colour* yellow, grey, brownish
Hardness 41/2-5	*Streak* white
Specific Gravity 5.9-6.1	*Lustre* greasy, adamantine
Cleavage imperfect	*Transparency* translucent
Fracture conchoidal, brittle	*Crystal system* tetragonal

Crystals dipyramidal, occasionally tabular, usually encrusting. Rarely in compact masses. Occurs in veins, particularly in pegmatites and skarns, sometimes as placers. LOCALITIES: Erzgebirge/Saxony/Germany, Cornwall and Lake District/England, Namibia, Nevada/USA. Important tungsten ore.

Stolzite [3] PbWO$_4$

Rare distinctly formed dipyramidal or thick tabular crystals. Mostly globular aggregates. Hardness 2.1/2-3, Specific gravity 7.9-8.2; colour reddish, yellow, green; streak white. Greasy lustre. Occurs in the oxidation zones of tungsten deposits. Of almost no importance as an ore of tungsten.

CHROMIUM ORE MINERALS

Only chromite is of importance as an ore mineral. Chromium is used for improving steel.

Chromite [4,5]

Composition (Fe,Mg)Cr$_2$O$_4$	*Colour* black
Hardness 51/2	*Streak* brown
Specific Gravity 4.5-4.8	*Lustre* metallic, greasy
Cleavage none	*Transparency* opaque
Fracture uneven, conchoidal	*Crystal system* cubic

Octahedral crystals, rare. Mostly compact clusters or disseminated grains. Occurs in peridotite and serpentinite, also in placers. LOCALITIES: Guleman/Turkey, Urals/Russia, Zimbabwe, Transvaal/South Africa, Stillwater/Montana and Colorado/USA.

---

1 Wolframite on zinnwaldite,
  Erzgebirge/Saxony/Germany
2 Scheelite on quartz,
  Erzgebirge/Saxony/Germany

3 Stolzite, New South Wales/Australia
4 Chromite, Guleman/Turkey
5 Chromite in serpentinite, Guleman/Turkey

COBALT ORE MINERALS

Asbolite, heterogenite, cobaltite, linnaeite, skutterudite belong in this group. Cobalt is used as an alloying metal for hard and tough steels and for magnets. In addition it is used in the manufacture of ceramics and glass.

Erythrite [1] Cobalt bloom $CO_3[AsO_4]_2\cdot8H_2O$

Mostly radiating-lamellar aggregates, globular, earthy, and as a tarnish. Hardness 2, Specific Gravity 3.07, peach blossom red, greenish-grey when mixed with annabergite. Streak pale red. Pearly to vitreous lustre. Of no importance as an ore but it is a significant indicator mineral to cobalt-rich mineral deposits.

Cobaltite [2] Cobalt glance, cobaltine

Composition CoAsS	*Colour* silver white with a reddish tinge
Hardness 5½	*Streak* grey-black
Specific Gravity 6.0-6.4	*Lustre* metallic
Cleavage imperfect	*Transparency* opaque
Fracture conchoidal-uneven, brittle	*Crystal system* cubic

Cubic crystals always embedded, with striated faces. Also granular aggregates. Occurs in different types of vein deposits and in metamorphic rocks. LOCALITIES: Siegerland/Rhineland/Germany, Boliden/Sweden, Cobalt/Ontario/Canada, Cornwall/England. Important cobalt ore but rarely occurs in large quantities.

Skutterudite [3] Smaltite

Composition (Co,Ni)As$_3$	*Colour* tin white, steel grey
Hardness 6	*Streak* black
Specific Gravity 6.8	*Lustre* metallic
Cleavage none	*Transparency* opaque
Fracture conchoidal, brittle	*Crystal system* cubic

Octahedral crystals, small. Frequently compact aggregates. Occurs in veins of cobalt-nickel-deposits. LOCALITIES: St Andreasberg/Harz, Erzgebirge/Saxony/Germany, Kongsberg/Norway, Ontario/Canada, Franklin/New Jersey/USA. Important cobalt ore.

Linnaeite [4]

Composition Co$_3$S$_4$	*Colou r* white, grey, reddish tinge
Hardness 4½ -5½	*Streak* black
Specific Gravity 4.8-5.8	*Lustre* metallic
Cleavage imperfect	*Transparency* opaque
Fracture uneven, brittle	*Crystal system* cubic

Octahedral crystals, frequently well formed. Mostly disseminated, rarely compact granular aggregates. Occurs in sulphide-rich ore deposits. Important cobalt ore if it occurs in large quantities as in Zaire and Zambia.

Asbolite Cobalt-bearing wad (p.108). Earthy, powdery aggregate.

Heterogenite CoOOH Cobalt-bearing, nodular, black, earthy masses.

1 Erythrite, Bou Azzer/Morocco
2 Cobaltite, Hakansboda, Sweden

3 Skutterudite, Schneeberg/Saxony/Germany
4 Linnaeite, Littfeld/Siegerland/Germany

VANADIUM ORE MINERALS

The most important vanadium ore minerals are carnotite, descloizite, patronite and vanadinite. Vanadium is used predominantly as an alloy metal for special steels, also for the manufacture of permanent magnets.

Carnotite [1]

Composition $K_2[(UO_2)_2|V_2O_8]\cdot 3H_2O$	*Colour* yellow, green-yellow
Hardness 4	*Streak* yellow to green
Specific Gravity 4.5-4.6	*Lustre* pearly, silky, dull
Cleavage perfect	*Transparency* translucent to opaque
Fracture brittle	*Crystal system* monoclinic

Crystals tabular and very small. Fine grained to dense aggregates; also earthy and powdery masses. Occurs in sedimentary rocks. LOCALITIES: Utah, Arizona, Colorado/USA, Turkestan/Kazakhstan, Australia, Morocco. Important vanadium and uranium ore.

Descloizite [2]

Composition $Pb(Zn,Cu)(OH|VO_4)$	*Colour* brown, brown red, black
Hardness 3½	*Streak* light brown, light green
Specific Gravity 5.5-6.2	*Lustre* resinous, adamantine
Cleavage none	*Transparency* transparent to opaque
Fracture conchoidal, brittle	*Crystal system* orthorhombic

Prismatic, pyramidal crystals. Crusty, botryoidal, stalactitic, also earthy masses. Occurs in oxidation zones of non-ferrous metal mineral deposits, in sandstone and in karstic depressions. LOCALITIES: Dahn/Rheinpfalz/Germany, Obir/Kärnten/Austria, Tsumeb/Namibia, Broken Hill/Zambia, Bisbee/Arizona and New Mexico/USA.

Patronite [3]

Composition VS_4	*Colour* lead grey
Hardness 1-2	*Streak* green-black
Specific Gravity 2.81	*Lustre* dull
Cleavage none	*Transparency* opaque
Fracture conchoidal	*Crystal system* monoclinic

Crystals unknown. Fine grained masses, coke- like, earthy. Occurs in bituminous shale and asphalt mixtures. LOCALITIES: Minas Ragra/Peru.

Vanadinite [4]

Composition $Pb_5[Cl|(VO_4)_3]$	*Colour* yellow, brown, orange red
Hardness 3	*Streak* light yellow
Specific Gravity 6.5-7.1	*Lustre* adamantine, greasy
Cleavage none	*Transparency* opaque
Fracture conchoidal brittle	*Crystal system* hexagonal

Crystals short-prismatic or pyramidal; rarely massive, reniform, fibrous. Occurs in the weathering zone of lead mineral deposits. LOCALITIES: Tsumeb/Namibia, Broken Hill/Zambia, Arizona/USA. Locally important vanadium ore.

---

1 Carnotite, Yavapai County/Arizona/USA
2 Descloizite, Ankas/Namibia

3 Patronite, Minas Ragra/Peru
4 Vanadinite, Mibladen/Morocco

TITANIUM AND TANTALUM-NIOBIUM ORE MINERALS

Ilmenite, rutile (p.56) and sphene are titanium minerals, columbite and pyrochlore are tantalum-niobium minerals. Titanium, tantalum and niobium are used for improving steel; also of importance in the electrical and armaments industries.

Sphene [1] Titanite

Composition CaTi[OlSiO$_4$]	*Colour* yellow, brown, green, black
Hardness 5-5½	*Streak* white
Specific Gravity 3.4-3.6	*Lustre* adamantine, greasy
Cleavage imperfect	*Transparency* transparent to opaque
Fracture conchoidal, brittle	*Crystal system* monoclinic

Crystals prismatic, tabular. Frequently twinned. Occasionally granular aggregates. Occurs as an accessory constituent in many rock types. Only occasionally workable as a titanium ore. LOCALITITES: Kola/Russia, Minas Gerais/Brazil, Renfrew/Ontario/Canada, Franklin/New Jersey and Brewster/New York/USA.

Ilmenite [2]

Composition FeTiO$_3$	*Colour* black with a violet tinge
Hardness 5-6	*Streak* brown black
Specific Gravity 4.5-5.0	*Lustre* metallic, dull
Cleavage none	*Transparency* opaque
Fracture conchoidal, uneven, brittle	*Crystal system* trigonal

Crystals tabular or rhombohedral. Massive granular aggregates, frequently disseminated. Occurs in igneous rocks and sands. LOCALITIES: Norway, Sweden, Quebec/Canada, Wyoming/USA. Important titanium raw material.

Columbite [3]

Collective name for complete isomorphous series between niobite and tantalite.

Composition Niobite (Fe,Mn)(Nb,Ta)$_2$O$_6$	*Fracture* conchoidal, brittle
Tantalite (Fe,Mn)(TaNb)$_2$O$_6$	*Colour* black, brown
Hardness 6-6½	*Streak* brown, black
Specific Gravity 5.2-8.1	*Lustre* metallic
Cleavage imperfect	*Transparency* opaque

Crystals (orthorhombic system) tabular, prismatic. Compact masses, disseminated grains. Occurs in granite pegmatites and in placers. LOCALITIES: Hazendorf/Upper Pfalz/Germany, Moss/Norway, Varuträsk/Sweden, Nigeria, Brazil, S Dakota and New England/USA, Londonderry/Australia.

Pyrochlore [4]

Composition (Na,Ca)$_2$(Nb,Ti,Ta)$_2$O$_6$ (OH,F,O)	*Colour* brown, black
Hardness 5-5½	*Streak* yellow-brown
Specific Gravity 3.5-4.6	*Lustre* adamantine, greasy
Cleavage none	*Transparency* translucent to opaque
Fracture conchoidal, uneven, brittle	*Crystal system* cubic

Crystals encrusting, cube, octahedron. Compact masses, disseminated. Occurs in pegmatites and carbonatites. LOCALITIES: Sweden, Kola/Russia.

---

1 Sphene, Minas Gerais/Brazil
2 Ilmenite, Norway

3 Columbite (black) Hagendorf/Oberpfalz/ Germany
4 Pyrochlore (brown) Brevik/Norway

MINERALS OF THE NON-FERROUS METAL ORES

To this group belong minerals from which non-ferrous, light and radioactive metals, bismuth, arsenic, antimony and mercury are extracted.

COPPER ORE MINERALS

Bornite, chalcanthite (copper vitriol), chrysocolla (p.182), covellite, cuprite, enargite, native copper, chalcocite, chalcopyrite and malachite (p.172) are members of this group. Copper is used predominantly in the electrical industry.

Native copper [1]
Cubic crystals, usually distorted. Mostly compact masses, grains, platy, filiform. Hardness 2½-3. Specific gravity 8.3-8.7. Occurs in basic igneous rocks and in the oxidation zones of copper deposits. LOCALITIES: Siegerland/Germany, Lake Superior/USA, Urals/Russia. Insignificant as an ore of copper.

Chalcopyrite [2]

Composition $CuFeS_2$	Colour brassy yellow with a green tinge
Hardness 3½-4	Streak green black
Specific Gravity 4.1-4.3	Lustre metallic
Cleavage imperfect	Transparency opaque
Fracture conchoidal, uneven, brittle	Crystal system tetragonal

Crystals small. Mostly compact masses. Occurs in igneous rocks and copper-bearing shales. LOCALITIES: Siegerland/Germany, Spain, Butte/Montana and Bingham/Utah/USA, South Africa. Important copper ore.

Covellite [3]

Composition CuS	Colour blue-black
Hardness 1½-2	Streak blue-black
Specific Gravity 4.68	Lustre metallic, greasy, dull
Cleavage very perfect	Transparency opaque
Fracture conchoidal	Crystal system hexagonal

Tabular crystals, rare. Mostly compact, earthy masses, also as tarnishings. Occurs in the weathering zone of copper ore deposits. LOCALITIES: Sangerhausen/Harz/Germany, Bor/Yugoslavia, Butte/Montana/USA. Important copper ore.

Chalcocite [4] Chalcosine

Composition Cu_2S	Colour lead grey
Hardness 2½-3	Streak dark grey
Specific Gravity 5.5-5.8	Lustre metallic, dull tarnish
Cleavage imperfect	Transparency opaque
Fracture conchoidal	Crystal system orthorhombic

Crystals thick tabular, short columnar, rare. Mostly compact masses, also disseminated. Occurs in vein deposits and as impregnations. LOCALITIES: Butte/Montana and Connecticut/USA, Tsumeb/Namibia, Transvaal/South Africa, Cornwall/England. Important copper ore.

Enargite [1]

Composition Cu₃AsS₄	*Colour* grey-black with violet tinge
Hardness 3½	*Streak* black
Specific Gravity 4.4	*Lustre* metallic
Cleavage perfect	*Transparency* opaque
Fracture uneven, brittle	*Crystal system* orthorhombic

Crystals short columnar, tabular, rare. Usually compact masses, also radiating and disseminated. Occurs in iron-poor copper ore veins. LOCALITIES: Bor/Yugoslavia, Bingham, Utah and Butte/Montana/USA, Tsumeb/Namibia. Important copper ore.

Bornite [2]

Composition Cu₅FeS₄	*Colour* reddish, variegated tarnish
Hardness 3	*Streak* grey-black
Specific Gravity 4.9-5.3	*Lustre* metallic
Cleavage imperfect	*Transparency* opaque
Fracture conchoidal	*Crystal system* cubic

Rarely well-developed crystals, distorted cubes. Usually compact masses or disseminated. Occurs in iron-poor copper deposits, in veins and as impregnations. LOCALITIES: Siegerland/Rhineland/Germany, Mansfeld/Germany, Butte/Montana/USA, Tsumeb/Namibia, Transvaal/South Africa, Cornwall/England. Important copper ore.

Cuprite [3] Red copper ore

Composition Cu₂O	*Colour* brown-red, grey
Hardness 3½-4	*Streak* brown-red
Specific Gravity 5.8-6.2	*Lustre* metallic, dull
Cleavage: perfect	*Transparency* translucent to opaque
Fracture conchoidal uneven, brittle	*Crystal system* cubic

Crystals mostly encrusting, octahedra. Aggregates compact, granular, dense. Occurs in the oxidation zone of sulphidic copper ores. LOCALITIES: Lyons/France, Arizona/USA, Tsumeb/Namibia, Cornwall/England. Locally important copper ore.
Chalcotrichite Hair-like variety of cuprite.
Tile ore Mixture of cuprite and powdery limonite.
Copper pecherz Dense mixture of cuprite, limonite and silica.

Aurichalcite [4]

Composition (Zn,Cu)₅[(OH)₃ǀCO₃]₂	*Colour* green, blue
Hardness 2	*Streak* green-blue
Specific Gravity 3.6-4.2	*Lustre* pearly, silky
Cleavage perfect	*Transparency* translucent
Fracture lamellar	*Crystal system* orthorhombic

Crystals acicular, tabular, mostly small, tufted aggregates, rosettes, crusts, also earthy. Occurs in the oxidation zone of non-ferrous metal deposits. LOCALITIES: Laurium/Greece, Monteponi/Italy, Tsumeb/Namibia, Bisbee/Arizona/USA. Not a copper ore but an indicator mineral of copper ores.

---

1 Enargite, Pasto Bueno/Peru
2 Bornite, Neue Hardt
   Quarry/Siegerland/Germany

3 Cuprite on cerussite, Tsumeb/Namibia
4 Aurichalcite, Mapimi/Durango/Mexico

LEAD ORE MINERALS

Anglesite, galena, cerussite and pyromorphite belong here. Lead is used for cables, pipes, accumulators, and for protection against radiation.

Crocoite [1] Red lead ore

Composition PbCrO$_4$	*Colour* yellowish red
Hardness 2½-3	*Streak* orange
Specific Gravity 5.9-6.1	*Lustre* greasy, adamantine
Cleavage perfect	*Transparency* translucent
Fracture conchoidal, uneven	*Crystal system* monoclinic

Crystals acicular. Rarely compact masses. Occurs in galena deposits. Localities: Dundas/Tasmania, Brazil, Russia, Lancaster Co/Pennsylvania/USA. No economic importance.

Anglesite [2]

Composition PbSO$_4$	*Colour* colourless, white, grey, black
Hardness 3-3½	*Streak* white
Specific Gravity 6.3-6.4	*Lustre* adamantine, greasy
Cleavage imperfect	*Transparency* transparent to translucent
Fracture conchoidal, brittle	*Crystal system* orthorhombic

Crystals mostly small, pyramidal, prismatic, tabular. Aggregates granular, earthy, crusty. Occurs in the oxidation zone of galena deposits. Localities: Bleiberg/Kärnten/Austria, Spain, Scotland, Phoenixville/Pennsylvania and Missouri/USA, Anglesey/Wales. Locally an ore of lead.

Cerussite [3] White lead ore

Composition PbCo$_3$	*Colour* colourless, grey, brownish
Hardness 3-3½	*Streak* white
Specific Gravity 6.4-6.6	*Lustre* adamantine, greasy, vitreous
Cleavage imperfect	*Transparency* transparent to opaque
Fracture conchoidal, brittle	*Crystal system* orthorhombic

Crystals tabular, prismatic. Aggregates dense, fine grained, tufted. Occurs in the weathering zone of carbonate- bearing galena deposits. Localities: Colorado/USA, Zambia, Tsumeb/Namibia. Locally an important lead ore.
Black lead ore Finely crystalline cerussite, dark coloured because of galena.
Earthy cerussite Very impure earthy variety of cerussite.

Galena [4]

Composition PbS	*Colour* lead grey with a reddish tinge
Hardness 2½-3	*Streak* grey-black
Specific Gravity 7.2-7.6	*Lustre* metallic, dull
Cleavage very perfect	*Transparency* opaque
Fracture conchoidal, brittle	*Crystal system* cubic

Crystals cubic, mostly encrusting. Aggregates compact, granular. Almost always intergrown with sphalerite. Occurs in veins, stocks, layers. Localities: Harz/Germany, Bleiberg/Kärnten/Austria, Pribram/Czechoslovakia, Zambia, Pennines/England, Missouri/Oklahoma/Kansas/USA. The most important lead ore.

---

1 Crocoite, Tasmania/Australia
2 Anglesite, Tsumeb/Namibia
3 Cerussite, Tsumeb/Namibia

4 Galena with calcite,
   Siegen/Westphalia/Germany

Mimetesite [1]

Composition Pb₅[Cl|(AsO₄)₃]	*Colour* yellow, green, brown, colourless
Hardness 3½-4	*Streak* white
Specific Gravity 7.1	*Lustre* adamantine, greasy
Cleavage none	*Transparency* transparent to translucent
Fracture conchoidal, uneven, brittle	*Crystal system* hexagonal

Composition $Pb_5[Cl|(AsO_4)_3]$

Crystals prismatic, barrel-shaped, pyramidal, encrusting. Aggregates globular, reniform, crusty, also earthy masses. Occurs in the oxidation zone of lead deposits. LOCALITIES: Erzgebirge/Germany, Cornwall/England, Langban/Sweden, Tsumeb/Namibia. Rare, no economic importance.

Pyromorphite [2,5]

Composition Pb[Cl|(PO₄)₃]	*Colour* green, brown, orange, white, colourless
Hardness 3½-4	*Streak* white
Specific Gravity 6.7-7.1	*Lustre* adamantine, greasy
Cleavage none	*Crystal system* hexagonal
Fracture conchoidal, uneven, brittle	*Transparency* transparent to translucent

Composition $Pb[Cl|(PO_4)_3]$

Crystals encrusting, prismatic, barrel shaped, also acicular, tabular. Aggregates botryoidal, disseminated, as encrustations rarely compact. Occurs in the oxidation zone of lead deposits. LOCALITIES: Freiberg/Saxony/Germany, Clausthal/Harz/Germany, Pribram/Czechoslovakia, Cornwall/England, Broken Hill/Australia, Phoenixville/Pennsylvania/USA. Locally important lead ore.
Brown lead ore Brown coloured variety of pyromorphite.
Variegated lead ore Brightly coloured variety of pyromorphite.
Green lead ore Green coloured variety of pyromorphite [2] or mimetesite.

Linarite [3]

Composition PbCu[(OH)₂|SO₄]	*Colour* azure blue
Hardness 2½	*Streak* light blue
Specific Gravity 5.3-5.5	*Lustre* vitreous, adamantine
Cleavage perfect	*Transparency* translucent
Fracture conchoidal	*Crystal system* monoclinic

Composition $PbCu[(OH)_2|SO_4]$

Crystals small, richly faceted, prismatic, rarely tabular. Crystalline crusts, felted aggregates. Occurs in the oxidation zone of copper/lead deposits. LOCALITIES: Spain, Kärnten/Austria, Namibia, Tiger/Arizona, Butte/Montana/USA. Never in large amounts.

Phosgenite [4]

Composition Pb[Cl₂|CO₃]	*Colour* yellow, white, grey, colourless, green
Hardness 2-3	*Streak* white
Specific Gravity 6.0-6.3	*Lustre* adamantine, greasy
Cleavage perfect	*Transparency* transparent to translucent
Fracture conchoidal	*Crystal system* tetragonal

Composition $Pb[Cl_2|CO_3]$

Crystals short columnar, often richly faceted, also thick tabular. Aggregates compact, granular. Occurs in the oxidation zone of lead ore deposits. LOCALITIES: Sardinia, Laurium/Greece, Tsumeb/Namibia. Never in very large amounts.

---

1 Mimetesite, Mexico
2 Pyromorphite, Freiburg/Oberpfalz/Germany
3 Linarite, New Mexico/USA

4 Phosgenite on galena, Monte Poni/Sardinia
5 Brown lead ore, Friedrichssegen/Bad Ems/Rhineland/Germany

ZINC ORE MINERALS

Franklinite, hemimorphite, smithsonite, willemite, sphalerite and zincite belong here. Zinc is used for zinc coating (zincing) and as an alloy-metal.

Hemimorphite [1] Zinc silicate ore

Composition $Zn_4[(OH)_2|Si_2O_7]\cdot H_2O$	*Colour* colourless, white, green, brown
Hardness 5	*Streak* white
Specific Gravity 3.3-3.5	*Lustre* vitreous
Cleavage perfect	*Transparency* transparent to translucent
Fracture conchoidal, brittle	*Crystal system* orthorhombic

Crystals usually small, mostly tabular, encrusting. Crystalline crusts, also globular and stalactitic masses. Occurs in the oxidation zone of lead-zinc deposits. LOCALITIES: Bleiberg/Kärnten/Austria, Chihuahua/Mexico, Transbaikal/Russia, Arizona, Virginia/USA, Cumberland, Derbyshire/England. Important zinc ore.
Galmei Collective name for carbonate-and-silicate bearing zinc ores of hemimorphite, hydrozincite, smithsonite, willemite.

Zincite [2] Red zinc ore

Composition ZnO	*Colour* red
Hardness 4½-5	*Streak* orange, yellow
Specific Gravity 5.4-5.7	*Lustre* greasy, adamantine
Cleavage perfect	*Transparency* translucent
Fracture conchoidal, brittle	*Crystal system* hexagonal

Crystals tabular, very rare. Granular and sparry aggregates or disseminated. occurs in marble. LOCALITIES: New Jersey/USA, Olkurz/Poland, Tuscany/Italy, Australia. Only in New Jersey/USA is it an important ore of zinc.

Sphalerite [4] zincblende, blende

Composition ZnS	*Colour* black, brown, yellow, red, whitish
Hardness 3½-4	*Streak* brown, yellowish white
Specific Gravity 3.9-4.2	*Lustre* adamantine, greasy
Cleavage perfect	*Transparency* transparent to translucent
Fracture uneven, brittle	*Crystal system* cubic

Crystals tetrahedral, dodecahedral. Aggregates granular, sparry, crusty, disseminated. Occurs in veins, in copper-bearing shales. LOCALITIES: Meggen/Westphalia/Germany, Bleiberg/Kärnten/Austria, Trepca/Yugoslavia, Alston Moor/England, Joplin/Missouri/USA. The most important zinc ore.

Colour varieties
Honey blende - yellow brown [4]
Ruby blende - red
Cleiophane - whitish
Marmatite - black
Christophite - black, iron rich

Schalenblende [3]
Finegrained – fibrous aggregate. Partly an aggregate of sphalerite, wurtzite and galena, partly of sphalerite and wurtzite.

---

1 Hemimorphite, Chihuahua/Mexico
2 Zincite (red) with franklinite (black)
  Franklin/New Jersey/USA

3 Schalenblende, Wiesloch/Baden/Germany
4 Sphalerite (honey blende), Casapalca/Peru

132

Smithsonite [1,2] Zinc spar

Composition $ZnCO_3$	*Colour* colourless, whitish, many colours
Hardness 5	*Streak* white
Specific Gravity 4.3-4.5	*Lustre* vitreous, pearly
Cleavage perfect	*Transparency* translucent to opaque
Fracture uneven, conchoidal, brittle	*Crystal system* trigonal

Crystals rare and small. Aggregates reniform, stalactitic, crusty. Occurs in the oxidation zone of sulphidic lead-zinc deposits. LOCALITIES: Bleiberg/Kärnten/Austria, Greece, Australia, Namibia, Magdelena/New Mexico/USA. Important zinc ore.

Hydrozincite [3]

Composition $Zn_5[(OH)_3|CO_3]_2$	*Colour* white, yellowish, pink, colourless
Hardness 2-2½	*Streak* white
Specific Gravity 3.5-3.8	*Lustre* silky, dull
Cleavage perfect	*Transparency* translucent to opaque
Fracture brittle	*Crystal system* monoclinic

Small, tabular crystals. Compact, dense masses, banded, crusty, stalactitic. Occurs in the oxidation zone of zinc deposits. LOCALITIES: Bleiberg/Kärnten/Austria, Spain, Nevada/USA, Western Australia. Sometimes locally an ore of zinc.

TIN ORE MINERALS

Only cassiterite and stannite are important. Tin is an alloying metal.

Stannite [4] Tin pyrites

Composition Cu_2FeSnS_4	*Colour* grey with olive green tinge
Hardness 4	*Streak* black
Specific Gravity 4.3-4.5	*Lustre* metallic
Cleavage imperfect	*Transparency* opaque
Fracture uneven, brittle	*Crystal system* tetragonal

Crystals tetrahedral and tabular, rare and small. Granular to dense aggregates, disseminated. Occurs in tin ore deposits. LOCALITIES: Saxony/Germany, England, Bolivia, E Siberia. Locally a tin and copper ore.

Cassiterite [5] Tin stone

Composition SnO_2	*Colour* brown, black, yellow, reddish
Hardness 7	*Streak* white, brownish
Specific Gravity 6.6-7.1	*Lustre* adamantine, greasy
Cleavage imperfect	*Transparency* translucent to opaque
Fracture conchoidal, brittle	*Crystal system* tetragonal

Crystals embedded and encrusting, acicular (needle tin). Compact masses, finely fibrous, globular (wood tin). Occurs in pegmatites, veins, as impregnations (mountain tin), as rolled grains (stream tin). LOCALITIES: Erzgebirge/Germany, Cornwall/England, France, Malaysia, Bolivia, Oxford Co/Maine and Custer/S Dakota/USA. The most important tin ore.

1 Smithsonite, Kelley Mine/New Mexico/USA
2 Smithsonite, Tsumeb/Namibia
3 Hydrozincite (white) Yazd/Iran

4 Stannite, St Agnes/Cornwall/England
5 Cassiterite (black crystals)
  Ehrenfriedersdorf/Erzgebirge/Germany

BISMUTH ORE MINERALS

Native bismuth, bismuthinite and bismuth ochre belong in this group. Bismuth is an alloying metal, also used in pharmacy and medicine.

Bismuthinite [1,3] Bismuth glance.

Composition Bi_2S_3	*Colour* white, grey, yellowish tarnish
Hardness 2	*Streak* grey
Specific Gravity 6.8-7.2	*Lustre* metallic
Cleavage very perfect	*Transparency* opaque
Fracture conchoidal, brittle	*Crystal system* orthorhombic

Crystals acicular, short columnar. Aggregates radiating, lamellar, granular, rarely compact masses. Occurs in tin, silver, cobalt, tungsten mineral deposits. LOCALITIES: Erzgebirge/Germany, Cornwall/England, Bolivia, Australia, Haddam/Connecticut/USA. Important bismuth ore.

Native bismuth [4]

Composition Bi	*Colour* reddish silver white, tarnishes
Hardness 2-2½	*Streak* grey
Specific Gravity 9.7-9.8	*Lustre* metallic
Cleavage perfect	*Transparency* opaque
Fracture brittle	*Crystal system* trigonal

Crystals very rare, cubic in appearance. Usually skeletal dendritic aggregates, also disseminated grains, rarely in very large masses. Occurs in cobalt-nickel-silver ore veins sometimes in placers. LOCALITIES: Erzgebirge/Germany, Cornwall/England, Ontario/Canada, Bolivia, Connecticut, Colorado/USA. Locally an important bismuth ore.

Bismuth ochre [3] Bi_2O_3

Bismuth ochre is a mixture of different rare bismuth minerals (eg. bismite, bismutite). Canary- to lemon-yellow or green, streak grey. Hardness 2½-3½. Specific gravity 6.7-7.4. Vitreous lustre. Earthy formation, crusty, globular. Occurs as the weathering product of cobalt-nickel-silver ore veins. LOCALITIES: Erzebirge/Germany, England, Bolivia, USA. Of no importance as an ore but a characteristic indicator of the occurrence of bismuth.

Schapbachite [5] Matildite

Composition $AgBiS_2$	*Colour* grey to black
Hardness 2½	*Streak* light grey
Specific Gravity 6.9-7.2	*Lustre* metallic
Cleavage none	*Transparency* opaque
Fracture uneven, brittle	*Crystal system* orthorhombic

Crystals rare, prismatic, usually compact or granular aggregates, intergrown with galena. Occurs on galena deposits. LOCALITIES: Schapbachtal/Schwarzwald/ Germany, Zinnwald/Erzebirge/Germany, Peru, Tasmania, Japan, Colorado, Arizona/USA. Although the bismuth content amounts to more than 50% it is of no economic importance as an ore of bismuth. Locally important as a carrier of silver.

---

1 Bismuthinite with pyrite, Vogtland, Germany
2 Bismuth ochre, San
  Domingo/Wickenburg/Arizona/USA
3 Bismuthinite, Colorado/USA

4 Native bismuth,
  Schneckenstein/Vogtland/Germany
5 Schapbachite, Matilda/Morococha/Peru

136

MERCURY ORE MINERALS

The most important ore mineral is cinnabar. Native mercury, calomel and schwazite are of lesser importance. Natural mixed crystals of gold or silver with mercury are called amalgam. Mercury is used in the electronics industry, for measuring instruments, in medicine and the armaments industry.

Cinnabar [3,5]

Composition HgS	*Colour* red, rarely bluish
Hardness 2-2½	*Streak* red
Specific Gravity 8.0-8.2	*Lustre* adamantine, metallic
Cleavage perfect	*Transparency* translucent
Fracture splintery, brittle	*Crystal system* trigonal

Crystals small and rare, thick tabular, rhombohedral, prismatic, often cruciform twinned. Mostly granular or compact masses, also disseminated and powdery encrustations. Occurs in veins in sedimentary rocks, in volcanic tuffs, occasionally also in placers. LOCALITIES: Almadén/Spain, Yugoslavia, Tuscany/Italy, Nevada/USA, Russia, Mexico, Peru.

Native mercury [5] Hg

Small, tin-white droplets, frequently covered with a grey skin, adhering only lightly to the parent rock, especially to cinnabar. Solidifies at -38.9°C to rhombohedron-like forms in the tetragonal system. Specific gravity 13.55. Metallic lustre. Very poisonous. Occurs in the weathering zone of mercury deposits. LOCALITIES: as cinnabar. Worked with cinnabar as an ore.

Calomel [1] Hornquicksilver

Composition Hg$_2$Cl$_2$	*Colour* yellowish, brown, grey, colourless
Hardness 1-2	*Streak* white
Specific Gravity 6.4-6.5	*Lustre* adamantine
Cleavage imperfect	*Transparency* translucent to opaque
Fracture conchoidal	*Crystal system* tetragonal

Small crystals, prismatic, tabular, pyramidal. Aggregates compactly hornlike, crusty, also earthy. Occurs in the weathering zone of mercury deposits. LOCALITIES: as cinnabar. Rarely in large amounts.

Schwazite [2,4] Hermesite

Composition (CuHg)$_3$SbS$_4$	*Colour* grey to black
Hardness 3-4½	*Streak* grey-black
Specific Gravity 5.1	*Lustre* metallic, dull
Cleavage none	*Transparency* opaque
Fracture conchoidal, brittle	*Crystal system* cubic

Schwazite belongs to the so called fahlerz group (p.142). Crystals tetrahedral, dodecahedral, cubic. Aggregates compact, granular, dense, also disseminated. Occurs in mercury-bearing ore veins. LOCALITIES: as cinnabar.

ARSENIC ORE MINERALS

Arsenic, arsenopyrite, orpiment, löllingite, realgar and tennantite belong here. Arsenic is used for pest control, in tanning, pharmacy and cosmetics. Some arsenic compounds are very poisonous.

Native arsenic [5]

Composition As	*Colour* tin-white tarnishing to black
Hardness 3-4	*Streak* black
Specific Gravity 5.4-5.9	*Lustre* metallic, dull
Cleavage perfect	*Transparency* opaque
Fracture uneven, brittle	*Crystal system* trigonal

Crystals rhombohedral, pseudo-cubic, rare. Mostly compact fine-grained masses, shell-like globular aggregates, also stalactitic. Occurs as a minor constituent in veins of arsenic-bearing ores. LOCALITIES: Erzgebirge, Wittichen/Schwarzwald/Germany, Vosges/France, Pribram/Czechoslovakia, Kongsberg/Norway, New Jersey/USA. Of scarcely any economic importance.

Scherbencobalt [5] Globular, shell-like arsenic aggregate.

Arsenopyrite [2]

Composition FeAsS	*Colour* tin-white, grey, tarnishing to yellowish
Hardness 5½-6	*Streak* grey-black
Specific Gravity 5.9-6.2	*Lustre* metallic
Cleavage imperfect	*Transparency* opaque
Fracture uneven, brittle	*Crystal system* orthorhombic

Crystals short- and long-columnar, octahedral, embedded and encrusting, frequently cruciform twinned. Aggregates compactly granular, radiating, disseminated. Occurs in ore veins. LOCALITIES: Fichtelgebirge, Erzgebirge/Germany, Mitterberg/Austria, Cornwall/England, Boliden/Sweden, Deloro/Canada, Connecticut. Colorado/USA. The most important ore of arsenic.

Löllingite [1,4]

Composition FeAs$_2$	*Colour* silver-white, tarnishing to grey
Hardness 5-5½	*Streak* grey black
Specific Gravity 7.1-7.5	*Lustre* metallic
Cleavage perfect	*Transparency* opaque
Fracture uneven, brittle	*Crystal system* orthorhombic

Crystals prismatic. Compact aggregates, disseminated. Occurs as a minor constituent in ore veins. LOCALITIES: Lölling/Kärnten/Harz/Germany, Falun/Sweden, Ontario/Canada, New York/USA. With other arsenic minerals worked as an ore of arsenic.

Gersdorffite [3] NiAsS

Colour silver-white to steel grey, tarnishing to dark grey, metallic to dull lustre. Streak grey-black. Hardness 5. Specific gravity 5.6-6.2. Crystals cubic, octahedral; granular rarely compact aggregates. Frequently has a green weathering skin (annabergite). Of no economic importance.

---

1 Löllingite in rhodonite, Australia
2 Arsenopyrite, Hartmannsdorf/Germany
3 Gersdorffite, Montana/USA
4 Löllingite, Reichestein/Silesia/Poland
5 Arsenic as scherbencobalt, St. Andreasberg/Harz/Germany

Orpiment [1,4]

Composition As_2S_3	*Colour* lemon-yellow to orange-yellow
Hardness 1½-2	*Streak* light-yellow to orange-yellow
Specific Gravity 3.48	*Lustre* pearly, greasy
Cleavage very perfect	*Transparency* transparent to translucent
Fracture conchoidal, flexible	*Crystal system* monoclinic

Well-formed crystals rare, mostly small, short- prismatic. Usually compact shapeless or reniform, columnar lamellar, coarsely sparry masses, also earthy encrustations. Occurs in vein deposits of arsenic-bearing ores and in argillaceous rocks. LOCALITIES: Macedonia/Yugoslavia, Kurdistan/Turkey, Rumania, Hungary, Utah/USA. Locally raw material for arsenic. Formerly frequently used as the yellow pigment in painting.

Realgar [2]

Composition As_4S_4	*Colour* red, red orange
Hardness 1½-2	*Streak* orange-yellow
Specific Gravity 3.5-3.6	*Lustre* adamantine, greasy
Cleavage imperfect	*Transparency* translucent
Fracture conchoidal	*Crystal system* monoclinic

Crystals richly faceted, prismatic, mostly small, encrusting. Aggregates compact, fine grained, also encrustations. Realgar disintegrates in daylight into earthy orpiment. Occurs in vein deposits of arsenic bearing ores, in mudstone and in limestone. LOCALITIES: Wallis/Switzerland, Macedonia/Yugoslavia, Turkey, Siebenbürgen/Rumania, Utah, Wyoming/USA, Mexico. Locally raw material for arsenic. Also used for red pigment (poisonous!)

Tennantite [3]

Composition $Cu_{12}A_4S_{13}$	*Colour* grey with olive coloured tinge
Hardness 3-4½	*Streak* black to brown to dark red
Specific Gravity 4.6-4.8	*Lustre* metallic, dull
Cleavage none	*Transparency* translucent, opaque
Fracture conchoidal, uneven, brittle	*Crystal system* cubic

Tennantite belongs to the "fahlerz" group. Crystals encrusting, usually tetrahedral, richly faceted, frequently interpenetration-twinned. Mostly compact, granular to dense on its own. Occurs in copper and lead deposits. LOCALITIES: Clausthal/Harz, Freiberg/Saxony/Germany, Pribram/Czechoslovakia, St Marie aux Mines/Alsace/France, Butte/Montana/USA, Boliden/Sweden. Occasionally a raw material for arsenic.

FAHLERZ GROUP

In the fahlerz group are sulphide minerals with typically "fahlem" (wan or pale) appearance i.e. with olive-grey-yellowish lustre. To this group belong, among others, the silver rich freibergite (silver fahlerz), the mercury rich schwazite (mercury fahlerz) [Nos 2 and 4, p.139], the arsenic rich tennantite (arsenic fahlerz) [3] the antimony rich tetrahedrite (antimony fahlerz) [No. 1, p.147]. The name fahlerz is an old German miners' term.

ANTIMONY ORE MINERALS

Antimony bearing minerals are native antimony, stibnite, berthierite, boulangerite, bournonite, jamesonite, senarmontite, tetrahedrite and valentinite. Stibnite is the only ore of importance. Antimony is used as an alloying metal and as raw material for pigment.

Stibnite [1] Antimonite, antimony glance.

Composition Sb_2S_3	*Colour* lead grey
Hardness 2	*Streak* lead grey
Specific Gravity 4.6-4.7	*Lustre* metallic, dull
Cleavage very perfect	*Transparency* opaque
Fracture conchoidal, flexible	*Crystal system* orthorhombic

Crystals acicular. Crystal aggregates, also granular and dense masses. Occurs in stibnite-quartz veins or in lead and silver deposits. LOCALITIES: France, Japan, South Africa, Bolivia. The most important ore of antimony.

Senarmontite [2]

Composition Sb_2O_3	*Colour* colourless, white, grey
Hardness 2	*Streak* white
Specific Gravity 5.50	*Lustre* adamantine, greasy
Cleavage imperfect	*Transparency* transparent to translucent
Fracture conchoidal, brittle	*Crystal system* cubic

Crystals octahedral. Aggregates compactly granular, dense, crusty. Occurs in the oxidation zone of antimony-bearing deposits. Rare.

Boulangerite [3]

Composition $Pb_5Sb_4S_{11}$	*Colour* grey black
Hardness 2½-3	*Streak* black
Specific Gravity 5.8-6.2	*Lustre* metallic
Cleavage perfect	*Transparency* opaque
Fracture uneven, flexible	*Crystal system* monoclinic

Crystals very rare, prismatic. Mostly finely-fibrous or finegrained aggregates, also compact masses. Occurs in lead-zinc deposits. Localities: Harz/Germany, Pribram/Czechoslovakia, Yugoslavia, Sweden, Hollister/California/USA, Hunan/China. Occasionally an ore of lead.
Plumosite Filiform boulangerite. Formerly considered to be a specific mineral.

Bournonite [4] Wheel ore

Composition $PbCuSbS_3$	*Colour* grey to black
Hardness 2½-3	*Streak* grey
Specific Gravity 5.7-5.9	*Lustre* metallic, dull
Cleavage imperfect	*Transparency* opaque
Fracture conchoidal	*Crystal system* orthorhombic

Crystals thick tabular. Aggregates compact, granular, dense, also disseminated. Occurs as a minor constituent in lead-zinc-copper deposits. LOCALITIES: Harz/Germany, Kärnten/Austria, Cornwall/England, Bolivia, Park City/Utah/USA. Locally a lead and copper ore.

---

1 Stibnite with quartz, Wolfsberg/Harz/Germany
2 Senarmontite, Djebel Hamimat/Algeria
144 3 Boulangerite, Müsen/Westphalia/Germany

4 Bournonite with siderite, Horhausen/
  Siegerland/Germany

Tetrahedrite [1] Antimony fahlerz

Composition $Cu_{12}Sb_4S_{13}$	*Colour* grey with olive coloured tinge
Hardness 3-4	*Streak* black to brown
Specific Gravity 4.6-5.2	*Lustre* metallic-dull
Cleavage none	*Transparency* opaque
Fracture conchoidal, brittle	*Crystal system* cubic

Crystals tetrahedral, often richly faceted, encrusting. Compact, granular, dense aggregates: also disseminated. Occurs in copper and lead deposits. LOCALITIES: Harz/Germany, Cornwall/England, Idaho/USA. Occasionally a copper ore.

Valentinite [2]

Composition Sb_2O_3	*Colour* colourless, white, grey, yellowish
Hardness 2½-3	*Streak* white
Specific Gravity 5.6-5.8	*Lustre* adamantine, pearly
Cleavage perfect	*Transparency* translucent
Fracture brittle	*Crystal system* orthorhombic

Crystals prismatic, tabular, richly faceted. Columnar-fibrous tufts, also compact aggregates. Occurs in the oxidation zone of antimony-bearing ore deposits. LOCALITIES: Harz, Saxony/Germany, Dauphiné/France, Algeria, Bolivia, Wolfe Co/Quebec/Canada. Together with stibnite it is used as an ore of antimony.

Berthierite [3]

Composition $FeSb_2S_4$	*Colour* steel grey, various when tarnished
Hardness 2-3	*Streak* brown grey
Specific Gravity 4.6	*Lustre* metallic
Cleavage imperfect	*Transparency* opaque
Fracture uneven, brittle	*Crystal system* orthorhombic

Crystals prismatic, acicular. Radiating-fibrous aggregates, also granular to dense masses. Occurs in antimony ore deposits. LOCALITIES: Auvergne/France, Cornwall/England, California/USA. Economically unimportant.

Jamesonite [4,5]

Composition $Pb_4FeSb_6S_{14}$	*Colour* lead grey, multi-colour tarnish
Hardness 2½	*Streak* grey-black
Specific Gravity 5.63	*Lustre* metallic, silky
Cleavage perfect	*Transparency* opaque
Fracture brittle	*Crystal system* monoclinic

Acicular crystals. Radiating, felted aggregates. Occurs in lead-zinc deposits. LOCALITIES: Harz, Saxony/Germany, Cornwall/England, Arkansas, South Dakota/USA. Rarely in workable masses.

Feather ore No standard definition. In general a felted aggregate of jamesonite, boulangerite, stibnite and other minerals.
Native antimony Tin-white, hardness 3-3½, specific gravity 6.7
Antimony ochre Yellowish weathering product of stibnite.

---

1 Tetrahedrite, Pasto Buno/Peru
2 Valentinite, Bösing/Czechoslovakia
3 Berthierite, Herja/Rumania

4 Jamesonite (metallic grey) in quartz, Neumühle/Thüringia/Germany
5 Jamesonite with pyrite, Zacatecas/Mexico

LIGHT-METAL RAW MATERIALS

Bauxite, the raw material for aluminium, and magnesite, raw material for magnesium, belong here. Aluminium is employed in vehicle construction and in electronics; magnesium in the making of components for aircraft, as an alloy-metal and for pyrotechnics.

Bauxite [3]

Bauxite is a mixture, particularly of the minerals gibbsite, diaspore, boehmite and alumogel. White to dark red-brown, dense, earthy, reniform. Originates as the weathering residuum of carbonate rock (calc bauxite) or, in a tropical climate, from silicate rock (silicate bauxite). LOCALITIES: Vogelsberg/Hessen/Germany, Les Baux/France, Gant/Hungary, Guyana, Arkansas/USA.

Gibbsite [1] Hydrargillite

Composition Al(OH)$_3$	*Colour* colourless, white, different tones
Hardness 2½-3½	*Streak* white
Specific Gravity 2.3-2.4	*Lustre* vitreous, pearly
Cleavage very perfect	*Transparency* transparent to translucent
Fracture flexible, tough	*Crystal system* monoclinic

Small, tabular crystals. Usually scaly, radially fibrous, botryoidal aggregates, nodular crusts. Occurs as a constituent of bauxite and tropical soils (laterite, terra rossa). LOCALITIES: as for bauxite.

Diaspore [2]

Composition AlOOH	*Colour* colourless, white, lightly tinted
Hardness 6½-7	*Streak* white
Specific Gravity 3.3-3.5	*Lustre* vitreous, pearly
Cleavage very perfect	*Transparency* transparent to translucent
Fracture conchoidal, brittle	*Crystal system* orthorhombic

Crystals small, tabular, rare. Lamellar, radiating aggregates, also compact masses. Occurs as a constituent of calc-bauxites, metamorphic rocks, tropical lateritic soils. LOCALITIES: Tessin/Switzerland, Greiner/Tyrol/Austria, Greece, Chester/Massachusetts/USA.

Boehmite (AlOOH) Similar to diaspore in many respects.
Alumogel (AlOOH+aq) Amorphous, white or coloured masses.

Magnesite [4] Bitter spar

Composition MgCO$_3$	*Colour* colourless, white, grey, brownish
Hardness 4-4½	*Streak* white
Specific Gravity 2.9-3.1	*Lustre* vitreous
Cleavage very perfect	*Transparency* transparent to translucent
Fracture conchoidal, brittle	*Crystal system* trigonal

Crystals rare. Aggregates granular-sparry or fine grained dense. Occurs in metamorphic rocks and dolomite rock. LOCALITIES: Kärnten/Austria, Tyrol, Czechoslovakia, Greece, Yugoslavia, Korea, China, Coast Range/California/USA. Raw material for high-temperature-resistant construction material, as insulation material and for the extraction of magnesium metal.

---

1 Gibbsite, Minas Gerais/Brazil
2 Diaspore, Mineral County/Nevada/USA

3 Bauxite, Istria/Yugoslavia
4 Magnesite, Tuscany/Italy

RADIOACTIVE MINERALS

The best known radioactive minerals are autunite, brannerite, carnotite (p.120), monazite (p.152), torbernite, thorite, uranocircite, uranophane and pitchblende. Uranium and thorium are used in the generation of nuclear energy.

Torbernite [1] Copper uranite

Composition Cu[UO$_2$|PO$_4$]$_2$·8-12H$_2$O	*Colour* grass green
Hardness 2-2½	*Streak* pale green
Specific Gravity 3.3-3.7	*Lustre* vitreous, pearly
Cleavage perfect	*Transparency* translucent
Fracture uneven	*Crystal system* tetragonal

Crystals thin-tabular. Scaly aggregates, also crusty. Occurs in the oxidation zone of uranium deposits. LOCALITIES: Erzgebirge/Germany, Massif Central/France, Zaire, Utah/USA, Cornwall/England. Indicator mineral for uranium ores.

Uranophane [2] Uranotil

Composition CaH$_2$[UO$_2$|SiO$_4$]·5H$_2$O	*Colour* yellow
Hardness 2½	*Streak* light yellow
Specific Gravity 3.8-3.9	*Lustre* vitreous, pearly
Cleavage perfect	*Transparency* translucent
Fracture brittle	*Crystal system* monoclinic

Acicular crystals. Radiating but also felted aggregates. Occurs in uranium deposits and in druses in granite. LOCALITIES: Oberpfalz/Germany, Erzgebirge/Czechoslovakia, Zaire, New Mexico/USA. Only rarely in workable quantity.

Autunite [3] Lime uranite

Composition Ca[UO$_2$|PO$_4$]$_2$·8-12H$_2$O	*Colour* yellow with greenish tinge
Hardness 2-2½	*Streak* yellowish
Specific Gravity 3.2	*Lustre* vitreous, pearly
Cleavage perfect	*Transparency* translucent
Fracture uneven, brittle	*Crystal system* tetragonal

Crystals tabular. Tufted aggregates. Occurs in uranium deposits. LOCALITIES: Erzgebirge/Germany, Autun/Saone/France, Zaire, Mount Spokane/Washington and Colorado/USA.

Pitchblende [4] Uraninite and pecherz

Composition UO$_2$	*Colour* black
Hardness 4-6	*Streak* black, brownish, greenish
Specific Gravity 9.1-10.6	*Lustre* greasy, dull
Cleavage none	*Transparency* opaque
Fracture conchoidal, uneven	*Crystal system* cubic

Crystals and crystalline aggregates (uraninite) exhibit cube and octahedron, massive forms (pitchblende) reniform, powdery ("uranium black"). Strongly radioactive. Occurs in acid rocks, pegmatites, sandstones. LOCALITIES: Oberpfalz, Erzgebirge/Germany, Ontario/Canada, Colorado/ USA. The most important uranium ore.

---

1 Torbernite, Poppenreuth/Oberpfalz/Germany
2 Uranophane, New Mexico/USA
3 Autunite on quartz, Erzgebirge/Germany
4 Pitchblende, Wölsendorf/Oberpfalz/Germany

Monazite [3]

Composition Ce[PO₄]	*Colour* yellow to dark brown
Hardness 5-5½	*Streak* white
Specific Gravity 4.6-5.7	*Lustre* resinous
Cleavage perfect	*Transparency* translucent to opaque
Fracture conchoidal, brittle	*Crystal system* monoclinic

Crystals thick tabular, embedded and encrusting, frequently twinned, almost always thorium-bearing and thus often radioactive. Disseminated grains in acid igneous rocks and their pegmatites, in gneiss and particularly in stream-placer and beach-placer deposits. LOCALITIES: Travancore/S India, Sri Lanka, Esperito Santo/Brazil, Cape Province/South Africa, Amelia Court House/Virginia and Alexander County/N Carolina/USA Important raw material for the extraction of thorium and cerium.

SULPHUR-BEARING MINERALS

Sulphur-bearing minerals are pyrrhotite, marcasite, pyrite and native sulphur. Sulphur is used for the production of sulphuric acid. The chemical and pharmaceutical industries, the rubber and paper industries consume large quantities of sulphuric acid.

Pyrrhotite [1,2] Pyrrhotine

Composition FeS	*Colour* brown yellow
Hardness 4	*Streak* grey black
Specific Gravity 4.6	*Lustre* metallic
Cleavage imperfect	*Transparency* opaque
Fracture brittle, uneven	*Crystal system* hexagonal

Crystals usually small, tabular, rare. Aggregates coarsely-lamellar, rosette-like, mostly massive granular to compact masses; frequently disseminated. Magnetic. Occurs in basic plutonic rocks, skarns, veins and stocks, rarely in metamorphic rocks. LOCALITIES: Bodenmais/ Bayerischer Wald/Germany, Freiberg/Saxony/ Germany, Trepca/Yugoslavia, Central Sweden, Minas Gerais/Brazil, Sudbury/ Canada, Standish/Maine and Brewster/New York/USA. Occasionally the raw material for the manufacture of sulphuric acid. In association with pentlandite (p.114) an important ore of nickel.

Native sulphur [4]

Composition S	*Colour* yellow, brownish with greenish tinge
Hardness 2	*Streak* white
Specific Gravity 2.0-2.1	*Lustre* adamantine, resinous, greasy
Cleavage none	*Transparency* translucent
Fracture conchoidal, uneven	*Crystal system* orthorhombic

Crystals pyramidal, common. Aggregates compact granular, fibrous, dense, also crusts, and impregnations. Frequently occurs in volcanic areas originating from gases and thermal springs; also in clayey, marly sedimentary rocks. LOCALITIES: Sicily/Italy, Texas, Louisiana/USA, Japan, Indonesia. Sulphur is the raw material for the production of sulphuric acid and is an important basic material for the manufacture of insecticides.

---

1 Pyrrhotite, Waldsassen/Oberpfalz/Germany
2 Pyrrhotite with ankerite, Mexico

3 Monazite in parent rock, Namibia
4 Sulphur on calcite, Sicily/Italy

1
2
3
4

Marcasite [1,2]

Composition FeS$_2$	*Colour* brassy yellow with a greenish tinge
Hardness 6-6½	*Streak* greenish black
Specific Gravity 4.8-4.9	*Lustre* metallic
Cleavage imperfect	*Transparency* opaque
Fracture uneven, brittle	*Crystal system* orthorhombic

Crystals embedded and encrusting, tabular, often intergrown, twinned. Frequently covered with a rust-coloured weathered skin. Aggregates as crystal groups or compact-radiating, crusty. Petrifying substance of animal and plant fossils. Occurs in pyrrhotite deposits, ore veins in limestone, as concretions in argillaceous rocks and lignite. Localities: Meggen/Westphalia/Germany, Upper Silesia/Poland, Brüx/Czechoslovakia, Galena/Illinois and Missouri/USA, Dover/England. Together with pyrite used as raw material for sulphur.

Marcasite can decompose and thus change into sulphurous acid and sulphur. Therefore marcasite in collections should be isolated from the air. There is no safe method of preservation. Sometimes a coating of lacquer or soaking in paraffin helps. Frequently the breakdown first starts after several years.

Cocks'-comb pyrites [1] Marcasite crystals in parallel growth which form aggregates like the comb of a chicken.
Spear pyrites [2] Marcasite crystals intergrown like the point of a spear.
Radiated pyrites Coarsely-to-finely-radiating marcasite aggregates.
Hepatic pyrites Compact, dense marcasite masses.
Marcasite nodules [3] Nut-to head-sized concretions with radiating structure. Most nodules said to be marcasite consist of pyrite.

Pyrite [3-5]

Composition FeS$_2$	*Colour* brassy yellow, tarnish multi-coloured
Hardness 6-6½	*Streak* greenish black
Specific Gravity 5.0-5.2	*Lustre* metallic
Cleavage imperfect	*Transparency* opaque
Fracture conchoidal, brittle	*Crystal system* cubic

Crystals embedded and encrusting. Cubes with characteristic striations, pentagonal dodecahedra, octahedra, many crystal combinations, interpenetration twins. Occasionally has a brown to rust-red weathering skin. Aggregates compact-granular, radiating, nodular, reniform, frequently disseminated. Occurs in deposits on its own, in association with other minerals in sulphide ore deposits, in argillaceous and calcareous rocks, in bituminous coal and lignite beds and as an accessory constituent in many igneous rocks. Localities: Meggen/Westphalia, Rammelsberg/Harz/Germany, Elba, Piemont/Italy, Greece, Spain, Sweden, South Africa, Leadville/Colorado Jerome/Arizona/USA.

Pyrite is the most important source of sulphur after native sulphur; because of its frequent association with gold and copper minerals it is locally a gold and copper ore.

Weathering of pyrite in sulphide deposits produces, in near-surface zones, the so-called iron hat, limonitic iron ore.

---

1 Marcasite as cockscomb pyrites, Indiana/USA
2 Marcasite as spear pyrite, Brüx/Czechoslovakia
3 So-called marcasite nodule, Calais/France
4 Pyrite aggregate, Huelva/Spain
5 Pyrite in crystalline form and as more massive

1

2

3

4

5

MINERALS AS GEMSTONES

STONES IN THE LIVES OF HUMANS

Gemstones have been known to man for at least 7000 years. Among the first known were amethyst, amber, garnet, jade, lapis lazuli, emerald and turquoise. They were reserved for the wealthy classes of the population and served as a status symbol. Princes demonstrated wealth and hence power with insignia studded with precious stones. Right up to modern times gemstones have been valued as amulets and talismans. They are supposed to ward off evil, sustain health, make one privy to princely favour and bring home seafarers safely. Gemstones even have their value as remedies in powdered form or placed in contact with the body. At an early stage gemstones were allocated to signs of the zodiac, and from these in turn birth-stones and month-stones were derived. Recently some states have identified themselves symbolically with gemstones which are to be found within their borders. Gemstones also have their established place in modern religions. The official shield of the high priest of the Jews was studded with four rows of precious stones. Gemstones adorn the tiara and mitre of the Pope and bishops as well as the monstrances, reliquaries and icons in Christian churches.

Today, jewellery is used to a much higher degree than was earlier the case as a source of personal gratification, providing pleasure in beauty and harmony. However, the gemstone is often stripped of all symbolic and aesthetic value and is regarded purely as a capital investment.

TERMINOLOGY

Precious stone There is no completely unambiguous definition of the precious stone. All precious stones have in common the fact that they are special and that they are beautiful. In former times only a few stones were designated as precious. Today there is an almost countless number of precious stones.

Most gemstones are minerals, rarely mineral aggregates. There are also a number of substances of organic origin (for example amber) which are included as precious stones. The variety of precious stones has increased even further through the production of artificial copies and through the creation of stones which have no natural counterpart.

Semi-precious stone In earlier times semi-precious stone was used to designate stones which were less valuable and not very hard. This term, still current in the trade today, ought not to be used, because it has a derogatory significance. There is no clear boundary between them and "genuine" precious stones.

Gemstone Collective term for all ornamental stones. Some people, on the other hand, use it to embrace the less valuable stones, similar to the term semi-precious stone. In actual fact there is no convincing way to distinguish these from the "more valuable" precious stones, and hence it is often quite simply used as a synonym for precious stones.

Coloured precious stone (coloured stone) Term used essentially in the trade for gemstones, with the exception of agate and diamond.

Toison of the Golden Fleece (1760/70) with diamonds, rubies and garnets; original size (Treasure chamber, Munich Residency)

Jewel In the wider sense every ornamental piece is a jewel. In the narrower sense a jewel is understood to be a piece of jewellery which contains one or several gemstones set in precious metal. Occasionally polished stones which are not in a setting are also described as jewels.

Gemmology (the science of gemstones) Scientific discipline which is concerned with gemstones, a branch of mineralogy.

Carat A unit of weight in the gemstone trade which has been generally used since ancient times, although in earlier days there were somewhat differing weight values. Since 1907 the valid measurement is the metric carat (mct). 1 carat = 200 milligrams or 0.2 grams. Subdivision of the carat is expressed in fractions (e.g. one-tenth of a carat) or in decimals to two places (e.g. 1.25ct).

The carat weight of gemstones must not be confused with the carat number used by goldsmiths. With gold the carat is not a unit of weight but rather a designation of quality. The higher the carat number, the more fine the gold present in the piece of jewellery, so that the weight can be different each time.

THE NOMENCLATURE OF GEMSTONES

The oldest names of gemstones go back to Oriental languages, to Greek and Latin. The Greek language in particular has left its stamp on the modern nomenclature of gemstones.

The names refer to outstanding characteristics (particularly colour), to locations and to mysterious powers which are allegedly innate within the gemstone. With the development of a scientific method of observation in mineralogy the science of gemstones becomes more objective. Occult and mystical ideas recede into the background. Nevertheless there is still something inexplicably special that surrounds gemstones. The many foreign-sounding names of gemstones, as they are frequently used in the trade, also contribute to this. Many "fantasy" names, often positively misleading, are supposed to increase the incentive to buy by giving the impression that the stones are of a greater value than is in fact the case and also by conjuring up an association with something mysterious.

In many countries there are legally binding regulations and recommendations concerning the naming of gemstones, but in the practice of selling such guidelines are frequently ignored.

IMITATIONS

Attempts to imitate gemstones are as old as the hills. The types of imitations can be divided into three groups. The oldest are imitations made from a different material substance than the stone in question. The so-called composite stones contain at least one part which is a genuine gemstone. Finally, synthetic gemstones are purely artificial products, but made from the same material as the stone being imitated.

Imitations (*sensu stricto*) The Egyptians were probably the first to fake valuable stones by using glass and glazing. In 1758 a Viennese man, Josef Strasser, developed a type of glass which could be ground and looks deceptively similar to diamonds. These diamond imitations, known as strass, made their way into the gemstone trade.

In the meantime many imitation gemstones have become widespread. Simple plate glass is sufficient for cheap fashion jewellery; for imitation gemstones which give the effect of being more valuable, lead glass or flint glass are used, because they have a high refractive index. Porcelain, artificial resins and plastic materials are also used in imitating gemstones.

All these imitations usually have only the colour in common with the original; the other physical characteristics, especially hardness and fire can never be satisfactorily reproduced.

Composite or assembled stones In this group of imitations at least one part is a natural gemstone, which is combined with other gemstones, with non-precious stones or with glass. If the newly constructed stone consists of two parts it is called a doublet, if there are three parts it is called a triplet. The desired colour tone is often achieved merely by using a coloured adhesive layer to bind the individual parts together. Stones which have been carefully assembled are difficult to recognise, especially if the seams are covered by the setting.
Reconstructed stones These are made by melting together small splinters of real precious stones to produce pieces of a larger format. They are mid-way between synthetics and doublets.

Synthetic gemstones (synthetics) For centuries men have had the dream of producing stones which look completely like genuine gemstones. At the end of the nineteenth century this hope was fulfilled when the French chemist, A.V. Verneuil, succeeded in producing the first commercially usable synthetic rubies. His flame fusion process is still used today on a large scale. The end product of this method is a body of a longish pear shape, approximately 1.5cm in diameter and up to 7cm in length. This artificial stone corresponds completely to the original with regard to its crystal structure, chemical composition and physical characteristics. A laymen would find it scarcely possible to distinguish between the natural gemstones and the synthetic.

Nowadays almost all precious stones have their good synthetic equivalents. In 1955 there was a successful attempt to produce synthetic diamonds in the USA and in Sweden simultaneously. In 1970 diamonds of gemstone quality and of usable size were achieved. However, production is so expensive that for the time being synthetic diamonds will not be able to establish themselves on the gemstones market. For industrial purposes synthetic diamonds which do not possess gemstone quality have become indispensable.

Since 1953 there have been in existence synthetic stones of gemstone quality which have no natural counterpart. They are impressive because of outstanding optical characteristics and often serve as diamond substitutes. Among these are fabulite (or diagem). YAG (or diamonair), galliant, djevalite and zirconia (or phianite, also known as fianite).

Synthetically produced gemstones are not included in the imitations but form an independent group alongside natural precious stones. In the trade they always have to be designated as "synthetic".

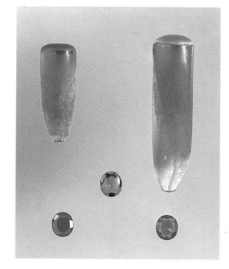

Boules and synthetic precious stones which have been cut from them.

WORKING OF GEMSTONES

Until about 1400 only natural crystal surfaces and cleavage surfaces of transparent stones were worked. When these surfaces were polished they acquired a higher lustre and better transparency. Even before this date opaque gemstones were ground on hard sandstone until they were smooth or curved (en cabochon) before the polishing took place. A highpoint in the working of stones was reached in the form of the facet cut, which appeared in the fifteenth century.

The purpose of grinding is to emphasise the colour of the gemstone, heighten the brilliance, intensify the dispersion, but also to suppress disadvantageous characteristics. We differentiate between en cabochon cut, plain cut and facet cut according to the type of surface shaping.

In the working of gemstones we nowadays differentiate between stone engraving, working of agate, of coloured stones and of diamond.

Stone engraving Stone engraving, also known as glyptography, embraces the cutting of reliefs as well as the production of small sculptures and ornamental objects. Engravings which cut down into the surface, those with a negative picture, used for seals, are called intaglios, those with raised pictures are called cameos. The term intaglio is also used as an umbrella term for both types of engraving. Multi-coloured agates are the usual raw material for intaglios. The main tool is a small lathe with a horizontally set shaft.

Working of agate Agate is first roughly shaped on a carborundum grinding wheel. The fine grinding is carried out on a sandstone wheel. The polishing takes place on slowly turning cylinders and wheels covered in wood, leather or felt. Recently automatic machines have been developed which ensure even grinding and evenly rounded shapes.

Working of coloured stones The coloured stone is cut to the required size with a circular saw set with diamonds, then formed into a rough shape with a coarse-grained carborundum wheel. Opaque stones are given an en cabochon cut on fine-grained carborundum wheels, transparent stones are given a facet cut on a horizontal grinding disc.

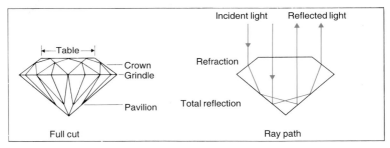

Diamond, brilliant cut

Working of diamond Formerly rough diamonds were initially all cleaved, nowadays they are sawn. The diamond acquires its rough shape by being rubbed against another diamond. Finally the facets are produced with a horizontally set steel disc smeared with powdered diamond and oil. For the brilliant cut the facet surfaces are calculated in such a way that light falling upon the crystal is repeatedly reflected inside the crystal and thrown back upwards. In this way the brilliance of the stone is achieved.

WELL KNOWN TYPES OF CUT OF GEMSTONES
(looking from above and from the side)

1 *Brilliant full cut* Possesses at least 32 facets plus the table on the upper part as well as at least 24 facets on the lower part. Since this cut was developed specifically for diamond it is also known as the diamond cut. The short term brilliant is only apposite for the diamond, all other brilliant-ground precious stones have to bear the name of the mineral (e.g. zircon-brilliant).

2 *Eight cut* In addition to the table it also has 8 facets on both upper and lower parts. Used for the smallest diamonds on which it is not possible or not worth carrying out a full cut.

3 *Step cut* Simple kind of facet cut, used especially for coloured gemstones. Several facets are cut parallel to the edges, the steepness of the facets increases towards the girdle. On the lower part the number of facets is usually greater.

4 *Emerald cut* Step cut with octagonal shape, especially for emeralds, but also used for other coloured stones.

5 *Rose cut* Facet cut without table or pavilion. Several variations, depending on number and arrangement of facets. Nowadays very rarely used because of low level of brilliance.

6 *Scissors cut* Variation of step cut. Facets are divided into four sub-facets by the "scissors".

7 *Table cut* Simplest form of step cut. The upper part is very flat, giving a large table. Used as seal-ring or gentleman's ring.

8 *Cabochon* Main representative of plain cut. Upper part domed, lower part level or slightly arched. With dark stones the lower part is hollowed out inside (chipped out), in order to lighten the colour.

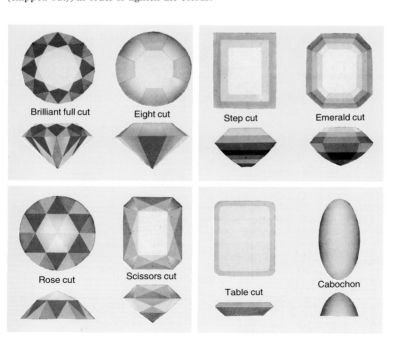

Brilliant full cut   Eight cut   Step cut   Emerald cut

Rose cut   Scissors cut   Table cut   Cabochon

Diamond [3,12,13]

Composition C	*Colour* colourless, all colours, also black
Hardness 10	*Streak* white
Specific Gravity 3.47-3.55	*Lustre* adamantine
Cleavage perfect	*Transparency* transparent to opaque
Fracture conchoidal, splintery, brittle	*Crystal system* cubic

Crystals embedded, octahedron, dodecahedron, cube. High refraction, strong dispersion. Globular, dense aggregates are called carbonado or bort. Colourless and fine coloured diamonds are cut for gemstones. The value of a diamond depends on purity, colour, cut and weight.

Only 20% of all diamonds are suitable for use in jewellery. The majority are used as industrial diamonds (bort) for drilling, cutting, and grinding-tools.

Occurs in old volcanic vents, pipes or in placer deposits. The largest producers of gem diamonds are South Africa, Russia, Namibia, Australia; the largest producers of natural industrial diamonds are Zaire, Russia, South Africa.

Diamond synthesis was successful in 1955 in the USA and Sweden. At the present time the production of synthetic diamonds, which are not suitable for jewellery, is greater then the output of natural diamonds.

Corundum [15-18]

Composition Al_2O_3	*Colour* colourless, different colours
Hardness 9	*Streak* white
Specific Gravity 3.97-4.05	*Lustre* vitreous
Cleavage none	*Transparency* transparent to opaque
Fracture conchoidal, splintery, brittle	*Crystal system* trigonal

Crystals mostly embedded, tabular, short columnar, barrel-shaped. Usually show asterism [1,4]. Crystalline aggregates and compact, sparry masses. Occurs in plutonic rocks and their pegmatites, in carbonate rocks and placers.

Common corundum Unattractively cloudy. Used as a grinding and polishing medium.
Schmirgel Mixture of crystalline corundum, magnetite, hematite and quartz, among others; used as a grinding material. Localities: Turkey, Greece, Massachusetts/USA

Gem corundum Corundum suitable for use in jewellery – ruby and sapphire.
Ruby [10,17,18] Red variety of corundum. Occurs in dolomitised marble and in placer deposits. Localities: Upper Burma, Thailand, Sri Lanka, Tanzania. Synthetic gemstone rubies [4,14] are on the market.
Sapphire [5-8,15,17] All gem quality corundums which are not red, particularly the blue varieties. Colourless sapphire is called leucosapphire, orange yellow is padparadscha [6]. Usually occurs in placer deposits. Localities: Australia, Burma, Sri Lanka, Thailand. Synthetic sapphires [1,2,11].

1 Synthetic star sapphire	10 Ruby, Thailand
2 Synthetic sapphire	11 Synthetic corundum
3 Diamond, South Africa	12 Diamond crystal, Ghana
4 Synthetic star ruby	13 Diamond crystal, Kinshase/Zaire
5 Synthetic sapphire-triplet	14 Synthetic ruby
6 Padparadscha sapphire, Ceylon	15 Sapphire crystals, Australia and Upper Burma
7 Sapphire, Mogok/Burma	16 Corundum crystal, Sri Lanka
8 Sapphire, Mogok/Burma	17 Ruby in matrix, Canada
9 Zirconia used as a diamond substitute	18 Ruby crystals, Burma

Beryl [10]

Composition Al₂Be₃[Si₆O₁₈]	*Colour* colourless, variously coloured
Hardness 7½-8	*Streak* white
Specific Gravity 2.63-2.91	*Lustre* vitreous
Cleavage imperfect	*Transparency* transparent to opaque
Fracture conchoidal, uneven, brittle	*Crystal system* hexagonal

Crystals embedded and encrusting, mostly long prisms, rarely tabular. Sometimes compact, granular aggregates. Occurs in pegmatite veins of granitic rocks and in placer deposits. LOCALITIES: S Korea, India, Brazil, W Australia, S Dakota, New Hampshire/USA. The most important ore for the extraction of beryllium.

Common beryl Unattractively cloudy, not of gemstone quality.
Precious beryl Beautifully coloured beryl variety suitable for jewellery.

Emerald [1,2,8] Green variety of beryl. Mostly cloudy because of inclusions. Occurs in or close to pegmatite veins. Worked almost entirely from the parent rock, rarely from placer deposits. LOCALITIES: Muzo and Chivor/Colombia, Brazil, Zimbabwe, Transvaal/South Africa, Habachtal, Salzburg/Austria. Synthetic emeralds have been on the market since the 1950s. There are also triplets [1] as imitations.

Aquamarine [3,4,12] Blue variety of beryl. Parent rocks are pegmatite and granite. LOCALITIES: Brazil, Nigeria, Australia, Burma, India, Sri Lanka. So-called synthetic aquamarines are in fact synthetic spinels.

Golden beryl [5] Gem beryl with lemon yellow to golden yellow colour.
Goshenite Colourless gem beryl.
Heliodor Gem beryl with light yellow green colour.
Morganite Gem beryl with soft pink to violet colour.

Chrysoberyl [6,11]

Composition Al₂BeO₄	*Colour* yellow, greenish, brownish
Hardness 8½	*Streak* white
Specific Gravity 3.7-3.72	*Lustre* vitreous, greasy
Cleavage imperfect	*Transparency* transparent to translucent
Fracture conchoidal, brittle	*Crystal system* orthorhombic

Crystals embedded, thick tabular. Occurs in pegmatites, schists and placers. LOCALITIES: Sri Lanka, Mogok/Burma, Urals/Russia, Minas Gerais/Brazil, Haddam/Connecticut/USA. Locally used as a beryllium ore. Fine coloured varieties as gemstones.

Alexandrite [7,9] Chrysoberyl of gemstone quality. Green in daylight but red in artificial light. Frequently shows interpenetration twinning. LOCALITIES: Sri Lanka, Zimbabwe, Burma, Brazil. Alexandrite-coloured imitations are known.

Chrysoberyl cat's eye (Cat's eye, cymophane) Chrysoberyl variety with a wavy-light effect. Localities: Sri Lanka, Brazil, China.

---

1 Emerald coloured beryl triplet
2 Emerald, Muzo/Colombia
3 Aquamarine, Madagascar
4 Aquamarine, Minas Gerais/Brazil
5 Golden beryl, Sri Lanka
6 Chrysoberyl, Minas Novas/Brazil

7 Alexandrite coloured synthetic corundum
8 Emerald in parent rock, Chivor/Colombia
9 Alexandrite, Novello Claims/Zimbabwe
10 Beryl in parent rock, Utah/USA
11 Chrysoberyl (yellow) with garnet (red) USA
12 Aquamarine in quartz, Brazil

Spinel [1-3, 15]

Composition MgAl$_2$O$_4$	*Colour* colourless, all colours
Hardness 8	*Streak* white
Specific Gravity 3.58-3.61	*Lustre* vitreous
Cleavage imperfect	*Transparency* transparent to opaque
Fracture conchoidal, brittle	*Crystal system* cubic

Crystals usually octahedral, embedded, mostly small, frequently twinned. Occurs in carbonate rocks, igneous rocks, schists, placers. LOCALITIES: Sri Lanka, Burma, Thailand, Orange County/New York and Ogdensburg/New Jersey/USA. Gemstone (precious spinel). Synthetic spinels are available [3,4].

Pleonaste [Ceylonite] Opaque, black spinel.

Topaz [5,10,13,16]

Composition Al$_2$(F$_2$SiO$_4$)	*Colour* colourless, yellow, brown, blue, green
Hardness 8	*Streak* white
Specific Gravity 3.53-3.56	*Lustre* vitreous
Cleavage perfect	*Transparency* transparent to translucent
Fracture conchoidal, uneven	*Crystal system* orthorhombic

Crystals prismatic, encrusting. Occurs in acid igneous rocks, in greisen, in placers. LOCALITIES: Saxony, Brazil, Sri Lanka, Burma, Pakistan, Colorado/USA, Cornwall/England. Gemstone (gem topaz). Colours are changed by heating.

Golden topaz Misleading trade name for amethyst turned yellow by heating.

Zircon [7,11,12,14]

Composition Zr [Si O$_4$]	*Colour* brown, red, green, blue, colourless.
Hardness 6½-7½	*Streak* white
Specific Gravity 3.9-4.8	*Lustre* adamantine, greasy
Cleavage imperfect	*Transparency* transparent to opaque
Fracture conchoidal, brittle	*Crystal system* tetragonal

Crystals short columnar, embedded or rounded grains. Occurs as an accessory constituent in many rock types, in placer deposits. LOCALITIES: Norway, Cambodia, Burma, Thailand, Sri Lanka, Florida and Litchfield/Maine/USA, Renfrew/Canada. The most important ore of zirconium. Gemstone. Heating produces colourless or blue stones [11].

Hyacinth Yellowish red to red brown zircon variety.
Starlite Blue zircon variety. [11] is heated zircon with starlite colours.
Jargon Colourless to pale yellow variety of zircon.
Zirconia [6] Synthetic gemstone, passed off as zircon and diamond

Garnet [8,9]

See also pp.80/81. Gemstone minerals which occur in all colours except blue.

1 Spinel, Mogok/Burma
2 Spinel, Sri Lanka
3 Synthetic spinel triplet
4 Topaz coloured synthetic spinel
5 Topaz, Minas Gerais/Brazil
6 Zirconia, a synthetic gemstone
7 Zircon, Sri Lanka
8 Garnet – pyrope variety, Bohemia/ Czechoslovakia
9 Garnet – almandine variety, Sri Lanka
10 Topaz crystal, Thomas Mts/Utah/USA
11 Heated zircon, Sri Lanka
12 Zircon crystal, Brazil
13 Topaz crystal, Minas Gerais/Brazil
14 Zircon with biotite in quartz, Norway
15 Spinel (pleonaste) in calcite, Madagascar
16 Topaz on quartz, Schneckenstein/Saxony/ Germany

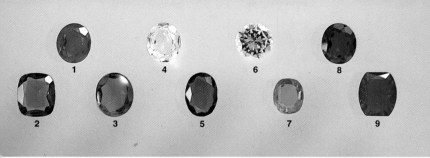

Tourmaline [2-6]

Composition (Na,Li,Ca)(Fe^2,Mg,Mn,Al)$_3$ Al$_6$[(OH)$_4$l(BO$_3$)$_3$lSi$_6$O$_{18}$]	*Fracture* Conchoidal, uneven, brittle
Hardness 7-7½	*Colour* colourless, all colours
Specific Gravity 3.02-3.26	*Streak* white
Cleavage none	*Lustre* vitreous
	Transparency transparent to opaque

Crystals (trigonal system) embedded and encrusting, elongated, vertical striations, three sided cross section. Compact columnar aggregates. Occurs in acid igneous rocks and their pegmatites, in calcareous rocks and schists, in placer deposits. LOCALITIES: Sri Lanka, Madagascar, Brazil, Mozambique, Maine, Pala/California, Hamburg/New Jersey, New York/USA, Cornwall/England.
Tourmaline comprises a group of mixed crystals:

Elbaite Lithium tourmaline **Buergerite** Iron tourmaline
Dravite Magnesium tourmaline **Tsilaisite** Manganese tourmaline
Schorl Iron tourmaline **Uvite** Magnesium tourmaline

Tourmaline is a widely used gemstone. Colour varieties have their own name.

Achroite colourless or almost colourless **Rubellite** pink to red
Dravite yellow brown to dark brown **Schorl** black
Indigolite all shades of blue **Verdelite** all shades of green

Spodumene [7,8]

Composition LiAl[Si$_2$O$_6$]	*Colour* grey-white, colourless, green, violet
Hardness 6-7	*Streak* white
Specific Gravity 3.16-3.20	*Lustre* vitreous, pearly
Cleavage perfect	*Transparency* transparent to translucent
Fracture uneven	*Crystal system* monoclinic

Crystals prismatic, tabular. Aggregates sparry, broad columnar. Occurs in granite pegmatites. LOCALITIES: Scotland, Sweden, Madagascar, Brazil, Burma, S Dakota & N Carolina/USA, Manitoba/Canada. Important lithium raw material. Fine coloured varieties used as gemstones.
Hiddenite Yellow green to green variety of spodumene. Gemstone.
Kunzite Pink to violet spodumene variety. Gemstone.

Jadeite [10]

Composition NaAl[Si$_2$O$_6$]	*Colour* green, also other colours
Hardness 6½-7	*Streak* white
Specific Gravity 3.30-3.36	*Lustre* vitreous
Cleavage imperfect	*Transparency* translucent to opaque
Fracture uneven, splintery, very tough	*Crystal system* monoclinic

Crystals very rare, short prismatic. Usually felted, fibrous aggregates. Occurs in crystalline schists and as pebbles. LOCALITIES: Burma, Yunan/China, Japan, California/USA. Used for *objets d'art*.
Chloromelanite [9] Green to black flecked variety of jadeite.
Jade Umbrella term for the similar minerals jadeite and nephrite (p.86)

---

1 Dark and light green jadeite, Taiwan
2 Green tourmaline, Brazil
3 Green and red tourmaline, Madagascar
4 Tourmaline crystals, Brazil
5 Tourmaline cross section, Mozambique

6 Rubellite tourmaline, California/USA
7 Hiddenite, Minas Gerais/Brazil
8 Kunzite, Brazil
9 Chloromelanite, Burma
10 Jadeite, China

Peridot [1-3] Chrysolite

Peridot or chrysolite is the term used by the trade for the gem variety of olivine. In mineralogy both names are synonymous with olivine. Mineralogical data for olivine are given on page 52.

The colour of peridot is yellow green, olive green or greenish brown. It occurs in basic igneous rocks, in serpentinite and as a derived mineral in sands. LOCALITIES: Volcanic island Zebirget (St. John)/Red Sea, Mogok/Upper Burma, Queensland/Australia, Brazil, South Africa, San Carlos/Arizona and Hawaii/USA.

Thulite [4]

Dense, red gem variety of zoisite. Mineralogical data for zoisite on page 82. Occurs in metamorphic rocks. LOCALITIES: Central and South Norway, Namibia, Western Australia, North Carolina/USA .

Tanzanite [5,6]

Blue transparent gemstone variety of zoisite. Mineralogical data for zoisite is on page 82. In good quality material the colour is ultramarine blue to sapphire blue, under artificial illumination more amethyst violet. Heating to 400-500°C deepens the blue colour. Occurs in veins and joint infillings in gneisses. Unique locality near Arusha in the north of Tanzania.

Tanzanite was first discovered in 1967 and was named after the country of origin by the jewellery firm of Tiffany in New York.

Moonstone [7]

Transparent to translucent gemstone variety of adularia with yellowish brown to bluish white sheen. Mineralogical data for orthoclase on page 40. Occurs in pegmatites. LOCALITIES: Sri Lanka, India, Madagascar, Australia, Brazil, USA. Moonstone is not a stone from the Moon! The name most likely derives from moonlight.

Moonstones with similar appearance are also known from other feldspars, among others, microcline, labradorite and albite.

Amazonite [8,9]

Green to bluish green opaque gemstone variety of microcline. The colour shade is generally not uniform. Mineralogical data for microcline on page 40. Occurs in granite rocks, granite pegmatites. LOCALITIES: Pike's Peak/Colorado/USA, Ilmengebirge/Urals/Russia, Madagascar, Namibia, India, Brazil.

Sunstone [10] Aventurine feldspar, aventurine.

Orange to red brown gemstone variety of oligoclase. Mineralogical data for plagioclase on page 42. The characteristic metallic glitter is caused by light interference from hematite or goethite platelets. Occurs in acid igneous rocks and gneisses. LOCALITIES: South Norway, Canada, India, Russia, USA.

Not to be confused with aventurine quartz [Nos 1 & 4, p.177] which in abbreviated form is known as sunstone aventurine.

---

1 Tumbled peridots, South Africa	6 Raw tanzanite, Arusha/Tanzania
2 Cut peridots, Burma	7 Polished moonstone, India
3 Rolled peridots, Arizona/USA	8 Cut amazonite, Namibia
4 Thulite spheres, Namibia	9 Cut amazonite, Norway
5 Cut tanzanite, Arusha/Tanzania	10 Polished sunstone, Norway

Rhodonite [1]

Composition CaMn$_4$[Si$_5$O$_{15}$]	*Colour* pink, red, black, flecks and veins
Hardness 5½-6½	*Streak* white
Specific Gravity 3.40-3.73	*Lustre* vitreous, pearly
Cleavage perfect	*Transparency* transparent to opaque
Fracture conchoidal,uneven, brittle	*Crystal system* triclinic

Crystals tabular, prismatic, rare. Coarsely sparry, dense aggregates. Occurs in schists and in manganese ore bodies. LOCALITIES: France, Urals/Russia, India, Madagascar, Franklin/New Jersey/USA. Used in the art trade. Occasionally an ore of manganese.

Lapis lazuli [2] Lazurite, lapis

Composition Na$_8$[Sl(AlSiO$_4$)$_6$]	*Colour* azure blue, violet, greenish blue
Hardness 5-6	*Streak* light blue
Specific Gravity 2.38-2.42	*Lustre* vitreous, greasy
Cleavage none	*Transparency* opaque
Fracture conchoidal, brittle	*Crystal system* cubic

Crystals embedded, very rare. Usually fine grained, dense masses. Frequently veined with calcite, disseminated pyrite. Occurs in calcareous rocks. LOCALITIES: Afghanistan, Russia, Chile, California/USA. Used as a gemstone and for ornamental objects.

Since lapis lazuli always contains several minerals (eg calcite diopside, mica, hauyne, pyrite, sodalite) some experts consider it to be a rock with the main constituent being lazurite.

Turquoise [3] Kallaite

Composition CuAl$_6$[(OH)$_2$|PO$_4$]$_4$·4H$_2$O	*Colour* sky blue, blue green
Hardness 5-6	*Streak* white
Specific Gravity 2.6-2.8	*Lustre* waxy, vitreous
Cleavage none	*Transparency* opaque
Fracture conchoidal, uneven, brittle	*Crystal system* triclinic

Crystals prismatic, very rare. Fine grained masses, botryoidal, also encrustations. Occurs as fissure fillings in joints in trachyte and sandstone. LOCALITIES: Iran, Samarkand/Russia, Sinai/Egypt, SW states of USA, Cornwall/England.
Bone turquoise (odontolite) Fossil ivory coloured turquoise-blue by vivianite.

Malachite [4]

Composition Cu$_2$[(OH)$_2$|CO$_3$]	*Colour* light green, black green
Hardness 3½-4	*Streak* light green
Specific Gravity 3.75-3.95	*Lustre* vitreous, silky, dull
Cleavage perfect	*Transparency* translucent to opaque
Fracture scaly, splintery, brittle	*Crystal system* monoclinic

Crystals acicular, rare. Aggregates compact, reniform, globular, banded, radiating. Occurs in the oxidation zone of copper ore deposits. LOCALITIES: Urals/Russia, Zaire, Australia, Chile, Namibia, Arizona/USA, Cornwall/England. Used as a gemstone and for ornamental objects.

1 Rhodonite, Franklin/New Jersey/USA
2 Lapis lazuli, Badakhschan/Afghanistan
3 Turquoise, New Mexico/USA
4 Malachite (cut) Katanga/Zaire

Rock crystal [5]

Colourless macrocrystalline variety of the quartz group. Mineralogical data on page 36. Even though its occurrence is worldwide material worth cutting is rare. For costume jewellery and as diamond imitations.

Amethyst [1,11]

Violet coloured macrocrystalline variety of quartz. Mineralogical data on page 36. The strongest shades of colour occur in the crystal terminations. Colours can fade. Heating gives rise to yellow, brown, green and colourless tones. LOCALITIES: Brazil, Uruguay, India, Madagascar, Montana and California/USA. Amethyst has recently been synthesized.

Amethystine quartz [2]

Compact formation of the violet quartz variety, amethyst. Frequently banded and streaked with milky quartz. Mineralogical data on page 36. LOCALITIES: Brazil, Uruguay, Madagascar, Namibia, Urals/Russia.

Citrine [3,4,12]

Yellow to brownish macrocrystalline variety of quartz. Mineralogical data on page 36. Natural citrines are pale yellow [4]. Most of the citrines on offer in the trade have a tinge of reddish [3,12]. Citrines can be produced by heating amethyst and smoky quartz. In the trade citrine is often misleadingly called topaz or Bahia-, Golden-, Madeira-, Palmyra-, Rio Grande-topaz. This should not be allowed. Naturally coloured citrine is rare. LOCALITES: Bahia, Minas Gerais/Brazil, Madagascar, Urals/Russia, Spain, France, Scotland, Colorado/USA.

Smoky quartz [6,7,10]

Smoke-coloured variety of macrocrystalline quartz. Mineralogical data page 36. Colour varies from brown to black. In the trade frequently but misleadingly called smoky topaz. At a temperature of 300-400°C smoky quartz can be made to lose its colour. LOCALITIES: Switzerland, Brazil, Madagascar, Colorado/USA.
Morion Very dark to black, opaque variety of smoky quartz.

Rose quartz [8,9]

Pink coloured mostly cloudy variety of quartz. Usually massive. Crystals very rare. Mineralogical data page 36. Colour, occasionally with a tinge of violet, can fade. Inclusions of rutile needles can, when the stone is cut en cabochon, give rise to a six-rayed star. LOCALITIES: Bayerischer Wald, Pleystein/Oberpfalz/Germany, Minas Gerais/Brazil, Madagascar, India.

Prasiolite

Leek-green variety of quartz whose colour can be derived by heating of violet amethyst or yellowish citrine. Only a few quartzes from Minas Gerais/Brazil and Arizona/USA are suitable for this heat treatment.

---

1 Amethyst, India
2 Amethystine quartz, Madagascar
3 Heated citrine, India
4 Natural citrine, India
5 Rock crystal, Japan
6 Smoky quartz, Brazil

7 Smoky quartz, India
8 Cut rose quartz, Madagascar
9 Rose quartz, Minas Gerais/Brazil
10 Smoky quartz, Graubünden/Switzerland
11 Amethyst, Rio Grande do Sul/Brazil
12 Heated citrine, Brazil

Aventurine [1,4] Aventurine-quartz

Massive variety of quartz with a metallic iridescence. Mineralogical data page 36. Inclusions of fuchsite mica impart to the stone a medium- to dark-green colour, hematite platelets give a red or brown colour. LOCALITIES: India, Brazil, Urals, Siberia, Tanzania. Not to be confused with sunstone [No 10, p.171] which like aventurine-quartz is also known as aventurine.

Prase [6]

Leek-green, massive variety of quartz. Mineralogical data page 36. The colour is due to actinolite inclusions. LOCALITIES: Erzgebirge/Germany, Salzburg/Austria, Finland, Scotland, North Carolina/USA, Western Australia.

Blue quartz Sapphire quartz

Usually a cloudy-blue coloured massive variety of quartz occasionally also clear, transparent to translucent. Mineralogical data page 36. The colour stems from inclusions of crocidolite- or rutile-fibres. LOCALITIES: Salzburg/Austria, Scandinavia, Brazil, South Africa, Virginia/USA.

Quartz cat's eye Cat's eye quartz

Massive quartz aggregates of white, grey, greenish or brownish colour with cat's eye effect. This latter is caused by inclusions of parallel oriented finely-fibrous amphibole asbestos and is clearly visible when cut en cabochon. Mineralogical data page 36. Irregular fracture. LOCALITIES: Sri Lanka, India, Brazil.

The abbreviated form cat's eye must not be used for quartz cat's eye since it always means the cat's eye of chrysoberyl (p.164).

Falcon's eye [3] Hawk's eye

Finely fibrous, opaque quartz aggregate with inclusions of crocidolite blue grey to blue green, with a surface schillerization with cat's eye effect when the en cabochon cut is used. The texture is a response to the partial pseudomorphism of quartz after crocidolite. Mineralogical data on page 36. Fracture is fibrous, lustre silky. LOCALITIES: Griqualand/Orange R/South Africa, Western Australia, Burma, India, California/USA.

Tiger's eye [2,5]

Finely fibrous, opaque variety of quartz, a pseudomorph of quartz after crocidolite formed from Hawk's eye by the silicification of crocidolite while keeping the columnar structure. Fracture fibrous, lustre silky. The golden yellow colour results from inclusions of limonite. Surface iridescence with cat's eye effect when cut en cabochon. Occurs together with Hawk's eye as platy cleft-fillings only a few centimetres thick. The fibres of the tiger's eye lie at right angles to the face of the cleft. LOCALITIES: Griqualand/Orange Republic/South Africa, Western Australia, Burma, India, California/USA.

1 Polished aventurine, South Africa
2 Polished tiger's eye, Griqualand/Orange R/South Africa
3 Hawk's eye, Orange R/South Africa
4 Unpolished aventurine, Warmbrunn, Silesia/Poland
5 Tiger's eye, Orange R/South Africa
6 Cut prase, Norseman/Western Australia

Chalcedony [1,2]

Bluish microcrystalline variety of the quartz group. Mineralogical data page 38. Natural chalcedony has no banding [1]. In the trade parallel-striped, artificial blue-coloured agate [2] is offered as chalcedony. LOCALITIES: Namibia, Brazil, Uruguay, India, Madagascar, Dolores County/Colorado/USA.

Agate [3]

Microcrystalline variety of the quartz group of varying colours, a chalcedony. Mineralogical data page 38. Usually translucent in thin slices, otherwise opaque. Occurs as spherical or almond shaped inclusions in basic volcanic rocks. The stripey appearance is the result of rhythmic crystallization. Under the influence of weathering a white crust forms on the outer layer and in the uppermost agate bands. In the interior of the agate-almonds there are frequently well-developed crystals (eg. rock crystal, amethyst, smoky quartz, calcite, hematite, siderite). LOCALITIES: Brazil, Uruguay, China, India, Madagascar, Mexico, USA.

Many agates are normally an unattractive grey colour and are only feebly patterned. They assume their brightly coloured appearance and striking structures only by being dyed. The extent to which the individual layers take on colour varies according to porosity, water content and crystallinity.

There are many varied uses for agate: *objets d'art*, ring-stones, brooches, pendants, as the base-stone for intaglios and cameos, and also a widely varied use in technology because of its toughness and chemical resistance. There are numerous variety names depending on colour and pattern.

Banded agate Layers parallel to the outer surface.
Enhydros (waterstone) Agate-almond full of water which shines through the walls. Quickly dries out in the air.
Fortification agate Patterned like the bastions of an old fortress.
Tubular agate Agate shot through with tube-like feeder canals.
Sard stone Agate with straight interior layers.
Brecciated agate Broken agate later naturally cemented.

Chrysoprase [5]

Green microcrystalline variety of the quartz group, a chalcedony. Mineralogical data on page 38. Larger broken pieces are often fissured with irregular colours. Colour can fade. In a moist environment the colours may recover. LOCALITIES: Queensland/Australia, Goyaz/Brazil, California/USA, South Africa, India, Madagascar.

Jasper [4]

Microcrystalline variety of quartz, a chalcedony. Mineralogical data on page 38. Contains up to 20% of foreign materials which determine the colour, streak (ochre yellow, brown to red, also white) and appearance. Uniformly coloured jasper is rare, usually it is multicoloured, striped, spotted or marbled. Many trade names; for example basanite (black), plasma (green), silex (brown/red). LOCALITIES: Baden, St Egidien/Saxony/ Germany, Dauphiné/France, India, Urals/Russia. Used for *objets d'art*.

Carnelian [1,2]

Red to brown-red microcrystalline variety of quartz, a chalcedony. Mineralogical data on page 38. Most of the carnelians on offer are coloured agates with a stripy structure [2]; true carnelians show cloudy colour distribution in transmitted light [1]. LOCALITIES: India, Brazil, Uruguay.

Sard [3]

Red brown variety of carnelian. No sharp distinction from true carnelian.

Heliotrope [4] Blood stone

Opaque, dark green variety of quartz with red spotty inclusions, a chalcedony. Mineralogical data page 38. Colours are not always constant. LOCALITIES: India, Australia, Brazil, China, USA.

Dendritic agate [1] Tree stone, Mocha stone

Colourless to whitish grey, translucent chalcedony with tree-like or fern-like images called dendrites which are brown to black iron-manganese markings on very fine fracture surfaces. Mineralogical data page 38. LOCALITIES: Rio Grande do Sul/Brazil, India, USA.

Onyx

In gemmology onyx is understood as a black chalcedony as is also the agate-like double layer of black lower layer and white upper layer. In sard-onyx the basal layer is brown, in carnelian onyx it is red. In the trade onyx is also used as an abbreviated term for onyx-marble, delicately coloured, translucent limestone, particularly calcareous sinter (p.286).

Opal

Opal belongs to the quartz group. There are three varieties: common opal, opalescent precious opal, and orange red fire opal. Mineralogical data page 38.

Precious Opal [8,9]

The special characteristic of precious opals is opalescence, a rainbow like iridescence which changes with the angle of observation. The reasons are the reflection and interference effects of very small spheres of the mineral cristobalite embedded in a siliceous jelly cement. When the water content is reduced the opalescence diminishes and the stone cracks. The ageing process can be avoided and the play of colours increased if the stone is stored in damp cotton-wool. LOCALITIES: Australia, Brazil, Guatemala, Honduras, Nevada/USA.
Opal has been synthesized since 1970.
White or milky opal [9] Precious opal with light or white base colour.
Black opal [8] Precious opal with dark ground colour.

Fire Opal [5,6]

Named because of the fire-red, orange colour. Shows no opalescence, is usually milky-turbid, only rarely clearly transparent. LOCALITIES: Hildalgo and Queretaro/Mexico, Brazil, Guatemala, Honduras, Western Australia.

---

1 Cut carnelian, India
2 Coloured carnelian, Uruguay
3 Cut sard, India
4 Cut heliotrope, Kathiavar/India
5 Cut fire opal, Mexico

6 Rough fire opal, Mexico
7 Cut dendritic agate, India
8 Black opal in matrix, Coober Pedy/South Australia
9 White opal, Queensland/Australia

1

2

3

4

5

6

7

8

9

Variscite [1] Utahlite

Composition Al[PO₄]·2H₂O	Colour yellow green, bluish, colourless
Hardness 4-5	Streak white
Specific Gravity 2.52	Lustre vitreous, waxy
Cleavage perfect	Transparency translucent to opaque
Fracture conchoidal, brittle	Crystal system orthorhombic

Crystals tabular or short prismatic, small, rare. Radiating nodules, crusts. Feels greasy. Occurs in clefts and as cavity fillings in aluminium-rich rocks. LOCALITIES: Plauen/Vogtland/Germany, Leoben/Steiermark/Austria, Utah, Arkansas/USA, Queensland/Australia.

Chrysocolla [2]

Composition CuSiO₃+aq	Colour green, blue
Hardness 2-4	Streak greenish white
Specific Gravity 2.0-2.2	Lustre vitreous, greasy
Cleavage none	Transparency translucent to opaque
Fracture conchoidal, brittle	Crystal system no crystals, amorphous

Gel-like aggregates, botryoidal, stalactitic. Occurs in the oxidation zone of copper deposits. LOCALITIES: California, Idaho/USA, Mexico, Chile, Zaire, Cornwall/England. Locally important copper ore. Occasionally used as a gemstone.

Eiiat stone Mixture of chrysocolla, turquoise and malachite; gemstone.

Azurite [3]

Composition Cu₃[OH|CO₃]₂	Colour deep blue
Hardness 3½-4	Streak light blue
Specific Gravity 3.7-3.9	Lustre vitreous, greasy
Cleavage perfect	Transparency transparent to opaque
Fracture conchoidal, uneven, brittle	Crystal system monoclinic

Crystals embedded and encrusting, short columnar, thick tabular, richly faceted. Aggregates radiating, reniform, earthy. Occurs in the oxidation zone of copper deposits. LOCALITIES: Lyons/France, Tsumeb/Namibia, Swerdlovsk/Urals/Russia, Katanga/Zaire, Arizona/USA. Occasionally used as a gemstone.

Azur-malachite Intergrowth of azurite and malachite. Gemstone.

Dioptase [4]

Composition Cu₆[Si₆O₁₈]·6H₂O	Colour emerald green
Hardness 5	Streak green
Specific Gravity 3.28-3.35	Lustre vitreous
Cleavage perfect	Transparency transparent to translucent
Fracture conchoidal, uneven, brittle	Crystal system trigonal

Crystals short prismatic, stumpy, grows on surfaces in druses, also appears as crusts. Occurs in the oxidation zone of copper deposits, in calcite-and dolomite-veins. LOCALITIES: Namibia, Katanga/Zaire, Kazakhstan/Russia, Chile, Tiger/Arizona/USA. Occasionally used as a gemstone.

1 Variscite, High Run Mine/W Australia
2 Chrysocolla, Zacatecas/Mexico
3 Azurite and malachite, Arizona/USA
4 Dioptase, Tsumeb/Namibia

Coral [4,5,7,8]

Composition CaCO$_3$	*Colour* white, pink, red
Hardness 3-4	*Streak* white
Specific Gravity 2.6-2.7	*Lustre* dull, vitreous, waxy
Cleavage none	*Transparency* opaque
Fracture uneven, splintery	*Crystal system* trigonal

Corals are the supporting framework of small polyps which precipitate calcareous material in their outer body wall and thus build up reefs, atolls and coral banks with many intertwining branches down to a depth of 300m. Only these branches are used for working as precious stones. In the unworked state coral is dull or has a waxy lustre, when polished it has a vitreous lustre. LOCALITIES: coasts of the W Mediterranean, Bay of Biscay, Canary Islands, Malaysian archipelago, Midway Islands, Japan.

Black and dark blue corals consist of an organic horny substance with a specific gravity of 1.34-1.46. LOCALITIES: Malaysian archipelago, Red Sea. Unimportant in the gemstone industry.

Amber [6] Succinite

Composition about C$_{10}$H$_{16}$O	*Colour* yellow to brown, also other colours
Hardness 2-2½	*Streak* white
Specific Gravity usually 1.05-1.09, max 1.30	*Lustre* greasy, resinous
Cleavage none	*Transparency* transparent to opaque
Fracture chonchoidal, brittle	*Crystal system* amorphous

Amber is the fossil resin of pine trees. Nodular homogeneous structure of shell-like formation. Usually turbid because of blisters and small cracks. Sometimes has inclusions of insects and parts of plants. Occurs in argillaceous rocks or as beach deposits. LOCALITIES: E Prussia. Countries around the Baltic Sea, Romania, Siberia, Burma, Canada.

Ambroid Pressed amber made up of small pieces.

Pearls [1-3]

Composition CaCO$_3$+C$_{32}$H$_{48}$N$_2$O$_{11}$+H$_2$O	*Colour* white, beige, silvery, all colours
Hardness 3-4	*Streak* white
Specific Gravity 2.60-2.78	*Lustre* pearly
Cleavage none	*Transparency* translucent to opaque
Fracture uneven	*Crystal system* orthorhombic/trigonal

Pearls are produced by shellfish, mainly by oysters and mussels, more rarely by snails; up to the size of a pigeon's egg. They consist of carbonate of lime (in the form of aragonite) and an organic horny substance (conchiolin). LOCALITIES: Persian Gulf, South coast of India, North coast of Australia, coast of Central America.

Cultured pearls have been produced on farms in sea inlets and fresh water lakes since the second decade of this century. Today cultured pearls account for 90% of the whole pearl trade. Producing countries: Japan, N and W Australia, several states in S E Asia.

1 Cream coloured cultured pearl, Japan
2 Silver coloured cultured pearl, Japan
3 Baroque (irregular) cultured pearl
4 Polished pink coral, Malaysia

5 Polished red coral, Taiwan
6 Amber, Palmnicken/Russia
7 White coral branches, S Italy
8 Red coral branches, Sicily

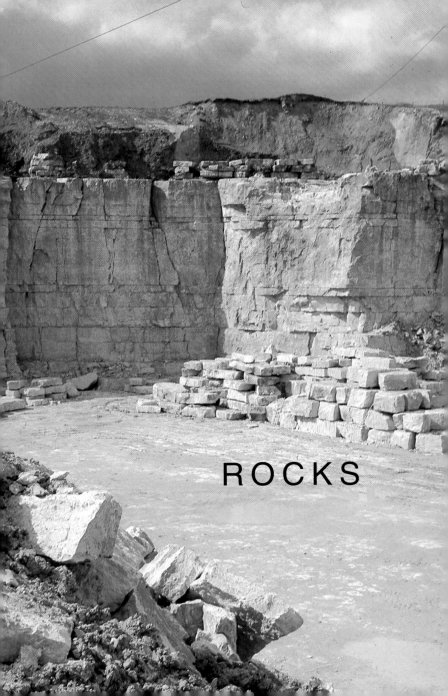

ROCKS

INTRODUCTION TO PETROLOGY

ROCKS IN THE LIFE OF MANKIND

From the beginning of human civilisation, for many thousands of years, stone (together with wood and bone) was the most important material for utensils and weapons. Metals remained unknown for a long time. In early times rocks were already being consciously sought for and used with quite specific aims. There is clear evidence of mining for flint 50,000 years ago.

The cultural history of many peoples is very closely connected with the rocks available in the area in which they live and which lend the landscape its dominant features. In rocky countryside the cultural development is different from that on the alluvial plains of the great rivers. Man soon learned to evaluate the differing possibilities of using rocks for construction, sculpture and ornamental purposes. In the architecture of many cities and villages the dependency on the bedrock or the surrounding countryside for construction materials can be seen quite clearly. In Northern Germany, where rock seldom reaches the surface, brick building methods predominate; the inner city area of Berne has the greenish-yellow colour of the local sandstone; buildings in the foothills of old and new volcanoes are constructed of dark lava-rock. Despite the availability of steel and concrete, natural stone still retains its importance today. Because there is a greater awareness of the use of stone and because it can be transported more easily than was the case in earlier times, it is moved across whole continents in order to be used as a decorative element in house facades, staircases and in prestigious buildings.

NAMES OF ROCKS

The nomenclature of rocks is much more confusing than that of minerals, gemstones and ores. Many derive their names from their external appearance, others from localities or landscapes, others according to the mineral composition. In addition to this the difficulty of gaining an overall view is increased by the flood of trade terms which are peculiar, not easily comprehensible, or even wrong and misleading. There is no generally accepted nomenclature for rocks. Endeavours to develop a valid and internationally accepted system have been in progress for years and are showing their first results. With the aid of the so-called "Streckeisen diagram", rocks from the plutonic groups were classified, defined and given established names by the International Union of Geological Sciences (Sub-commission of the IUGS) in 1972; in 1976 rocks in the volcanic group were similarly treated. There certainly do exist in practice generally accepted names for many groups of rocks, but the way in which they are differentiated from similar rocks varies. In contrast to minerals there is no clear natural dividing line between individual types of rock. On the contrary there are all manner of transitions to rocks which are genetically related. It is only man who applies standards here and sub-divides a rock mass into individual rock types.

Limestone quarry in the Franconian Jura

TERMINOLOGY

Rock Natural mixture of several kinds of mineral, occasionally also consisting of a single mineral. Forms separate geological bodies of rather large extent. In geological sciences we only use the term rock, not stone and stones.

Primitive rock Erroneous collective term for plutonic rocks and some metamorphic rocks. Formerly these rocks were considered to be the oldest formations.

Fels German term for a largish compact rock mass cropping out on the Earth's surface. Also used as a term for some non-schistose metamorphic rocks (p.318).

Solid and loose rock Consolidated rock mass (e.g. sandstone) or, conversely, loose accumulation of rock (e.g. sand and gravel).

Natural stone Term for rock which occurs naturally and is used for technical purposes in the construction industry. The opposite of this is artificially manufactured building stone, artificial stone, like brick or concrete blocks.

Ornamental stone Natural stone used in building which has been shaped by hand by a stone mason.

Hard and soft stone Term used by stone-masons and technicians in the building industry. There is no general agreement on where to draw the line between the two. Hard rocks have compressive strength values above approximately 1800 kg/cm^2 and include igneous rocks, amphibolite, quartzite and greywacke, also gneiss. Soft rocks are those with a compressive strength below $800kg/cm^2$; sandstones, limestones and basalt lavas belong in this group. Rocks with compressive strengths between 800 kg/cm^2 and $1800kg/cm^2$ are known as medium-hard rocks.

CLASSIFICATION OF ROCKS

In scientific petrology the main classification of rocks is based on their mode of origin, i.e. by the way in which the rocks develop: igneous rocks, sedimentary rocks, and metamorphic rocks.

Igneous rocks (magmatites) Develop when liquid molten rock, magma, solidifies in the Earth's crust or on the Earth's surface (p.190).

Sedimentary rocks (sedimentites) Develop at the Earth's surface from the weathering products of other rocks (p.260).

Metamorphic rocks (metamorphites)Develop through the transformation of other rocks in the Earth's crust as a result of great pressures and high temperatures (p.304).

Proportions of rocks forming the Earth's crust		**Proportions of minerals** forming the Earth's crust	
	Volume %		Volume %
Igneous rocks	65	Plagioclase feldspar	39
Sedimentary rocks	8	alkali feldspar	12
Metamorphic rocks	27	quartz	12
of these:			
granite	10	pyroxene	11
granodiorite, diorite	11	amphibole	5
basalt	43	mica	5
		olivine	3
		clay minerals	5
		calcite	1
		others	7

THE ROCK CYCLE

The genetic relationship of the main rock groups to one other and to the magma is shown by the following diagram.

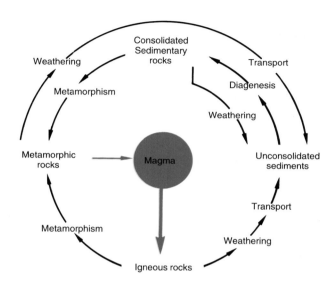

Magma Molten rock mass below the solid Earth's crust.

Weathering Reworking, i.e. comminution or solution of rocks under the influence of elements of the weather.

Transport Horizontal transportation of reworked rock material.

Diagenesis Low intensity transformation of a rock, especially resulting in greater compactness. Usually refers to sediments.

Metamorphism High intensity transformation of a rock through great pressure and high temperature. Only used for metamorphic rocks.

Melting Transformation of a solid rock into the molten state.

IGNEOUS ROCKS

ORIGIN

The material from which igneous rocks form is the magma, the viscous molten material from the interior of the Earth. If this fluid magmatic material penetrates into the lower parts of the Earth's crust plutonic rocks develop after a period of slow cooling. If magmatic material pours out directly onto the Earth's surface volcanic rocks form as the material cools down relatively quickly. Between these two groups lie the dyke or hypabyssal rocks as transitional members. Because the igneous rocks begin the rock cycle (p.189) they are termed primary rocks.

SYNONYMS

The following terms are used as synonyms for igneous rock: magmatic rock, pyrogenic rock, fusion rock, flow rock, massive rock and eruptive rock. The last term is not a particularly useful phrase since the name itself is not quite correct, that is to say, a real eruption only creates volcanic rocks, which therefore in many cases can equally be described as eruptive rocks.

SILICA CONTENT

The silica content (SiO_2) of igneous rocks determines their appearance to a very large extent. Silica-rich rocks, known as acid rocks, have, in general, a light appearance, silica-poor, termed basic, have a dark appearance.
Acid rocks Igneous rocks with a silica content above 65%.
Intermediate rocks Igneous rocks with a silica content of 52%- 65%.
Basic rocks (basites) Igneous rocks with a silica content below 52%. At values below 45% we speak of ultra-basic rocks.

Forms of occurrence of ascending magma and the igneous rocks formed

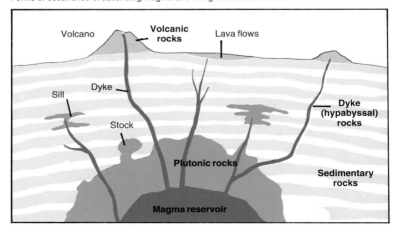

CLASSIFICATION AND NOMENCLATURE OF IGNEOUS ROCKS

Only since 1972 or 1976 has there been an internationally agreed nomenclature in science for igneous rocks (p.187). Some names which until then were scarcely current in the trade or industry are now gaining in significance, whilst on the other hand well-known terms are to disappear completely. As far as scientific petrology is concerned the new nomenclature, with its clear definition of terms, should be given an unqualified welcome. For the person involved in the stone industry and for all those with no prior training in mineralogy and petrology the new classification certainly does not mean that it will be easier to combine theory and practice. Those who are working with stone and who are responsible for using stone usually lack the specialist knowledge required to understand the basis on which the definitions are arrived at. For this reason an attempt has been made in the explanations which follow in this book to simplify the scientific nomenclature by forming groups of rocks (called rock families) and at the same time to bridge the gap between the new terms and the old rock names. As with every generalisation, this simplification demands numerous compromises.

The basis for the new classification and nomenclature of igneous rocks is the so-called "Streckeisen diagram", a double triangle, from which the individual types of rock can be derived according to the percentage of the main constituents. The Streckeisen classification distinguishes 16 groups of plutonic rocks and 15 volcanic rocks with further subdivisions of the main groups. For the sake of simplification these numerous types of rock are grouped in the classification used in this book into 5 rock families. The corresponding graphics and text can be found on pages 192-3.

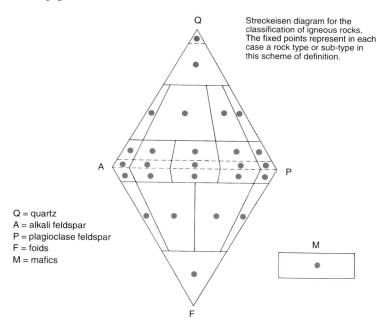

Streckeisen diagram for the classification of igneous rocks. The fixed points represent in each case a rock type or sub-type in this scheme of definition.

Q = quartz
A = alkali feldspar
P = plagioclase feldspar
F = foids
M = mafics

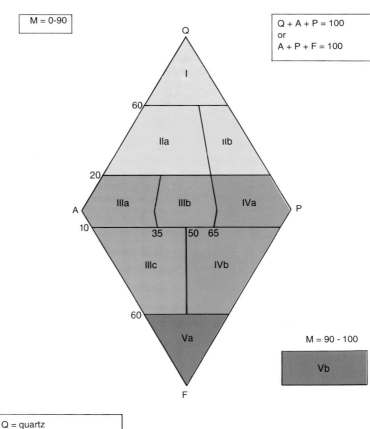

Igneous rocks and their rock-families

M = 0-90

Q + A + P = 100
or
A + P + F = 100

Q

I

60

IIa   IIb

20

IIIa   IIIb   IVa   P

A

10

35   50 65

IIIc   IVb

60

Va

F

M = 90 - 100

Vb

Q = quartz
A = alkali feldspar
P = plagioclase feldspar
F = foids
M = mafics

All figures denote %

Streckeisen diagram (simplified and modified)

	Plutonic rocks	Volcanic rocks	Major constituents
I	Quartzolite family	–	quartz
II	granite family (a) granite (b) granodiorite	rhyolite family (a) rhyolite (b) dacite	feldspars + quartz
III	syenite family (a) syenite (b) monzonite (c) foyaite	trachyte family (a) trachyte (b) latite (c) phonolite	feldspars
IV	diorite/gabbro family (a) diorite and gabbro (b) essexite	andesite/basalt family (a) andesite and basalt (b) tephrite	feldspars + foids
V	peridotite family (a) foidolite (b) ultramafic rocks	picrite family (a) foidite (b) ultramafic rocks	foids

MAJOR CONSTITUENTS OF THE STRECKEISEN DIAGRAM

Quartz quartz, tridymite, cristobalite (p.36).

Alkali feldspars orthoclase, microcline, perthite, anorthoclase, including albite with An_{0-5} (p.40).

Plagioclase feldspars albite-anorthite, except albite An_{0-5} (p.40).

Foids leucite, analcite, nepheline, sodalite, nosean among others (p.42).

Mafics Term for dark-coloured silicate minerals with magnesium (Ma) and iron (Fe), hence the name; for example biotite, hornblende, olivine, garnet, melilite. In German texts rocks which are made of dark minerals are also termed mafites. Adjective: mafic (also femic).

Felsics Term for light coloured minerals e.g. quartz, feldspars, foids. The names feldspar and silicate are not derived from the term "fels". In German texts all light rocks consisting of feldspars and/or quartz are sometimes called felsics. Adjective: felsic (also sialic or salic).

HYPABYSSAL ROCKS
(DYKE ROCKS)(TRANSITIONAL IGNEOUS ROCKS)

In the new classification using the Streckeisen diagram hypabyssal rocks, which hitherto have been regarded as a transitional group between plutonic and volcanic rocks, are no longer regarded as a group in their own right. They should be allocated either to plutonic or to volcanic rocks. Indeed in each of these two main groups there are dyke-shaped rock formations.

In the classification used in this book hypabyssal rocks have continued to be treated as a group in their own right (p.256), a concession to the degree to which the old classification scheme was well known to those who use and work with rocks. In some countries the hypabyssal rocks are likewise retained as an independent group.

The classification of igneous rocks follows the same scheme for both plutonic and volcanic rocks. First of all the volume per cent proportions of the minerals of the unknown rock are determined. A first elimination then results. The sub-division in the double-triangular diagram is valid only for those rocks whose mafic content (that is the amounts of dark minerals) amounts to between 0 and 90%. The remaining rocks are classified differently.

The determination of the position of the points in the double-triangular diagram is considered only in terms of quartz (Q), alkali feldspar (A), plagioclase (P) and foids (F). The mafics are discounted at this stage. Then the Q+A+P or A+P+F are recalculated to 100%. Since quartz and foids cannot occur together in a rock they are mutually exclusive in the double-triangular diagram.

The quartz or foid value so determined is plotted on the diagram parallel to the baseline A-P.

The A and P values determined for the rock are recalculated to 100% and are plotted on the line A-P. The line joining this point to the apex of the triangle at Q or F respectively intersects the horizontal "quartz line".

This is the plotted position of the rock specimen in the Streckeisen diagram.

Example

A rock specimen has
40% quartz (Q)
30% alkali feldspar (A)
20% plagioclase feldspar (P)
8% biotite and 2% ore

8% biotite and 2% ore are not taken into account at this stage.

Recalculation gives
44Q + 33A + 23P = 100

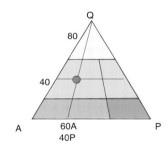

Recalculation of 30A and 20P gives
60A + 40P = 100

The rock specimen is therefore a granite.

Mafics in the classification system   The dark rocks with over 90% mafics, not shown in the diagram, are differentiated according to the content of olivine, pyroxenes and melilite.

With plutonic rocks, which are completely crystalline and coarse-grained, the constituents can be relatively simply recognised, if necessary in thin section under the microscope. Determination is difficult with fine-grained or glassy volcanic rocks. Here comparable mineral values have to be calculated from chemical analyses. This is a job for specialists only.

Nomenclature in the classification system   Standard names of rocks can be supplemented by being preceded by mineral terms. The expert recognises the fine classification of rock types by the manner of writing (noun, adjective) and the order of arrangement.

Rock varieties which are lighter than is generally the case are characterised by the prefix "leuco" and those which are darker than usual by the prefix "mela".

PLUTONIC ROCKS

ORIGIN

Plutonic rocks, named after Pluto, the god of the underworld in Greek mythology, originate deep down in or below the Earth's crust.

Magma penetrates over a wide area into the lower part of the solid Earth's crust and gradually solidifies there to form relatively coarse-grained rocks, the plutonic rocks. Because they cool down very slowly under thick overlying beds, several thousand metres thick, the minerals can crystallize out well and reach grain sizes which are recognisable with the naked eye. The pressure of the overlying rock bodies prevents the formation of gas cavities, and hence the plutonic rocks have a very compact appearance and possess only a low pore volume. The crystals are jumbled up without any directional arrangement. The separation out of types of mineral from the molten magma takes place in a certain sequence. First of all minor constituents like apatite, sphene, magnetite, zircon and ores are formed, then follow the dark constituents olivine, augite, hornblende and biotite, last of all quartz. The feldspars crystallize out gradually during the whole cooling phase, first of all the plagioclases (anorthite to albite) and finally the orthoclases.

The minerals which are precipitated first of all can develop their crystal shape fully because of the amount of space available, the last ones can only fill the spaces remaining. For this reason feldspars show their characteristic shape only occasionally as constituents of the rock; quartzes never do so. Through this differentiation in crystal formation the heavier, usually mafic, minerals sink down in the magma, so that a spatial separation of the minerals, and hence the rocks, takes place. At the bottom lies peridotite, in the middle area gabbro, diorite and syenite, in the upper area of the former magma body granite develops.

If we find plutonic rocks nowadays at the Earth's surface and even in high mountain regions then this means that the overlying cover rocks have, in the course of time, been removed.

SYNONYMS

The following terms are used as synonyms for plutonic rock: plutonite, intrusive rock, deep seated rock. The term massive rock is used both for igneous rocks in general and for plutonic rocks only.

Plutonic rock with characteristic random granular texture (two-mica granite, Fichtelgebirge/Germany: Half natural size.

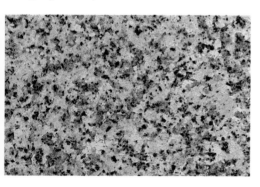

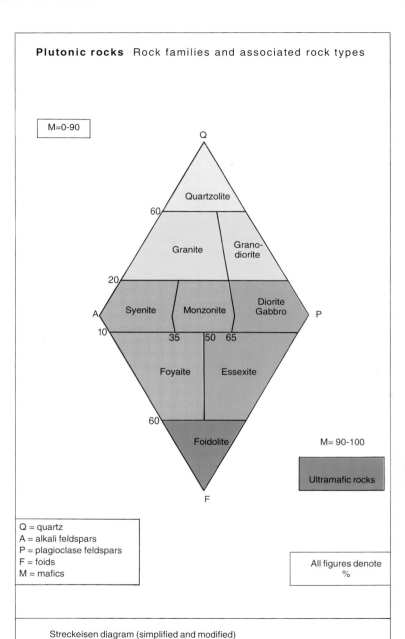

Plutonic rocks Rock families and associated rock types

M=0-90

Q

Quartzolite

60

Granite Grano-diorite

20

A Syenite Monzonite Diorite Gabbro P

10

35 50 65

Foyaite Essexite

60

Foidolite

M= 90-100

Ultramafic rocks

F

Q = quartz
A = alkali feldspars
P = plagioclase feldspars
F = foids
M = mafics

All figures denote %

Streckeisen diagram (simplified and modified)

	Plutonic family	Sub-division of plutonic family	Well known rock types (a selection)
	Quartzolite family		greisen, peracidite, arizonite, reef quartz*
	Granite family	granite	granite, orbicular granite, rapakivi
		granodiorite	granodiorite, trondhjemite, tonalite
	Syenite family	syenite	syenite, pulaskite, larvigite
		monzonite	monzonite
		foyaite	foyaite, shonkinite
	Diorite/gabbro family	diorite	diorite, orbicular diorite
		gabbro	gabbro, norite
			troctolite anorthosite
		essexite	essexite, theralite
	Peridotite family	foidolite	ijolite
		ultramafic rocks	dunite, peridotite, pyroxenite
			hornblendite, carbonatite

* pfahl quartz

Diagnostic features of plutonic rocks

1 Holocrystalline, the whole mass crystallised
2 Large crystals recognisable with the naked eye
3 Orientation can usually not be recognised in hand specimen, minerals randomly distributed, rare flow texture
4 Very compact, virtually no cavities
5 Never fossiliferous
6 Joints at right angles to each other
7 Tor structure (pillow jointing) is the typical weathering form
8 Topography generally smooth and rolling.

QUARTZOLITE FAMILY

Those rocks which fall into the uppermost part of the Streckeisen diagram are collectively known as the quartzolite family. A synonymous group name is peracidite. In a more restricted sense quartzolite is the term for rocks with a quartz content of more than 90%.

> Major constituents: quartz 60-100%
> Medium constituents: mica, feldspars, topaz, fluorite, apatite

The genesis of quartzolites is a matter of some controversy. There do not appear to be any plutonic bodies. In most cases their origin is connected with pegmatites and vein infillings. Volcanic equivalents are not known. Main representatives: greisen, peracidite, arizonite, reef quartz.

Greisen [4]

Light grey, granular, sometimes coloured brown because of the presence of iron. Formed by the replacement (metasomatism) of feldspars in acid igneous rocks (e.g. granite) or metamorphic rocks (gneiss). Occasionally contains deposits of tin, tungsten and molybdenum.

Greisen usually occurs as a vein infilling extending over only a few hundred metres and also, in certain cases, in irregular stocks. LOCALITIES: Fichtelgebirge/Germany, Saxony, Erzgebirge/Germany, Skiddaw and Cornwall/England, Galicia/Spain, Portugal.

Zwitter [1]

Formerly a term for the fine grained variety of greisen. Nowadays this distinction is not always applied and zwitter is understood as synonymous with greisen.

Peracidite [3] Silexite

A quartzolite with more than 90% quartz. The rock which gives it its name is a pegmatite from New York/USA.

Occasionally peracidite is also used as the group name instead of quartzolite.

Arizonite

Milky grey quartzolite with a quartz content of more than 80%, with mica as a minor constituent and orthoclase feldspar and apatite as medium constituents.

Reef quartz (Pfahlquartz) [2]

Turbid white or grey quartz rock, also coloured brownish yellow to reddish because of the presence of iron, from Pfahl in the Bayerischer Wald/Germany (illustration on p.256).

The Pfahl (original name) is essentially a vein infilling 150km long, up to 120m wide which in places towers as a residual hill 100m above its surroundings. It is associated with numerous small quartz veins.

Formerly widely used as road metal but now preserved from further destruction as a landscape conservation area.

1

2

3

4

GRANITE FAMILY

Granite and granodiorite are members of the granite family. Occasionally members of this group are also called granitoids or quartz-feldspar-plutonic rocks. They are the most widely-distributed plutonic rocks.

Whereas formerly the origin of granitic rocks was explained as differentiation of magma from inside the Earth, nowadays the tendency is to see the formation of granitic magma as a result of processes of melting or partial melting of pre-existing rocks.

Granite

The name granite derives from the Latin ("granum" = grain) and refers to the granular texture.

Light coloured minerals: 80-100%	
of which: quartz 20-60%	
feldspars 40-80%	of which: alkali-feldspar 35-100%
	plagioclase feldspar 0-65%
Dark minerals: 0-20%	
Medium constituents: biotite, augite, hornblende, muscovite, apatite, zircon, magnetite	

Feldspar, quartz and mica are popularly, though rather simplistically, considered to be the essential constituents of granite.

The general impression of granite is always that of a light coloured rock, regardless of whether it looks grey, yellowish, brownish, bluish or reddish; this is because of the high percentage of light coloured constituents. The dark minerals never exceed 20%.

The different colours derive from the feldspars. Quartz in granite does not appear colourless as it does on its own, but is a grey colour caused by the darkness of cavities shining through the glassy quartz.

The dark mica (biotite) is evenly distributed or occurs as nestlike accumulations. Where they occur as close accumulations several minerals which generally appear as medium constituents can become minor constituents and thus become the characteristic feature of granite varieties.

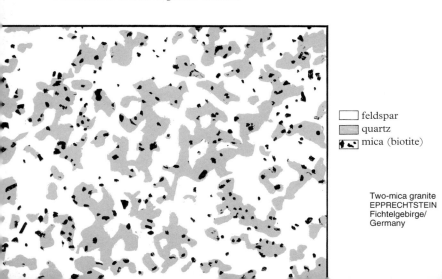

☐ feldspar
▨ quartz
◼ mica (biotite)

Two-mica granite
EPPRECHTSTEIN
Fichtelgebirge/
Germany

Texture The size of the individual constituents is very varied. However, the grains are always developed enough to be recognised by the naked eye, in other words they are at least a millimetre in diameter. Feldspars, especially potassium feldspar, are occasionally well-formed and up to several centimetres long (porphyritic texture). In granite, quartz never occurs with its typical crystal form since it is the last mineral to be precipitated from the melt as it solidifies and can therefore only fill in those spaces which are left in the rock.

Essential recognition characteristics for granites (as for all other plutonic rocks) are the randomness of the mineral grains and the compact structure; there are almost no recognisable cavities.

Distribution Granite can occur both in large rock complexes and in stocks and veins. LOCALITIES: Schwarzwald, Harz, Erzgebirge/Germany, Scandinavia, Finland, Central Alps, Vosges and Brittany/ France, Pyrenees, Canada, Scotland, Cornwall/England, California, Rocky Mountains, New Hampshire/USA.

Nomenclature In scientific petrology the granites are subdivided according to their significant constituents, in the building trade according to colour and locality. Trade names are written in capital letters.

Alkali feldspar granite Usually light coloured granite with dominant alkali feldspars in addition to quartz. The plagioclase content is below 10%.

Augite-hornblende-granite Augite and hornblende give a darker overall impression than is usually the case with granite

Biotite granite Biotite as minor constituent can reach up to 20% by volume.

Flaser granite Comes somewhere between granite and gneiss. As a result of tectonic forces the feldspars are flattened into a somewhat elongated shape resulting in a feebly schistose i.e. parallel texture.

Porphyritic granite Large grey, white or reddish feldspars with fully developed crystal form in a finer grained matrix.

Tourmaline granite Black tourmaline which is otherwise only rarely found in granite is the characteristic feature of this rock.

Two-mica granite In addition to biotite which is almost always present in granite, muscovite, which is otherwise present in only trace amounts, can be clearly recognised. Because of this the granite has many lustrous, silvery reflecting surfaces.

Uses Granite is a widely used stone for buildings and decorative work. Because of its high quartz content it wears extremely well and is highly resistant to weathering. Joint systems at right angles in conjunction with the high proportion of feldspars (which have cleavages at 90°) enable the winning of rectangular blocks and makes it possible to work with planes of splitting perpendicular to one another.

Grey varieties are used for cobble-stones, kerb-stones and boundary stones and broken-up as aggregates and road chippings. Coloured granites are used as raw material for sculpture and, when cut and polished, as cladding for buildings, for floor coverings and similar surfaces. Equigranular texture is desirable for cutting and polishing whereas a high mica content is disadvantageous.

---

1 Two-mica-granite, Schwarzwald/Germany
2 Alkali granite, Angermanland/Sweden

3 Biotite granite, Brocken/Harz/Germany
4 Biotite granite, Vosges/France

Orbicular granite [1]

A very rare granite in which single or multi-layer forms are embedded in a medium- to fine-grained ground mass. The orbicules, whose diameter can be up to 10cm and occasionally even more, are built up in a radiating and concentric fashion. They usually consist of the same minerals as the parent rock. Whitish plagioclase feldspar (oligoclase) occurs radially, dark mica (biotite) tangentially. Rhythmic enrichment of the minerals mentioned results in the shell-like structure of the orbicules. Usually an innermost core is formed of feldspar crystals but occasionally of rock particles.

The process of formation of the orbicules has not yet been elucidated with any certainty. The rhythmic crystallization is obviously connected to alternations in water vapour pressure in the easily-volatilized constituents of the magma. Partial melting and recrystallization probably also play a part. Orbicular granites are usually of only a few square metres in extent.

LOCALITIES: Finland, Sweden, Waldviertel/Austria, Riesengebirge/Poland, Peru, Japan, New Zealand, Vermont/USA. Used for small monuments.

Similar formations Orbicular rock formations are to be found in other plutonic rocks in addition to granite e.g. diorite, granodiorite, syenite and gabbro. In collecting circles the orbicular diorite of Corsica is probably the most well-known.

Orbicule Spherical rock formation.

Orbiculite Rock with spherical forms in a groundmass.

Esboite Local name for Finnish orbicular granite in which a clearly definable core is not recognisable.

Corsite Orbicular diorite from Corsica in which the concentric structure is determined by whitish plagioclase feldspar and green hornblende.

Rapakivi [2] Rapakivi granite

The name rapakivi (rotten rock) which originates from the Finnish is a porphyritic hornblende granite. It does have a certain similarity to an orbicular granite but in no sense does it belong to the group of orbiculites.

Alkali feldspar crystals (orthoclase) with a maximum diameter of 2-3cm lie in a medium grained groundmass of abundant quartz and biotite, or sometimes hornblende; the crystals are roundish to egg-shaped, generally of salmon- to flesh-colour but they can also be grey. They are surrounded by plagioclase (mostly oligoclase or albite or maybe andesine) of a light grey to yellowish grey and sometimes green colour. Occasionally several zones can be recognised. The genesis of rapakivi granite is a subject of dispute. Certainly the orthoclases were first of all precipitated from the magma. The crystallization of the other constituents appears to have taken place more or less simultaneously, so that they become arranged around the orthoclase cores. There are, however, schools of thought which suggest that certain anatectic processes occur in the development of rapakivi granite.

LOCALITIES: S Finland, near St Petersberg/Russia, Maine/USA, Brazil. Large blocks are used for monumental purposes, polished slabs for house facades. Some types are prone to decay since the oligoclase skin weathers relatively easily and the orthoclase crystals crumble away because of this disintegration.

1. Orbicular granite (? orbicular diorite), Corsica   2. Rapakivi BALTIC BROWN Ylamaa/Finland

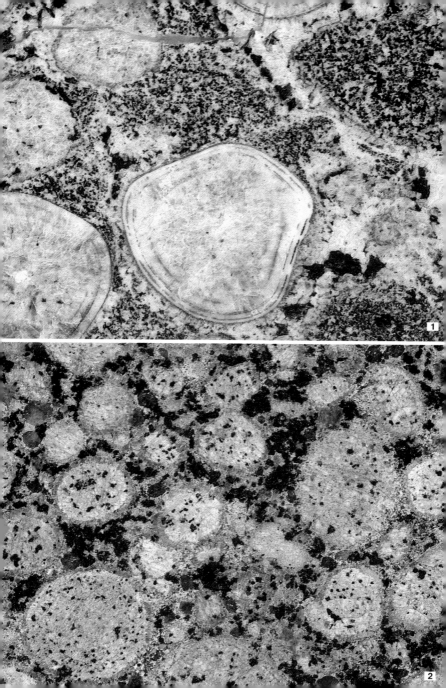

Granite massifs showing soft, rounded forms (Vosges/France).

GRANITE TRADE NAMES

There is an almost endless number of trade names for granite which is one of the most used rocks. Some of these trade names are completely false and misleading. Others are not scientifically correct but the rocks named are more or less closely related to granite and therefore possess similar properties.

Finally there is a host of trade names for genuine granite varieties. The habit of writing in capital letters when characterising trade types, which has become usual in most recent times, is increasingly becoming the standard practice.

Misleading trade names which include the term "granite"

BELGIAN GRANITE: grey-black, bituminous limestone, Belgium.
ROCQ GRANITE: grey limestone, France.
GRANITE MARBLE: grey limestone, Upper Bavaria/Germany.
GRANITO NERO: black limestone, Tessin/Switzerland.
PETIT GRANIT: black limestone, Belgium, sometimes synonymous with BELGIAN GRANITE.

False trade name using the term "granite"

CALANCA GRANITE: finely schistose paragneiss, Tessin/Switzerland.
FELSBERG GRANITE: black and white speckled granodiorite, Schwarzwald/Germany.
GRANITO AZUL: blue-grey foyaite, Brazil.
GRANITO DORATO: yellow flecked paragneiss, Piemonte/Italy.
GRANITO PRETO TIJUCA: dark green diorite, Brazil.
GRANITO VERDE: grey-green monzonite, S Tyrol/Italy.
GRANITO VERDE UBATUBA: blue-olive coloured charnockite, Brazil.
LAUSITZER GREEN GRANITE: black-green andesite or diabase, Saxony/Germany.
SHANDONG GRANITE: green orthogneiss, Graubünden/Switzerland.
SPALT GRANITE: several types of mica-rich paragneisses. Tessin/Switzerland.
SS GRANITE: almost black gabbro or diabase, Sweden: SS = Schwedisch Schwarz (Swedish black).
YELLOW JUPARANA GRANITE: yellowish orthogneiss, Brazil

---

1 Granite MEISSEN Saxony/Germany
2 Granite ISERGEBIRGE Isergebirge/ Czechoslovakia
3 Granite CLAIR DU TARN, France
4 Granite GUILT PALACIOS, W Spain
5 Granite KÖSSEINE, Fichtelgebirge/Bavaria/ Germany
6 Granite TRANAS, Central Sweden

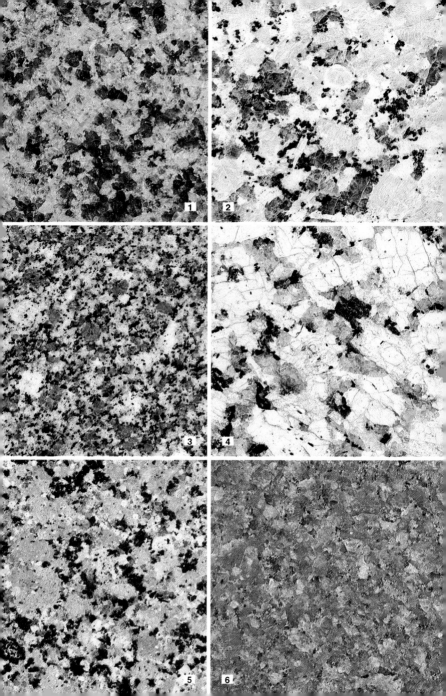

Tafoni, Corsica

Boulder field, Bayerischer
Wald/Germany
Exfoliation Fichtelgebirge/Germany

WEATHERING STRUCTURES OF GRANITIC ROCKS

Granite and similar rocks (granodiorite, diorite, syenite) display characteristic weathering structures.

Tafoni (top illustration). Weathering out of massive rocks resulting in many holes. Occurs in periodically wet coastal regions (Mediterranean, Central America, Namibia). Frequent wetting followed by drying-out results on the one hand in a hard skin and on the other in the development of holes.

Boulder Exfoliation (lower illustration). Onion-skin-like formation around a compact core covered with loosened residual rock. Formed by the combined effects of the release of pressure on the originally homogeneous rock, heating and cooling, as well as the chemical effects of circulating saline solutions.

Boulder field (middle illustration) (Felsenmeer). Accumulation of angular blocks on the summits of upland regions. Formed in mountain massifs by solution along mutually perpendicular joint systems because of earlier deeply penetrative weathering. The fine-grained material is washed away but the blocks loosened from the parent rock are left behind in a chaotic jumble.

Pillow jointing (Tor) (Upper and lower right illustrations p.209). Rounded weathering forms in massive rock. Particularly evident on free-standing rock domes which have cushion-like blocks piled up on top of each other. They develop by the crumbling away of rock particles along joints which intersect at rights angles to one another.

Exfoliation (spalling off) (illustration bottom left p209). Loosening of thin scales of granite exposed on rock outcrops. Leads to so-called bell- or sugar-loaf mountains. The causes are short-term changes of temperature, variably wet climate and/or the expansion of the rock when the pressure of the over burden is reduced, as well as the hardening of the outer scales by migrating mineral solutions.

Weathering structures in granite, Tafraout Oasis/Morocco

Left: Exfoliation, Kapland/South Africa Right: Pillow jointing (Tor) Bayerischer Wald/Germany

EXTRACTION OF GRANITE

Granite blocks are detached in the quarry by means of wedges, with the help of hydraulic equipment, by blasting or with a thermic lance.

Wedging off Splitting off by means of wedges takes place where large blocks are to be extracted for ornamental stone. Six-cm deep holes at intervals of 5-10cm are first of all cut by a pneumatic hammer into the rock surface along the required line of splitting. Angular wedges are placed in the holes and then driven in by hand using a medium weight hammer. This method is only possible with rock layers of no great thickness.

If round wedges are driven into drilled holes the depth of penetration is considerably greater, but the disadvantage is that unattractive grooves made by the drills are left in the sides of the blocks; there is also the higher use of equipment to consider.

Wedge-splitting is only possible if there are three free surfaces surrounding the block being worked; these can either be joint surfaces or fissures. If these are not present then similar slits have to be artificially produced. The widening of the fissures and the lifting off of the joint surfaces is carried out hydraulically.

Hydraulic splitting Far superior to wedge splitting by hand is that effected by hydraulic equipment using deeply drilled holes, albeit at the cost of considerable investment in equipment. Grooves in the sides of the block caused by the drilling are a disadvantage.

Shot splitting When breaking off large pieces of rock which are not necessarily going to be used for ornamental stone it is usual to use explosives. Relatively few drill holes suffice to take the explosive charges. Vertical quarry walls are dynamited when broken rock is extracted.

Thermic lance process Only in the last few decades has it been possible to remove granite blocks from the surrounding rock by using a directed flame which reaches over 1200°C. The application of the heat continually breaks off small slabs of rock so that the flame repeatedly hits fresh rock and thus digs its way into the rock body in the form of a slit. In this way large blocks can be extracted which are free from damage due to pressure or shock.

Right hand page: Removal of a block of rock using the thermic lance process.
Below: Wedging (left) and levering (right) of a granite block.

SURFACE WORKING OF GRANITIC ROCKS

Coloured granites are often cut into slabs and then used as ornamental stone for interior decoration or for the cladding of facades. The cutting is done with frame saws similar to the ones used in wood working.

The granite slabs which are produced in this way and then further cut to shape are then subjected to different types of surface dressings.

Rock faced [1] A natural freshly fractured surface, not further worked, and more or less rough depending on the grain-size.

Rough picked (punched). Stone surface with deep or shallow pits made by using a pick of hardened steel.

Fine axed (bush hammered) [2] Surface, texture and colour contrast are roughly evened-out. The tool used originally is a bush-hammer equipped with toothed points. Increasingly the hammers used are mechanised.

Tooled Roughened by using a comb-hammer equipped with rows of teeth.

Sand-blasted [3] Stone surface which has been rendered matt by using sand-blasting equipment.

Flamed [4] Rough surface which has strong texture and colouring as a result of the splitting-off of small platelets produced by the use of a directed hot flame.

Ground (rubbed) [5] Colours and textures are accentuated on a smooth matt surface by grinding away all unevennesses.

Polished [6] The surface of the stone acquires a high lustre as a result of fine grinding and special treatment with a polishing paste. By this process texture and colours are highlighted and richly contrasted. The harder and more compact the rock the more effective is the polish. Quartz and feldspar (and hence granite) are particularly suitable for polishing. The polished rocks allow the individual constituents to be picked out more clearly, and are generally darker than similar rocks with a natural fracture (rock-faced).

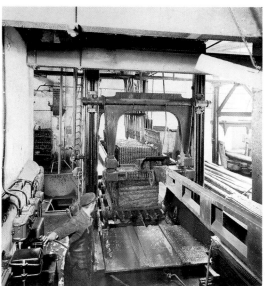

Frame saw in operation

Surface dressing using granite as an example, KAPUSTINO, Ukraine
1 Rock faced
2 Fine axed
3 Sand-blasted
4 Flamed
5 Rubbed
6 Polished

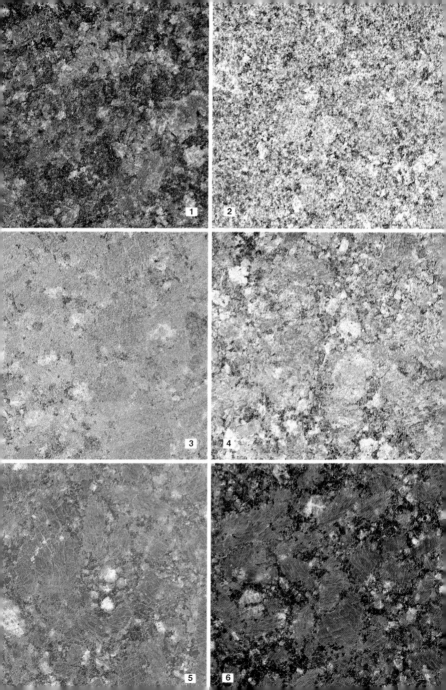

Granodiorite [1-4]

Granodiorite belongs to the granite family. The name indicates an intermediate position between granite and diorite.

Light minerals: 60-95%	
of which: quartz 20-60%	
feldspars 40-80%	of which: plagioclase feldspar 65-100%
	alkali feldspar 0-35%
Dark minerals: 5-40%	
medium constituents: biotite, hornblende, muscovite, pyroxene, zircon, apatite, magnetite	

Macroscopically it is difficult to distinguish granodiorite from granite although the overall impression is that it is always darker. Whereas in granite the alkali feldspars are dominant it is the plagioclase feldspars which predominate in granodiorite. Biotite is predominant among the dark constituents. Because of its higher mafic content granodiorite is distinctly darker than granite.
Occurs as relatively small rock complexes either on its own or within granitic massifs. LOCALITIES: Bayerischer Wald, Harz, Schwarzwald, Odenwald/Germany, Upper Austria, Bornholm Island/Denmark, South Norway, Coast Range/USA, Southern Uplands/Scotland. Used, like granite, as cobblestones and kerbstones, for gravestones, and in polished slabs as flooring and for cladding facades.

Trondhjemite [2] Biotite-granodiorite, quartz-mica-diorite.
A quartz-rich variety of granodiorite. Named after the locality in Central Norway. Trondhjemite contains very little or no alkali feldspar whereas the quartz content is clearly more than 20%. Biotite and hornblende are the dark constituents; they are regularly distributed and make up less than 15% of the whole. The rock is therefore characteristically light coloured. Zircon, apatite and magnetite are present as subsidiary medium constituents. LOCALITIES: Norway, Alaska, Andes. Used as road metal and for steps; polished slabs are used for interior decoration and for facades.

Tonalite [4] Variety of granodiorite. Named after the Tonale district of the South Tyrol. Contains only a little or, more usually, no alkali feldspar. Plagioclase feldspar is therefore the only feldspar present; this is the essential difference from granite and granodiorite. Quartz content is about 20%. Tonalite varies from lighter to darker appearance acccording to the proportion of mafic minerals (10-40%). Minor constituents are biotite and hornblende as well as accessory apatite, magnetite, zircon, augite and muscovite. Hornblende and biotite frequently occur as phenocrysts in an otherwise light coloured groundmass. Hence the flecked appearance of tonalite. LOCALITIES: S Tyrol/Italy, Graubünden/Switzerland, S Norway, Finland, Sweden, California/USA, British Columbia/Canada. Used as construction material for road surfaces or, when ground and polished, as slabs and material for steps.

Quartz diorite Usually a synonym for tonalite. Occasionally also an umbrella term for a series of similar varieties.

1 Granodiorite NEUHAUS, Upper Austria
2 Trondhjemite SOGNEFJORD, Norway
3 Grandiorite RÖNNE, Bornholm Island/Denmark
4 Tonalite BIANCO AURINIA, S Tyrol/Italy

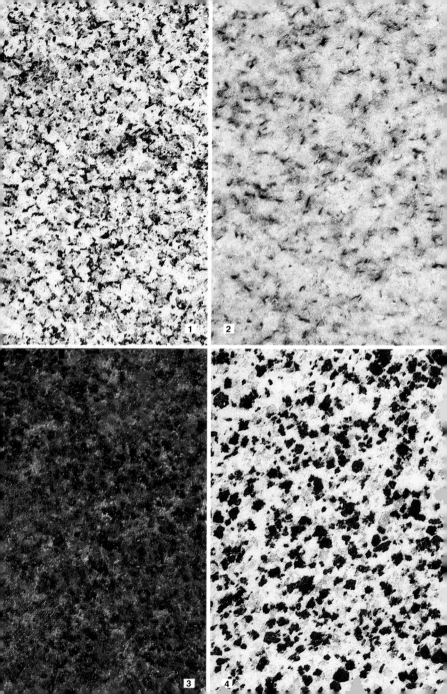

SYENITE FAMILY

Syenite, monzonite and foyaite belong to the syenite family

Syenite [1-4]

The name is derived from Syene, a place in Upper Egypt, nowadays called Aswan. In ancient times a much valued building stone, which is not actually a syenite but a hornblende granite, was quarried there.

Light minerals: 60-100%
      of which: feldspar 80-100%   of which: alkali feldspar 65-100%
                                                   plagioclase feldspar 0-35%

              quartz 0-20% or foids 0-10%
Dark minerals: 0-40%
Medium constituents: biotite, pyroxenes, zircon, apatite, magnetite, ilmenite.

Syenite is light to dark grey, also bluish or red, its texture is medium to coarse grained, rarely porphyritic. It can be distinguished from granite, which looks similar, by virtue of the fact that normal syenite contains little or no quartz. Either quartz or foids are present, the two mineral groups are mutually exclusive. Of limited occurrence, associated with diorite and granite. LOCALITIES: Fichtelgebirge, Saxony/Germany, Western Alps, S Portugal, Norway, New Hampshire and Massachusetts/USA, Sutherland/Scotland. Used as ornamental stone, gravestones, floor slabs and facade cladding.

False trade names using the term "syenite"

FRIEDERSDORF SYENITE: dark grey green lamprophyre/Germany.
LAUSITZ SYENITE: dark green lamprophyre, Germany.
ODENWALD SYENITE: dark grey diorite, Odenwald/Germany.
SCHREMS SYENITE: dark tonalite, Lower Austria.
WÖLSAU SYENITE: dark green diorite, Oberfranken/Germany.

Pulaskite [4]

Light-to dark-blue grey variety of syenite, an alkali syenite containing foids; also known as nepheline syenite since nepheline is the most important foid mineral. The foids can reach up to 5%. No quartz. Occasionally porphyritic because of somewhat enlarged potassium feldspar. Named after Pulaski County, Arkansas/USA.

Larvikite [2]

Bluish grey to dark green variety of syenite. Major constituent up to 90% anorthoclase feldspar together with augite and biotite. Quartz or nepheline can make-up up to 2% of the rock. The cause of the typical blue-green schiller, wrongly called labradorescence (by reference to labradorite feldspar) is the so-called unmixing process in the anorthoclase. LOCALITY: Vicinity of Larvik (hence the name of the rock) on Oslo fjord, Norway. Larvikite is much valued as a decorative stone, particularly for facades, floors and gravestones. Several trade types are differentiated by colour, tone and lustre effect.

---

1 Hornblende syenite BALMA, Piemont/Italy
2 Larvikite LABRADOR, S. Norway
3 Augite syenite KARDINAL, Transvaal/S. Africa
4 Pulaskite, Serra de Monchique/S. Portugal

Monzonite [1,2]

Monzonite is a member of the syenite family; named after the Monzoni Mountains in the South Tyrol

Light minerals: 55-90%		
	of which: feldspars 80-100%	of which: alkali feldspar 35-65%
		plagioclase feldspar 35-65%
	quartz 0-20% or foids 0-10%	
Dark minerals: 10-45%		
Medium constituents: pyroxenes, hornblende, biotite		

In normal monzonite alkali and plagioclase feldspar are present in roughly equal amounts; in the monzonites trending towards diorite/gabbro, plagioclase is predominant. In general quartz is below 5% or completely absent. Rare foids (nepheline and sodalite). Pyroxenes sometimes up to 20%.
Texture usually medium grained. Colour normally light to dark grey, also greenish, brownish and red. Sometimes has tabular alkali feldspars (microcline). Flow texture indicated by minerals with a preferred orientation. Occurs in close relation to granite and granodiorite bodies. LOCALITIES: S Tyrol/Italy, Saxony/Germany, S Norway, Nevada/USA Quebec/Canada, Ardnamurchan and Inverness/Scotland. Used locally as building stone. Some types are valued as ornamental stone.
Syenodiorite Older name for monzonite.

Foyaite [3,4] Foid syenite

Foyaite belongs to the syenite family. Named after Foya, a hill in Portugal.

Light minerals: 55-100%		
	of which: feldspars 40-90%	of which: alkali feldspar 50-100%
		plagioclase feldspar 0-50%
foids 10-60%		
Dark minerals: 0-45%		
Medium constituents: leucite, sodalite, nosean, hauyne, hornblende, pyroxenes, biotite.		

Plagioclase proportion clearly diminishes and may be completely absent. Quartz never present. Nepheline is the dominant foid. Pyroxenes and hornblendes determine the characteristic colour of the dark foyaites. The many varieties are distinguished according to the typical foid present. The texture is medium to coarse grained. Tabular potassium feldspars and columnar hornblendes as well as pyroxenes sometimes have a preferred orientation. The usually light coloured rocks acquire a more or less intensively mottled appearance according to the proportion of mafic minerals. Foyaites are rare; they occur in smallish intrusive bodies and stocks. Localities: Odenwald/Germany, Norway, Portugal, S Tyrol/Italy, Kola/Russia, Canada, Maine/USA. Used locally as building stone and road metal; some types are also used as ornamental stone because of their mottled appearance. Foid bearing rocks are more significant for their use as alkali raw material for the ceramic industry.
Shonkinite [3] Dark grey to almost black variety of foyaite with more than 50% dark constituents – pyroxenes (aegirine, augite), hornblende and often olivine. Named after the place where it was first found in Montana/USA.
Nepheline syenite and **elaeolite syenite** Earlier terms used as synonyms for foyaite.

1 Monzonite VERDE PELLEGRINO, S Tyrol/Italy
2 Monzonite SCHIPAIO, Ivory Coast
3 Shonkinite, Odenwald/Germany
4 Sodalite foyaite AZUL BAHIA, Brazil

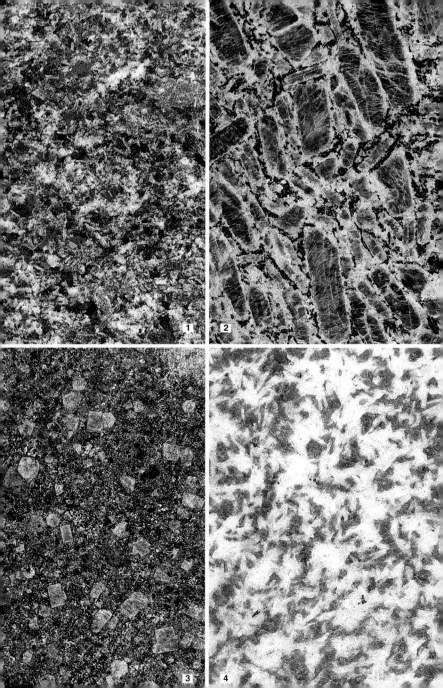

DIORITE/GABBRO FAMILY

Diorite, gabbro and essexite are members of the diorite/gabbro family. The differences between diorite and gabbro are only slight, hence the double name of this family.

Diorite [1 and No. 4, p.223]

The name (Greek "to distinguish") refers to the major constituents.

Light minerals: 50-85%
of which: feldspars 80-100%   of which: plagioclase feldspar 65-100%
alkali feldspar 0-35%

quartz 0-20% or foids 0-10%
Dark minerals: 15-50%
Medium constituents: hornblende, pyroxenes, sphene, apatite, zircon, garnets.

In diorite the lighter plagioclases (oligoclase and andesine) are predominant with the anorthite content being less than 50%. In the similar gabbro the darker plagioclases (labradorite and bytownite) become more significant. Hornblende and augite are the major dark constituents. Macroscopically, diorite can hardly be distinguished from gabbro. Alkali feldspar and quartz content usually amount to less than 5%. Foid bearing (and quartz free) diorites are rare. Texture fine to medium grained occasionally porphyritic. Colour light to dark grey, greenish grey; types transitional to gabbro are black-grey.

Occurs in smallish stocks and dykes as well as at the margins of large granitic intrusions. On the whole not very widespread. LOCALITIES: Bayerischer Wald, Harz, Odenwald, Schwarzwald/Germany, Finland, Argyll/Scotland, Jersey/England Washington and Massachusetts/USA. Used as aggregates and as cobble stones; also used as ornamental material because it takes a good polish. Many trade names of dioritic rocks bear the name SYENITE.

Orbicular diorite Appearance and origin as orbicular granite (p.204) The orbiculites of Corsica (Corsite) and of Finland (Esboite) are variously described as orbicular diorite or orbicular granite.

Gabbro [2 and No. 3, p.223]

Named after an Italian town in Tuscany

Light minerals: 35-80%
of which: feldspars 80-100%   of which: plagioclase feldspar 65-100%
alkali feldspar 0-35%

quartz 0-20% or foids 0-10%
Dark minerals: 20-65%
Medium constituents: pyroxenes, hornblende, olivine, biotite, magnetite, ilmenite, pyrrhotite.

In gabbro the darker plagioclases (labradorite and bytownite) predominate; the anorthite content is greater than 50%. In the similar diorite the lighter plagioclases (oligoclase and andesine) are more important (see above). Gabbro has a somewhat darker appearance than diorite. The major dark constituents are pyroxenes, hornblende and olivine. Alkali feldspars, quartz or foids are rarely present.

1 Diorite ITOACA, Espirito Santo/Brazil
2 Gabbro VIITASAARI, Finland
3 Norite IMPALA, Transvaal/South Africa
4 Anorthosite SPECTROLITE, Finland

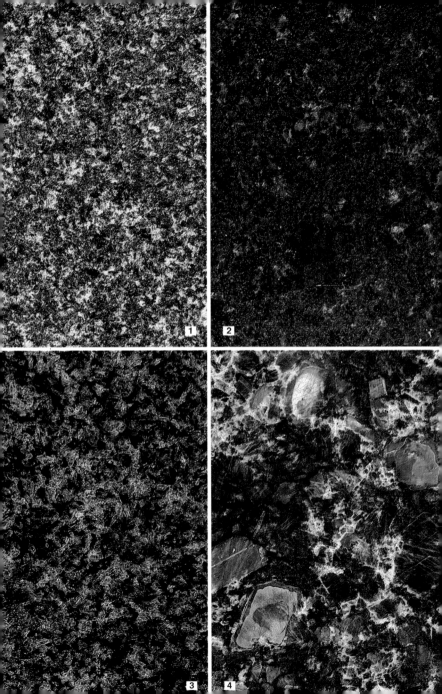

The texture can be fine to coarse grained. Colour bluish, medium to dark grey, sometimes almost black. Gabbro acquires a greenish colour (c.f. greenstones, p.248) when some minerals are altered to chlorite. Occurs in largish intrusions, stocks and dykes. LOCALITIES: Odenwald, Harz/Germany, Wallis/Switzerland, Transvaal/South Africa, Montana and Minnesota/USA, Aberdeen, Skye and Ardnamurchan/Scotland, Lake District/England. Used as building and ornamental stone. Some types are used for high quality railway ballast on account of their tough, bulky and felted texture. Gabbros which can take a high polish are used as gravestones and cladding for facades.

Norite [No. 3, p.221]
Dark grey variety of gabbro which contains hypersthene as the dark constituent. Occasionally can be recognised macroscopically by the bronzy colour of some of the pyroxenes, otherwise cannot be distinguished from gabbro. LOCALITIES: Norway, Transvaal/South Africa, Montana/USA Aberdeen and Banff/Scotland. The important nickel deposits of Sudbury/Canada are associated with norites.

Troctolite [1] Trout stone
Rare variety of gabbro with light coloured plagioclase and olivine as the dark component. The speckle-like olivines are green or when they occur as serpentine alteration products they are yellow, brownish, reddish and black. LOCALITIES: Harz/Germany, Silesia/Poland, Oklahoma and Montana/USA, Scotland.

Anorthosite [No. 4, p.221]
Light grey to almost black variety of gabbro made up of plagioclase with a mafic content of less than 10%. Medium constituents are pyroxenes, olivine, magnetite and ilmenite. LOCALITIES: Norway, Labrador and Quebec/Canada, Montana and New York/USA, Transvaal/South Africa.

SPECTROLITE [No. 4, p.221] Trade name for a variety of anorthosite from Finland with labradorescent feldspar. Used for decorative purposes and for costume jewellery.

Essexite [2]
Essexite, named after a locality in the USA, belongs to the diorite/gabbro family.

Light minerals: 30-80%		
of which: feldspars 40-90%	of which: plagioclase feldspar 50-100%	
	alkali feldspar 0-50%	
foids 10-60%		
Dark minerals: 20-70%		
Medium constituents: hornblende, biotite, magnetite, sphene, ilmenite, apatite		

Texture fine to medium grained, sometimes porphyritic. Dark grey to almost black because of the high content of pyroxenes. Occurs in small bodies and dykes, rare. LOCALITIES: Kaiserstuhl/Baden/Germany, Czechoslovakia, S Tyrol/Italy, Lanarkshire and Ayrshire/Scotland, Massachusetts/USA. Used locally as building stone. The stones used in the game of curling come from a porphyritic essexite in Scotland.

Theralite
Variety of essexite with plagioclase, nepheline and pyroxene, rare. LOCALITIES: Czechoslovakia, Auvergne/France Ayrshire/Scotland, Quebec and Ontario/Canada, Montana/USA.

1 Troctolite FORELLENSTEIN, Radautal/Harz/Germany

2 Essexite, Kaiserstuhl/Baden/Germany
3 Gabbro, Odenwald/Hessen/Germany

PERIDOTITE FAMILY

Foidolites and ultramafic rocks (ultramafitolites) belong to the peridotite family.

Foidolite [1]
Umbrella term for all plutonic rocks with a very high foid content.

Dark minerals: 0-90%	
Light minerals: 10-100%	of which: foids 60-100%
	feldspars 0-40%

Most of the foidolites are dark because of the high proportion of mafic minerals; some are virtually black. Quartz is totally lacking. There is a host of rock names on account of the very variable composition of the individual members. In contrast to the usual way of characterising a rock more specifically by prefixing the main name with a mineral name, foidolites are named exclusively according to geographical localities (such as italite, missourite, algarvite). Occurs only in small bodies; rare.

Ijolite [1] Variety of foidolite. The foid mineral nepheline is a major constituent making up roughly 50%. Mafic minerals also account for roughly 50%, of which pyroxenes constitute 40%. Accessory minerals are apatite, sphene and calcite.

Ultramafic rocks [2,4]
Collective term for plutonic rocks with more than 90% of dark minerals. Major constituents are olivine, pyroxenes, hornblende and melilite. Colour grey to black, also with green tones. Subdivision according to olivine content and the predominant mineral species.

	Dunite	Peridotite	Pyroxenite	Hornblendite	Melilitite
Olivine %	More than 90	40–90	less than 40	less than 40	less than 40
Other major constituents		pyroxene	pyroxene	hornblende	melilite
Varieties		harzburgite wehrlite lherzolite	enstatitite bronzitite hypersthenite		

Peridotite Sometimes used as an umbrella term for dunite and peridotite in a more restricted sense.

Carbonatite [3]
A light coloured rock consisting of calcite and/or dolomite which can be of both plutonic and volcanic origin. Since it is to be found in close association with foid rocks and is also transitional to them carbonatite is generally grouped with the ultramafitolites. Carbonate minerals make up at least 50%. Medium constituents are barite, apatite, magnetite, nepheline, biotite and phlogopite. Sometimes similar to a marble. Occurs in small plutonic bodies, stocks, dykes or streaks. LOCALITIES: Kaiserstuhl/Baden/Germany, Sweden, Norway, East African Rift, Arkansas/USA.
Ultramafites Either a synonym for ultramafic rocks or a collective term for ultramafitolite and ultramafitite (p.252).

---

1 Ijolite, Finland
2 Dunite, Aheim/Norway
3 Carbonatite, Telemark/Norway
4 Harzburgite, Bad Harzburg/Harz/Germany

1 2 3 4

VOLCANIC ROCKS

ORIGINS

Volcanic rocks develop when molten magma pushes its way up to the Earth's surface because of volcanic forces. The molten substance pouring like a river of mud out of a volcanic vent or along a fissure is called lava. If blobs of lava, mixed with remnants of rock from the former filling or the sides of the vent are first of all hurled through the air before they come to be deposited they are referred to as pyroclastic rocks.

The chemical composition and mineral constitution of volcanic rocks are roughly similar to those of the corresponding plutonics (cf. p.193). As the silica content decreases, so, like plutonic rocks, volcanics become darker and heavier.

Essential differences between volcanic and plutonic rocks are to be found in the rock texture. Because volcanic melts cool down relatively quickly the processes of crystallization and mineral formation follow a different course than with plutonics. The crystals of volcanics are usually small, in most cases microscopically small; not recognisable to the naked eye. We refer to an aphanitic rock texture.

Only individual crystals can develop to an advanced stage and take on their own individual shape. These then lie like strangers in the otherwise uniform ground mass. This is called porphyritic texture.

If the cooling down of volcanic rock melts takes place particularly quickly, for example, at the surface of a lava flow or when they plunge into the sea, no crystals at all can form. The mass is amorphous, a rock glass. In volcanic rocks there are often small cavities which have arisen as the fluid rocks have given off their gases.

Porphyritic texture with crystals showing their true shape
Flow texture with oriented crystals
Flow texture with oval-shaped cavities

Sometimes these cavities have an oval or elongated form and thus show an orientation in the rock, along the flow direction of the lava flow. Minerals, too, which crystallize out early can, by their preferred orientation, indicate a flow texture in volcanic rocks.

A characteristic feature particularly of dark, basic volcanic rocks is the presence of columnar joints which can be recognised in nature only where rock faces are exposed (steep slopes or quarries). Such four- to eight-sided columns are not crystal forms but rather elements of the rock which have been separated off from the main formation. They are formed by contraction as the lava cools down. The columns are at right angles to the former cooling surfaces.

In general fossils are not found in volcanic rocks. Hot lava normally destroys all life. Traces of life can be found very occasionally in volcanic tuff deposits.

Diagnostic features of volcanic rocks (vulcanites)

1 Only isolated crystals are well formed (porphyritic texture)
2 Dense groundmass (microcrystalline) or amorphous (non-crystalline, glassy)
3 Numerous small cavities
4 Often have flow structure
5 Frequently columnar jointed
6 Very rarely contain fossils

SYNONYMS

The following terms are used as synonyms for volcanic rocks: vulcanite, effusive rock, extrusive rock, eruptive rock. The last term should not be used in order to avoid any possible confusion with igneous rocks in general which are frequently referred to as eruptive rocks.

Prismatic joints in basalt, Auvergne/France

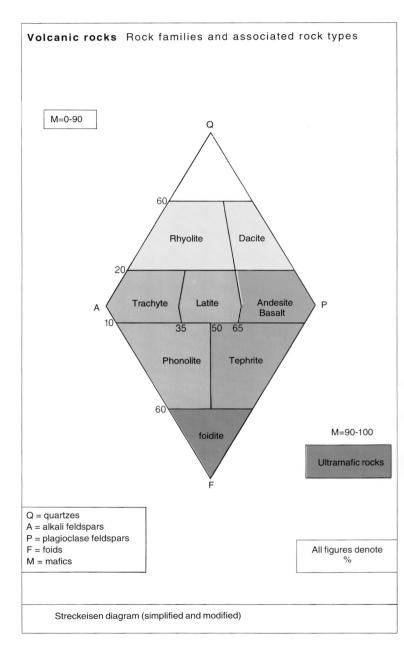

Volcanic rocks Rock families and associated rock types

M=0-90

Q

60

Rhyolite   Dacite

20

A Trachyte Latite Andesite P
                       Basalt

10

35 50 65

Phonolite Tephrite

60

foidite

F

M=90-100

Ultramafic rocks

Q = quartzes
A = alkali feldspars
P = plagioclase feldspars
F = foids
M = mafics

All figures denote
%

Streckeisen diagram (simplified and modified)

CLASSIFICATION OF VOLCANIC ROCKS

Depending on the way in which they have been formed we can distinguish between ejection products, pyroclastics, and the formations arising from the cooling down of lava flows, known as lavas.

Pyroclastic rocks are normally classified according to grain size, lavas according to the Streckeisen diagram (p.230).

The subdivision of volcanic rocks, which is used in Central Europe, into older (Palaeozoic) or younger (Neozoic) origins should no longer be used. However, in practice, some of the rock terms which should now be discarded are so firmly entrenched that it is doubtful if the trade will ever give them up. In this book the old and new rock terms are given equal weighting.

Old classification of lavas

Group name	New term	Old term
Quartz porphyry	Rhyolite (Liparite)	Quartz porphyry
Trachyte	Trachyte	Orthophyre
		Keratophyre
Porphyrite	Andesite	Porphyrite
Basalt	Basalt	Melaphyre
	Dolerite	Diabase
Picrite	Picrite	Palaeopicrite

New classification of volcanic rocks

	Volcanic rock family	Subdivision of volcanic family	Selection of well known rock types
	Rhyolite	Rhyolite	Rhyolite, Quartz porphyry
		Dacite	Dacite, Quartz porphyrite
	Trachyte	Trachyte	Trachyte, Keratophyre
		Latite	Latite
		Phonolite	Phonolite
	Andesite/Basalt	Andesite	Andesite, Porphyrite
		Basalt	Basalt, Dolerite, Melaphyre
			Diabase, Tholeiite
		Tephrite	Tephrite, Basanite, Limburgite
	Picrite	Foidite	Nephelinite, Leucitite
		Ultramafics	Melilitite, Picrite, Kimberlite

PYOCLASTIC ROCK (Tuff)

Pyroclastic rocks (from the Greek "fire- breaking") are volcanic rocks which consist of ejected products (lava blobs, remains of vent fillings or vent walls). Since the nature of deposition resembles the sedimentary rocks pyroclastic rocks are sometimes also classified with the sedimentary rocks.

Pyroclastic rocks are subdivided according to origin and appearance: tuff, tuffstone, tuffite, ignimbrite. Nomenclature is not always standardized.

Volcanic ash at the foot of Popocatepetl, Mexico

Tuff [1-5] volcanic tuff, tephra

By tuff (Latin: "porous stone") in a more restricted sense is understood the loose products of pyroclastic rocks, in a wider sense (especially in older literature) all pyroclastic rocks. The name tuff is also an abbreviated term for calcareous tufa, a sinter rock (p.286). This latter has nothing to do with the volcanic tuff discussed here.

Volcanic tuffs (in the narrower sense) are grouped according to the parent lava (e.g. andesite tuff) or to the grain size. The finest grained ejected material is called dust tuff; grains up to 2mm in diameter are called sand tuff; both groups together are called volcanic ash or ash tuff. Pebbles from bean to nut size (2-64mm) are known as lapilli [1,2].

Large ejecta (more than 64mm in diameter) in angular form are known as blocks or, if rounded, bombs [4,5]. Blocks are usually derived from solidified lavas and adjacent rock of volcanic vents and fissures. Bombs, usually fist to head size, are shaped lava blobs. As they rotate during their flight through the air the still-hot magma takes on roundish, twisted or spindle shapes. Before deposition they congeal to form solid rock. Scoria are porous, frothy magma blobs. The texture of tuffs is finely crystalline, amorphous, in individual cases porphyritic and usually very porous.

Occurrence: Coarse grained pyroclastic rocks are only found close to a volcano, within a radius of a few kilometres. Ashes, on the other hand, can be carried hundreds of kilometres away from the volcano by the wind.

1 Lapilli, Popocatapetl/Mexico
2 Lapilli, Hohentwiel/Hegau/Germany
3 Volcanic scoria, Tenayuca/Mexico
4 Volcanic bomb, Mauna Loa/Hawaii
5 Volcanic bomb, twisted spindle shape, Vesuvius/Italy

Tuffstone [1-4] (Tuff)

Tuffstone (abbreviated as "tuff") is solidified volcanic tuff. There is fine grained, coarse grained and mixed grained tuff, according to the type and sorting of the individual grains; it is usually riddled with cavities. The solidification of the originally loose material occurs through pressure and cementation. It is cemented by lime or silica. The bonding cement is transported by ground-water, interstitial water, circulating fluids and rain.

Tuffs can be layered because of grain size, grading in sedimentation or by repeated deposition. Unlike the sedimentary rocks, which have parallel-sided layers, the layer surfaces in tuffs are frequently impacted by large ejecta (bombs and blocks) which have fallen onto them. In hand specimens it is often difficult to distinguish between fine grained varieties and sedimentary rocks. Very old tuffs can be so strongly solidified that they resemble extruded lava or volcanic rocks. Occurrence: coarse grained tuffs in the vicinity of volcanoes, fine grained types at considerable distances from the source of eruption. LOCALITIES: Eifel, Neuwieder Bekken, Rhineland/Germany, Kaiserstuhl, Baden/Germany, Saxony/Germany, Auvergne/France, Pozzuoli/Italy, Snowdonia/Wales, Lake District/England, California, Oregon/USA. Because of their porosity they are used for heat insulation and as a lightweight building stone. Not very resistant to weathering.

Trass [4] Trachytic or phonolitic variety of tuff. On account of its hydraulic qualities when ground and added to cement it is used especially in underwater construction work. Because of its low setting temperature it raises the safety level against cracking and makes cement denser and chemically more resistant. Trass cement is especially suitable for mass concrete. LOCALITIES: Eifel, Siebengebirge, Rhineland/Germany, S France, Krim/former USSR.

Volcanic tuff beds impacted by bombs of differing sizes, Niedermendig/Eifel/Germany

Tuffite

Rock mixture of pyroclastic materials and sedimentary rocks. The deposition of both rock types took place at the same time or in alternating succession, often in layers.

Ignimbrite Welded tuff

Ignimbrites (Latin: "fire cloud") are deposits of glowing hot clouds, which reach the ground as mobile fluids, that is to say, in a molten condition. Here they fuse together to form a compact rock which looks like lava and is frequently very difficult to distinguish from it. LOCALITIES: Large areas in New Zealand, Alaska, Andes. Also Snowdonia/N Wales, Lake District/England, Oregon and Montana/USA.

1 Selbergite tuff, Eifel/Germany
2 Limburgite tuff, Kaiserstuhl/Baden/Germany
3 Phonolite tuff, ETTRINGER, Eifel/Germany
4 Trass, Brohltal/Eifel/Germany

VOLCANIC GLASS

Volcanic glass is a volcanic rock, but it is a term for a rock texture rather than an actual rock type. This texture is amorphous, as with artificial glasses. Only in individual cases are very small crystals formed within the rock. Volcanic glasses originate when the magma forcing its way up to the Earth's surface cools down very quickly. The time up to the point where the molten material solidifies is too short to allow the whole mass to crystallize out.

Where lava is rich in gases and viscous a highly porous rock forms, known as frothy glass; where lava is poor in gases or is unusually stiff a volcanic glass forms which is not very porous and is compact.

Pumice [1,2]

Pumice (Latin: "foam") is a frothy volcanic rock. As in a bath sponge the whole mass is riddled with pores of irregular or oval shape which are usually not connected with one another. Because of the high pore volume, which can reach 85%, pumice floats on water. Its colour is usually light grey to yellowish, rarely red or in dark tones.

Pumice develops in lava which is rich in gases and viscous. The gases, released because of a sudden diminution of pressure at the Earth's surface, create the many cavities. Shortly afterwards the lava solidifies. Since acidic lavas are especially viscous they are favourable for the formation of pumice. Accordingly most pumices have a high silica content and light colours. They are thus assigned to the rhyolite family. LOCALITIES: Lipari Islands/Italy, Iceland, Auvergne/France. Used in the production of lightweight building stones. The advantage of these stones lies in their light weight and in the good heat insulation they provide. The use of pumice as a grinding material in technology, and for cosmetic purposes, is due to the fact that it has no sharp-edged crystals which could have a damaging effect, and that the rock surface always remains rough and has a good grip.

Because of the varying granularity and hardness of natural pumice, pumice-like materials manufactured artificially out of quartz sand, which have constant qualities, are becoming increasingly important in grinding technology.

Scoria [3]

Pumice-like crusts full of holes on lava flows. They are more compact than pumice stone, weather-resistant and usually reddish.

Perlite [4] Pearl stone

Volcanic glass which is composed of small to pea-size concentric shell-like forms. When struck lightly perlite splits into pearl-like particles. Colour dark, bluish, green or brown. Waxy lustre. Probably develops through a loss of tension and the expansion associated with it, also by a shattering of originally compact obsidians or pitchstones. Because of their chemical composition they are usually designated as rhyolite glass. LOCALITIES: Hungary, New Mexico/USA. On heating perlite can be made to froth up and is then used as lightweight building and filter material; also as a filler and as insulating material.

1 Artificial pumice with equal-sized pores
2 Pumice, Lipari Island/Italy

3 Tephrite scoria, Vogelsberg/Hessen/Germany
4 Perlite, Fuzer/Hungary

Obsidian [1,2,4]

Obsidian is a compact natural glass. Named after the Roman Obsius (usually incorrectly named Obsidius or Obsidianus) who in ancient times first brought a piece of obsidian from Ethiopia to Rome.

When its composition is silica-rich obsidian belongs to the rhyolite family. There are also trachytic, andesitic and phonolitic obsidians.

Despite the high silica content the colour is dark; grey, brown to deep black. This is the result of extremely finely distributed magnetite or hematite or other colouring elements. Tiny pores are the cause of the gold-like reflections which are occasionally seen. Colour is uniform or stripy. Even black obsidian has a grey translucence at the edges while small splinters are even lighter coloured and transparent. Vitreous lustre and conchoidal fracture with sharp edges are characteristic.

It develops because of the rapid cooling of melts which are usually gas rich but so viscous that the gases (and up to 3% water) cannot escape and are still trapped within the rock. When heated to about 1000°C the gases are driven off and they inflate the obsidian to the point where it becomes pumice.

Occurs as crusts on lava flows, as ejecta or as the outer layer of swollen volcanic domes. LOCALITIES: Lipari Islands/Italy, Anatolia/Turkey, Iceland, Hungary, New Mexico and Wyoming/USA, Java, Japan.

In the Stone Age obsidian, together with flint, was a much valued raw material for utensils and weapons on account of its sharp edged fracture and its great hardness (Mohs' hardness 5-5½). In Mexico it was used into the sixteenth century for knives, scrapers and arrow heads among other things. Nowadays it is worked for sculptures, cult objects and costume jewellery.

Snowflake obsidian [1] Trade term for spherical inclusions, the so-called spherulites. These structures, consisting of radially arranged minerals (e.g. feldspars, cristobalite), may reach nut size. The crystals have grown radially from a crystallizing centre into the still hot viscous melt until the process is brought to an end by the cooling down and solidification of the lava. LOCALITIES: New Mexico and Utah/USA, Mexico

Apache tears [2] Trade term for nodular obsidian fragments. The rounding is due to transport by rivers and polishing by the sand. The polishing is often completed artificially. LOCALITIES: Texas/USA. According to popular tradition the nodules are to be found where an Amerindian died.

Pitchstone [3]

Palaeo-volcanic natural glass with a resinous or pitch-like lustre. Colour grey, black, greenish or brown, sometimes speckled and striped. Frequently large disseminated crystals of quartz and feldspars. Poor in volcanic gases, rich in water (up to 10%) which can be driven off at temperatures of 200-300°C. Classified with the rhyolites because of the chemical composition. Develops from obsidian by devitrification i.e. through a gradual crystallizing out, hence a transition from the glassy to the crystalline state. LOCALITIES: S Tyrol/Italy, Saxony/Germany, Colorado/USA, Eigg/Hebrides and Arran/Scotland.

Wildes Ei Nodular pitchstone formations in Palaeozoic rhyolites (quartz porphyries). Can reach football size.

1

2

3

4

RHYOLITE FAMILY

Rhyolite and dacite belong to the rhyolite family.

Rhyolite [3,4] Liparite

Rhyolite (Greek "flowstone") is a silica-rich volcanic rock.

Light minerals: 80–100%			
of which:	quartz 20–60%		
	feldspars 40–80%	of which:	alkali feldspar 35–100%
			plagioclase feldspar 0–65%
Dark minerals: 0–20%			
Medium constituents: aegirine, biotite, zircon, apatite, magnetite.			

Usually porphyritic texture. Phenocrysts are quartz, sanidine, plagioclase, rarely biotite. Very compact. Groundmass with varying amounts of glass, also dense and fine grained. Frequently flow textured caused by preferred orientation of phenocrysts. The colour of young rhyolite is light, white, grey, yellowish, reddish. Older rhyolites have a darker appearance. Since silica rich lavas are viscous, rhyolites (more than 70% SiO_2) are to be found in swollen volcanic forms such as blisters and domes. Rarely columnar jointed. LOCALITIES: Schwarzwald/Germany, Saxony/Germany, Vosges/France, Lipari and Tuscany/Italy, Iceland, Rocky Mountains/USA, Andes, Lake District/England, Snowdonia/Wales. Used as aggregates and chippings, for paving stones, as decorative material.
Quartz porphyry [1] (Palaeorhyolite) Palaeozoic volcanic rock of rhyolitic composition (porphyritic texture). The name quartz porphyry (Greek "purple colour") should be replaced by the term palaeorhyolite. Because of its great age the rock is somewhat altered and is coloured red, brown and sometimes greenish. The most important locality in Europe is South Tyrol/Italy.

Dacite [2]

Silica rich volcanic rock. Named after a Roman province in Rumania.

Light minerals: 70-95%			
of which:	quartz 20-60%		
	feldspars 40-80%	of which:	plagioclase feldspar 65-100%
			alkali feldspar 0-35%
Dark minerals: 5-30%			
Medium constituents: pyroxenes, hornblende biotite, zircon, apatite, magnetite.			

Plagioclase, quartz, rather rarely alkali feldspar, hornblende and biotite are phenocrysts in a fine grained often glassy groundmass. Often flow texture. Dacite natural glasses are known. Colour light to medium grey, generally somewhat darker than rhyolite with which dacite is often associated. LOCALITIES: Saar-Nahe district, Schwarzwald/Germany, Siebenbürgen/Romania, Massif Central/France, Rocky Mountains/USA. Used as aggregates and chippings, also as ornamental and decorative stone.
Quartz porphyrite (Palaeodacite) Palaeozoic volcanic rock of dacitic composition. The name quartz porphyrite should be replaced by palaeodacite. Colour is frequently reddish or greenish.

TRACHYTE FAMILY

Trachyte, latite and phonolite belong to the trachyte family.

Trachyte [1,2]

Trachyte (Greek "rough") is a feldspar-rich, light coloured volcanic rock.

Light minerals: 60-100%		
	of which: feldspars 80-100%	of which: alkali feldspar 65-100%
		plagioclase feldspar 0-35%
	quartz 0-20% or foids 0-10%	
Dark minerals: 0-40%		
Medium constituents: pyroxenes, hornblende, biotite, apatite		

Colour light to medium grey, yellow, brown, reddish in the older formations. Groundmass dense, fine grained, glassy, porous; always porphyritic. Phenocrysts of plagioclase, pyroxenes, hornblende and, above all, sanidine. Frequently shows flow texture. Occurs in lava domes and cumulo volcanoes. LOCALITIES: Siebengebirge, Westerwald/Germany, Auvergne/France, North Wales, Devon/England, Texas and Colorado/USA. Many trachytes are susceptible to frost.
Keratophyre [2] Palaeozoic trachyte with less than 40% mafic minerals.

Latite [3] Trachyandesite

A feldspar rich volcanic rock. Named after the country around Latium in Italy.

Light minerals: 65-95%		
	of which: feldspars 80-100%	of which: alkali feldspar 35-65%
		plagioclase feldspar 35-65%
	quartz 0-20% or	
	foids 0-10%	
Dark minerals: 5-35%		
Medium constituents: pyroxenes, hornblende, biotite, olivine, apatite, magnetite		

Feldspars are the major constituents, minor constituents nepheline and pyroxenes. Porphyritic texture with plagioclase, pyroxenes and sanidine phenocrysts. Groundmass fine grained and glassy. Flow texture. Colour light to medium grey. Occurs in lava sheets. LOCALITIES: Auvergne/France, Italy, Colorado and California/USA.

Phonolite [4]

Phonolite (Greek "ringing stone" or "clinkstone") is a feldspar and foid rich volcanic rock.

Light minerals: 60-100%		
	of which: feldspars 40-90%	of which: alkali feldspar 50-100%
		plagioclase feldspar 0-50%
	foids 10-60%	
Dark minerals: 0-40%		
Medium constituents: aegirine, hornblende, melanite, olivine.		

Texture dense to fine-grained, rarely glassy. Porphyritic with phenocrysts of sanidine and nepheline. Parallel texture which can lead to platy jointing. Colour grey, greenish, brownish. Occurs in dammed up lava flows rarely in sheets. LOCALITIES: Hegau, Kaiserstuhl/Baden/Rhone/Germany, Auvergne/France, Haddington/Scotland, Wolf Rock/England, Montana and South Dakota/USA.

---

1 Alkali trachyte, Auvergne/France
2 Quartz keratophyre, Westphalia/Germany

3 Nepheline latite, Siebengebirge/Rhineland/Germany
4 Phonolite, Hohentwiel/Hegau/Germany

1 2

3 4

ANDESITE/BASALT FAMILY

Andesite, basalt and tephrite belong to the andesite/basalt family. It is often not possible, macroscopically, to distinguish the individual members within this family nor to separate them from genetically related rocks.

Andesite [1]
Named after the Andes mountains in South America.

Light minerals: 60-85%				
	of which: feldspars 80-100%		of which: plagioclase feldspar 65-100%	
			alkali feldspar 0-35%	
	quartz 0-20% or foids 0-10%			
Dark minerals: 15-40%				
Medium constituents: hornblende, pyroxenes, biotite, olivine, magnetite, apatite, zircon.				

Andesite is a relatively pale rock with porphyritic texture. Phenocrysts are plagioclases (particularly andesine), hornblende, pyroxenes, and biotite. Groundmass fine grained and glassy. A tough and interweaved texture is the result of the felting of the tabular and lath-shaped major and minor constituents. Quartz makes up scarcely more than 5% of the groundmass. The colours of andesite are grey, brownish, reddish; older varieties mostly greenish. Occurs in lava flows and stocks together with basalt, latite, and trachyte. LOCALITIES: Rheinpfalz, Westerwald, Siebengebirge/Rhineland/Germany, Vosges and Auvergne/France, Glencoe/ Scotland, Lake District/England, Snowdonia/N Wales, Romania, Rocky Mountains, Oregon, California/USA.

Because of its felted texture it is suitable for high quality road metal and chippings. Andesite is the most important volcanic rock after basalt. The distinction between andesite and basalt is made according to the colour index i.e. according to the volume per cent of mafic constituents whereas in the plutonic equivalents, diorite and gabbro, it is made on anorthite content. An identification of the feldspar minerals is very difficult because of the porphyritic texture and the fine grained to glassy texture. In andesite the dark minerals make up less than 40% by volume of the total rock whereas in basalt they total more than 40%.

Porphyrite [2] Term for the usually greenish andesite formed in the Palaeozoic; it should be replaced by the term palaeoandesite.

Basalt [3,4]
Named after a place in Syria. Already known in antiquity.

Light minerals: 30-60%				
	of which: feldspars 80-100%		of which: plagioclase feldspar 65-100%	
			alkali feldspar 0-35%	
	quartz 0-20% or foids 0-10%			
Dark minerals: 40-70%				
Medium constituents: hornblende, pyroxenes, biotite, olivine, magnetite, ilmenite, apatite.				

Basalt is a dark rock, grey to black, also brownish; older varieties are greenish or browny red.

---

1 Hornblende andesite, Almeria/Spain
2 Augite porphyrite, Lemberg/Rheinlandpfalz/ Germany

3 Porphyritic basalt, Vogelsberg/Hessen/ Germany
4 Nepheline basalt, Odenwald/Hessen/Germany

1
2
3
4

All dark volcanic rocks look similar and can frequently only be identified with the aid of precise mineral identification tables and thin sections. Even this is not always successful because crystal formation in volcanic rocks is in part somewhat different from that in plutonic rocks.

The distinction of basalts from andesites (p.244) which are in the same rock family and which have almost the same mineral content is based on the colour index i.e. the proportion of mafic minerals. In basalt the dark constituents make up more than 40%, in andesites less than 40%.

The texture of basalt is usually fine grained to dense, only very occasionally coarse grained or glassy. Porphyritic texture with phenocrysts of pyroxenes, plagioclase, hornblende (rare) and olivine; frequently with preferred orientation. Occasionally cavities caused by former gas bubbles but seldom strongly porous. An interweaved texture results from the irregular dovetailing of lath-like plagioclases; this texture makes the basalt appear particularly tough, solid and weather resistant.

Basalt is the most widely distributed of all volcanic rocks. Since basaltic lavas are very fluid because of the low silica content they form lava flows of wide extent from fissure eruptions; these are the so-called plateau basalts, also called trap. Thicknesses may reach 3000m. Examples of these are the Deccan basalts of India, the Karroo basalts of South Africa, sheets in the Columbia Plateau of Oregon/USA, and further in Argentina and Siberia. There are also basalt cones and plug formations; Eifel, Westerwald, Rhone, Rheinpfalz/Germany, Auvergne/France.

As with all basic volcanic rocks columnar jointing is characteristic (p.229). Platy jointing seldom occurs. Basalt has many varied uses as a natural stone because of its good qualities and its wide distribution. It rates as the natural stone which is most resistant to weathering. Basalt with a preferred orientation has less good qualities. Used in earlier times as stone for walls and roads its main importance nowadays lies in its use as high grade aggregate e.g. for building railway lines and as chippings (for coating with bitumen). It should not be used as paving stones for carriageways because it becomes slippery when wet.

Large blocks of basalt cannot be extracted because of columnar jointing at outcrop. On the other hand squared blocks of virtually any required size can be extracted from porous basaltic lava developed at the surface of a lava flow and therefore not very well jointed. Melted basalt (melt basalt) is a raw material used in the production of mineral wool as well as the base material for highly resistant flooring slabs and linings.

Basalt varieties

Basalt varieties are usually further distinguished according to age and grain size without there being clear definitions or a uniform nomenclature.

Age	fine grained	coarse grained
young	basalt	dolerite
old	melaphyre	diabase

Basalt *sensu stricto* [Nos 3 and 4, p.245] Anamesite. Unaltered fine grained basalt of Tertiary or younger age. Colour usually grey, blue-grey to black.

1 2

3 4

Melaphyre [No. 3, p.247] Fine grained basalt of pre-Tertiary age. Former gas bubbles are filled with quartz, agate, chalcedony, zeolites, or chlorite (melaphyre mandelstein (almond stone). Colour dark grey, or, as a result of alteration of minerals, reddish to brown. Of only limited use in the construction industry. The term melaphyre should no longer be used and should be replaced by palaeobasalt. In earlier times old andesites were also very occasionally called melaphyre.

Dolerite [3 and No. 1, p.247] Coarse grained, unaltered, usually young basalt.

Diabase [1 and No. 4, p.247] Old Palaeozoic basalt. Chlorite and serpentine developed from dark minerals as a result of secondary alteration; the colour is consequently greenish (greenstone). We speak of the "greening" of basalts. Although such material alteration does not have to be a function of age but can depend on tectonic processes and circulating waters, most diabases are, in fact, probably of a considerable age. The term palaeobasalt should be used for diabases, as in the case of melaphyres.

In more recent times diabase is understood as a green variety of basalt as also of its plutonic counterpart gabbro. Some authors on the other hand regard diabase as being essentially a dyke rock.

Used as aggregates and because of the greenish colour as striking architectural stone for internal decoration as well as for the cladding of facades.

Tholeiite [No. 2, p.247] Olivine-free basalt; olivine basalt is its counterpart. This two-fold sub-division of basalts is recommended nowadays instead of the earlier distinction according to grain size and age.

Basalt lava [No. 4, p.251] A basalt lava riddled with many gas bubbles. Originates at the surface of a lava flow.

Basaltic rock Collective name for dark volcanic rocks (e.g basalt, tephrite, basanite, foidite, mafitite) which can scarcely be distinguished macroscopically and are difficult to determine even with the aid of a thin section and a microscope.

Sunburn basalt False name for a tephrite (p.250)

Trade names of basaltic rocks
BLACK SWEDISH [3]: black dolerite, Sweden
PORFIDO VERDE ANTICO: greenish andesite, Greece
BLACK PORPHYRY: dark andesite, Lugano/Switzerland
HESSIAN NEWGREEN: green diabase, Marburg/Hessen/Germany
TIBERIAS: flecked basalt, Israel
BODAFORS: dark green diabase, Sweden
VERDE INDIA [1]: greenish diabase, Karnataka/India

False trade names with basaltic connotation
HESSIAN DIABASE [4]: picrite, Dill area/Hessen/Germany
GREEN PORPHYRY: lamprophyre, Fichtelgebirge/Germany
LOBENSTEIN DIABASE: picrite, Thuringia/Germany
SOLVAG-GABBRO: Norwegian term for a peridotite, Norway
LAUSITZ GREEN GRANITE: black-green andesite or diabase, Saxony/Germany
GRANITE PATRIA: term for a greenish diabase, Fichtelgebirge/Germany.

1 Diabase VERDE INDIA, Karnataka/India
2 Lamprophyre GRENZLAND, Lausitz/Germany
3 Dolerite BLACK SWEDISH, Sweden
4 Picrite HESSIAN DIABASE, Hessen/Germany

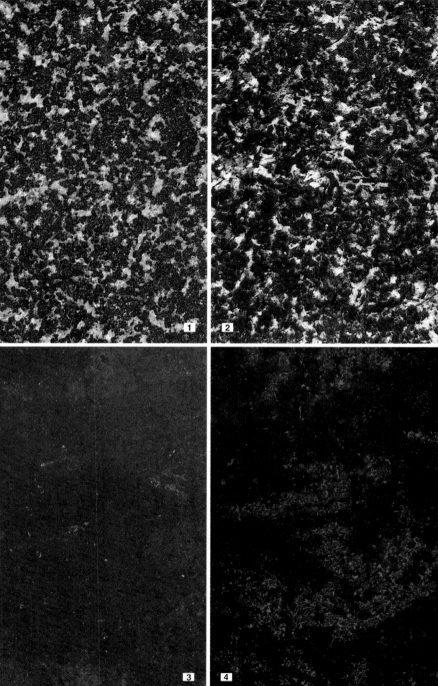

Tephrite [1]

Tephrite (Greek "ashstone") belongs to the basalt family.

Light minerals: 30-80%		
of which: feldspars 40-90%		of which: plagioclase feldspar 50-100%
		alkali feldspar 0-50%
foids 10-60%		
Dark minerals: 20-70%		
Medium constituents: pyroxenes, hornblende, olivine		

Tephrite has a more or less dark appearance depending on the proportion of mafic minerals. Texture is almost always porphyritic with phenocrysts of pyroxenes and hornblende. Plagioclase laths have a randomly felted arrangement (intersertal texture) in the fine grained, dense or glassy groundmass. Pyroxenes are the dominant minor constituent.

Can be distinguished from the similar looking basalt by the high content of foids. Nepheline and leucite are always represented, quartz is never present. Occurs only in geologically young formations. Secondarily altered tephrites become completely new rocks, because of the newly developed minerals, so that the tephritic origin is no longer recognisable. Columnar and platy jointing as with other silica- poor volcanics. LOCALITIES: Vogelsberg, Rhone, Eifel/Germany, Steiermark/Austria, Auvergne/France, Vesuvius/Italy.

Exploitation is limited under certain circumstances because foids weather easily (see below with sunburn basalt). Weather resistant types are used as road metal, chippings, fused basalt and in the production of mineral wool.

Basanite [2] Olivine rich variety of tephrite. Dark grey to black because of the high proportion (40-70%) of mafic minerals. Porphyritic texture, usually crystalline groundmass. The numerous cavities are often filled with zeolites. Localities: Eifel/Germany, Viterba/Italy, Canary Islands, Tassili Mountains/Algeria, Montana/USA, Ayrshire/Scotland. Only used locally as a construction stone.

Limburgite [3] Variety of tephrite with more than 50% of glass, more than 30% pyroxenes and up to about 10% olivine which can occur as phenocrysts. Zeolites are often deposited in the cavities.

Millstone lava [4] Term for a leucite-nepheline-tephrite, also (wrongly) called millstone trachyte. A similar solid rock is used worldwide as a grinding stone (especially for paper mills). Because of the innumerable pores throughout the rock it always remains rough and retains a good grip even when worn down. LOCALITIES: Niedermendig/Eifel/Germany where it can be worked in opencast workings as well as underground. The use of these quarries for the extraction of millstones goes back to the Stone Age.

Sunburn basalt (Sunburn) Vernacular term for tephrites and nephelinites which are susceptible to weathering. The alteration of nepheline into analcite results in a volume increase (of about 5%) which leads to the decay of the rocks. Wrongly considered to be due to the effects of the sun (hence the name). If such rocks are to be used in the building industry and in technology then an initial laboratory test is urgently advised.

1 Tephrite, Kaiserstuhl/Baden/Germany
2 Leucite basanite, Vesuvius/Italy
3 Limburgite, Kaiserstuhl/Baden/Germany
4 Millstone lava, Niedermendig/Eifel/Germany

1

2

3

4

PICRITE FAMILY

Foidites and ultramafic rocks (ultramafitites) are members of the picrite family.

Foidite

Collective term for all volcanic rocks with a very high foid content. Best known examples nephelinite and leucitite.

Dark minerals: 5-70%	
Light minerals: 30-95%	of which: foids 60-100% feldspars 0-40%

Foidites are similar to basalts in their external appearance. The most essential characteristic for distinguishing between them are the foids which are usually present in very considerable quantities. The individual types are named according to the dominant foid mineral.

Nephelinite [1] Light to medium-grey with nepheline and pyroxene as major constituents. Hornblende, apatite, melilite and sphene are present in smaller quantities. Olivine can make up up to 20%. Texture fine grained to dense, glassy and porphyritic. Sometimes the rocks decay because of the secondary alteration of nepheline to analcite (see sunburn basalt p.250). Occurs in dykes and small stocks. LOCALITIES: Eifel/Rhone, Erzgebirge/Germany, Auvergne/France, Hawaii/USA.

Leucitite [2] Because of the high proportion of leucite, which frequently forms large phenocrysts in a particularly fine grained to dense groundmass, leucitite has a very light appearance. If pyroxenes are more abundant then the colour is darker. LOCALITIES: Eifel, Kaiserstuhl/Baden/Germany, Bohemian Mittegebirge/Czechoslovakia, Vesuvius/Italy, Arizona/USA.

Ultramafic rocks (ultramafitites)

Ultramafic rocks are very dark volcanic rocks in which the proportion of dark minerals is greater than 90%. Melilitite and picrite are the best known representatives.

Melilitite The mineral melilite is the constituent which gives the rock its name. It must make up at least 10% but can amount to more than 30%. Other major constituents are diopside and phlogopite.

Picrite [3 and No. 4, p.249] Fine to medium grained, porphyritic texture. Major constituents are pyroxene and olivine; hornblende, biotite and magnetite are also present. Because of the secondary alteration of some minerals to serpentine and chlorite the originally grey to black picrite takes on a more greenish tint. Occurs in small bodies, rare.

Kimberlite [4]

Kimberlite (named after the town Kimberley in South Africa) is considered to be either a picrite or picrite derivative or on occasions as being a dyke rock. Texture fine to medium grained, also porphyritic, the rock often has a fragmentary appearance. Colour greenish to grey-bluish. Major minerals usually olivine, pyroxenes and phlogopite. Pyrope, chrome diopside and spinel are medium, sometimes minor, constituents. Occurs in dykes or in diatremes, the so-called pipes. LOCALITIES: South Africa, Zaire, India, Jakutien/former USSR. Uniquely diamond bearing.

1 Olivine nephelinite, Eifel/Rhineland/Germany
2 Nepheline leucitite, Eifel/Rhineland/Germany
3 Picrite, Fichtelgebirge, Bavaria/Germany
4 Kimberlite, Transvaal/South Africa

TECHNICAL PROPERTIES OF VOLCANIC ROCKS

| | Bulk density | Grain density | True porosity | Water | Apparent |
| | Density | Specific gravity | Total porosity | absorption | porosity |
	g/cm^3	g/cm3	Volume %	Weight %	Volume %
Quartz porphyry, porphyrite, andesite keratophyre	2.55–2.80	2.58–2.83	0.4 – 1.8	0.2– 0.7	0.4– 1.8
Basalt, melaphyre	2.95–3.00	3.00–3.15	0.2 – 0.9	0.1– 0.3	0.2– 0.8
Basalt lava	2.20–2.35	3.00–3.15	20 –25	4 –10	9 –24
Diabase	2.80–2.90	2.85–2.95	0.31–1.1	0.1– 0.4	0.3– 1.0
Pyroclastics	1.80–2.00	2.62–2.75	20 –30	6 –15	12 –30
Rhyolite, dacite	2.35–2.70	2.58–2.73	0.4–14.5	0.1– 4.7	
Trachyte	2.42–2.75	2.52–2.78	1.0–10.0	0.3– 4.0	
Andesite	2.50–2.75	2.58–2.80	0.8–14.0	0.3– 4.6	
Basalt	2.74–3.20	2.84–3.22	0.3–4.5	0.1– 1.7	
Phonolite, tephrite	2.37–2.64	2.50–2.67	1.3–12.5	0.3– 4.4	
Pyroclastics (rhyolitic, trachytic)	0.88–2.20	2.50–2.75	20.0–65.0	6.0–25.0	
Basalt lava	2.20–2.45	2.95–3.15	18.0–28.0	4.0– 10.0	

	Dry compressive strength kg/cm^2	Tensile strength in bending kg/cm2	Impact strength – number of blows to destruction	Abrasion resistance – loss in cm^3 from 50cm^2	
Quartz porphyry, porphyrite, andesite, keratophyre	1800–3000	150–200	11–13	5– 8	
Basalt, melaphyre	2500–4000	150–250	12–17	5– 8.5	
Basalt lava	800–1500	80–120	4– 5	12–15	
Diabase	1800–2500	150–250	11–16	5– 8	
Pyroclastics	200– 300	20– 60			

HYPABYSSAL (DYKE ROCKS)

Hypabyssal (also called transitional igneous rocks) were considered to be the third independent rock group within the igneous rocks. They occupy a midway position between plutonic and volcanic rocks with regard to genesis, texture and occurrence (c.f. illustration p.190). The origin was explained as the differentiation of partial melts into small rock bodies, the dykes. In more recent times the tendency is to assign the hypabyssal rocks more to the plutonic rocks but some of the types on the other hand might be considered to be volcanic. The nomenclature has altered to keep pace with the new ideas on the subject. Whereas formerly in naming hypabyssal rocks the name was derived from the equivalent plutonics and volcanics, nowadays they should be characterized by the prefix micro with the corresponding plutonic term as the main stem. Microplutonite or microplutonic rock is consequently in this sense the modern name for hypabyssal rock.

Nomenclature of hypabyssal rocks/microplutonites

	New nomenclature	Old nomenclature
Plutonic rocks	Microplutonics	Hypabyssal rocks
Granite	Microgranite	Granite porphyry
Granodiorite	Microgranodiorite	
Syenite	Microsyenite	Syenite porphyry
Monzonite	Micromonzonite	
Foyaite	Microfoyaite	
Diorite	Microdiorite	Diorite porphyrite
Gabbro	Microgabbro	Gabbro porphyrite
Essexite	Microessexite	
Foidolite	Microfoidolite	
Ultramafics	Microultramafitcs	

UNDIFFERENTIATED HYPABYSSAL ROCKS

The hypabyssal rocks named in the table above have the same chemical composition as the parent rock but the texture is different. Such hypabyssal rocks were formerly termed undifferentiated together with a little known special expression aschistic (Greek "unsplit").

The weathered out quartz vein in Pfahl/Bavarian Forest/Germany rises like a wall

1 Granite porphyry, Odenwald/Hessen/Germany
2 Graphic granite, Hitterö/Norway

3 Granite pegmatite with orthoclase crystals, tabular albite and smoky quartz, Fichtelgebirge/Germany

1

2

3

Granite porphyry (microgranite) The best known example of normal (i.e. undifferentiated) hypabyssal rocks with typically porphyritic texture. Large phenocrysts of feldspar and quartz in a fine mineral groundmass.

DIFFERENTIATED HYPABYSSAL ROCKS

Very occasionally the mineral content and texture of hypabyssal rocks are completely different from those of the related plutonic and volcanic rocks. In this case we speak of differentiated or diaschistic (Greek "Split") rocks. The coarse grained pegmatite, light coloured aplite and the dark lamprophyre belong to this group. Some of the quartzolites (p.198) must certainly be placed under this heading.

Pegmatite [No. 3, p.257] Light coloured coarse grained rock (Greek "solid stone"); it can be assigned to both the hypabyssal rocks and to the plutonics. It occurs in dykes (veins), stocks, and lenses or at the edge of large plutonic bodies, usually in association with the plutonic rocks. Many crystals have perfectly developed crystal forms. Giant crystals are known.

Since pegmatites often contain rare minerals they can be of significance economically. The pegmatites are named after the appropriate plutonic rock (e.g. granite pegmatite) or after the useful minerals (mica pegmatite, feldspar pegmatite, gemstone pegmatite). Pegmatite is understood to be not only the coarse grained rock type but also, in a wider sense, the whole pegmatite rock body.

Graphic granite [No. 2, p.256] Pegmatite variety with regular intergrowth of potash feldspar (microcline) and quartz with a columnar form. The dark grey quartzes lie in a light coloured grey-white or brownish feldspar matrix in forms like Arabic graphic characters or Germanic runes. The ratio of potash feldspar to quartz is approximately 70:30.

Aplite [1,2] Light coloured fine grained dyke rock (Greek "simple stone") All minerals are granular with no individual shape and with saccharoidal texture. Often a granite composition (granite aplite) with alkali feldspar and plagioclase in equal amounts. There are however aplites which correspond to other plutonic rocks (e.g. syenite aplite, diorite aplite, essexite aplite) Rock colour white, yellowish or red. Occurs in dykes up to several metres thick. Present in almost every granite complex frequently in proximity of pegmatites.

Lamprophyre [3,4 and No. 2, p.248] Dark dyke rock (Greek "gleaming mixture") with extraordinarily fine-grained or glassy groundmass and usually porphyritic texture. Micas on the fracture surfaces create a certain lustre. Mineral content and texture are very different in the individual lamprophyres. Occurs in dykes scarcely more than one metre thick. Well known varieties are: kersantite, minette, monchiquite, spessartite, vosgesite. Some authors also place kimberlite (p.252) under this heading.

Minette [3] Lamprophyre variety of syenitic composition. More potash feldspar than plagioclase. Biotite and pyroxenes present in large quantity. Should not be confused with the oolitic iron ores which are also called minette (p.294).

Spessartite [4] Lamprophyre variety of dioritic composition. More plagioclase than potash feldspar. Hornblende or augite are the dark constituents which produce the colour. Quartz can be present.

---

1 Aplite, Odenwald/Hessen/Germany
2 Tourmaline aplite, Fichtelgebirge/Bavaria/Germany

3 Minette, Vosges/France
4 Spessartite, Oberpfalz/Bavaria/Germany

1

2

2

3

SEDIMENTARY ROCKS

Sedimentary rocks constitute only about 8% of the Earth's crust. They are distributed mainly at or near the Earth's surface where, as unconsolidated or solid rock, they cover 75% of the continents and probably still more of the ocean floors.

ORIGIN

Sedimentary rocks are secondary rocks. They originate on the Earth's surface from the weathered debris of other rocks, namely igneous, metamorphic and older sedimentary rocks. Normally there is a fairly long transport path between the site of the original rock and the area of deposition of the weathered products. In this way, by the agents of water, ice, wind and gravity, the rock debris being carried along and the constituents present in solution are so mixed together, separated out or chemically altered that a completely new rock is formed at the site of deposition.

Layering (bedding) Almost all sedimentary rocks are layered. They possess boundary planes which pervade the whole mass and are present at both sides of the variable rock material. Such layers develop as a result of variable deposition from water either as a result of grain sorting or interruption of sedimentation. If the sedimentation is in a delta where deposition, because of variation of the flow of the river, results in layers which cross one another, so-called cross-bedding is formed.

In small hand specimens the characteristic feature of layering is, under some circumstances, not always visible. In the field however, sedimentary rocks with large scale bedding can be identified with little doubt. Boundaries between layers (bedding planes) are usually surfaces of easy splitting.

The layer thicknesses vary between fractions of a millimetre to several metres. In the millimetre domain we speak of laminations, at the centimetre level of thinly bedded and for decimetre thickness of thickly bedded rocks.

Limestone with concordant bedding   Cross bedding with discordances

Unstratified strongly jointed reef limestone,
Eichstätt/Bavaria/Germany

Earthpillars developed in unstratified moraine,
S Tyrol/Italy

In some sedimentary rocks joints (very small fissures) run mainly at right angles
to the bedding surfaces. After weathering, this results, especially in sandstones, in
the formation of block-shaped segmentation of individual rock layers. In
limestone, on the other hand, bizarre, sharp ridged topography is formed because
of the relatively easy solubility (p.282).

Reef limestones are, as a rule, unbedded. They develop as an atoll or as a
fringing reef, because of continuous deposition of lime by very small coral
animals. Reef limestones in some areas only form individual knolls within
otherwise well-bedded limestone massifs.

Moraines, deposits from glaciers, are also always unstratified. Characteristic
features of glacial sedimentation are no sorting, all grain sizes present, deposition
of even platy components without any preferred orientation, large blocks possibly
up to more than one metre in size.

Diagenesis Most sedimentary rocks are initially deposited as unconsolidated
material called sediments. Consolidation sets in only gradually because of
dewatering and/or because of cementation with a binding material (clayey,
calcareous, siliceous). All these processes of rock alteration which lead to
consolidation are called diagenesis.

Rocks which have become solid in this way should be described by the suffix
"stone" (eg sand- sandstone, clay- claystone (mudstone)).

There are also sedimentary rocks which immediately they are formed become
solid rock; examples of these are calcareous tufa, reef limestone and saline rocks.

Fossil content Fossils are an essential distinguishing feature of sedimentary rocks;
these include any traces of life such as the hard parts of animals, imprints of
plants and boring, browsing and walking traces of small living creatures.
Most fossils are found in sedimentary rocks but not all these rocks need contain
them. Nor are fossils exclusively restricted to sedimentary rocks; traces of life can
just as well occur in volcanic tuff deposits. Nevertheless, the fossil content
together with the characteristic layering is usually a convincing indication of a
sedimentary rock.

Soils Very occasionally soils are numbered among sedimentary rocks but in this
book they are not treated as a group in their own right. Everything which is of
petrological interest in soils is mentioned under the corresponding rocks (clay,
marl, limestone etc).

CLASSIFICATION OF SEDIMENTARY ROCKS

There is no obligatory or generally recommended classification of sedimentary rocks; in consequence a uniform nomenclature is lacking. The main groups are usually divided according to their mode of origin. Further subdivision is based on chemical properties, technical measurements or genetic principles.

Main groups of sedimentary rocks

Clastic sediments	Chemical-biogenic sediments	Residual rocks	Carbonaceous rocks
Psephites	Limestones	Kaolin	Peat
Psammites	Siliceous rocks	Bauxite	Lignite
Pelites	Saline rocks		Bituminous coal
	Phosphate rocks		Anthracite
	Ferriferous rocks		

SYNONYMS

The following terms are used as synonyms for sedimentary rocks: sedimentite, deposited rock, layered rock and sediment. Only the term sedimentary rock is entirely unambiguous because volcanic tuffs and very occasionally even lavas develop by deposition from above.

The term "layered rock" is also not a completely valid substitute for sedimentary rock. It is certainly true that most sedimentary rocks are layered but there are those (e.g. reefs or moraines) which have no layering. On the other hand non-sedimentary rocks can also be layered (volcanic tuff, some metamorphic rocks).

The term sediment was formerly used instead of sedimentary rock. Nowadays, some authors apply the term "sediment" solely to unconsolidated deposits; only solid rocks are called sedimentary rocks by some authors.

Characteristic features of sedimentary rocks

1 Mostly well developed layering (bedding)
2 Often fossiliferous
3 Topography often rugged and bizarre
4 Moraines never stratified, no grain sorting
5 Reef limestones almost never stratified

Weathering using granite as an example

1 Fresh granite not yet attacked by weathering
2 Brown coloration as a result of chemical reactions causing iron compounds to go into solution
3 Feldspars are decomposed by water containing carbonic acid, in depth weathering
4 The texture is made looser because of a combination of chemical and physical weathering, little cracks pervade the rock
5 Granite has broken down into coarse grained friable pieces
6 Fine grained tilth with clay minerals developed as the final phase of weathering

PSEPHITE FAMILY

This category includes both loose unconsolidated and lithified coarse clastic sedimentary rocks with a grain size of more than 2mm in diameter.

Fragment [3]

Angular rock debris resulting from the mechanical breakdown of rock bodies is called a fragment if it is an individual piece, or rubble if it is en masse. It is deposited not far from the parent rock.

Rubble

Larger accumulations of angular fragments. Only found close to the source rock, usually on the sides of hills as so-called screes.

Pebble [1]

A piece of rock rounded in the coarse of transport by rivers or by breakers on the shore as a result of rolling or pushing movement; also rounded by the individual pieces striking against each other. Sandstones and limestones are rounded after 1-5km of river transport, granite and quartzite after 10-20km.

Drift [4]

If glaciers are the transporting agent the individual fragments acquire a flat shape with rounded edges and straight scratch lines from contact with other rock debris (striated pebbles).

Rock fragments transported by ice can be almost any size. There are pieces a cubic metre in size – so called foundlings, erratic blocks or erratics for short which have sometimes been transported 1000km or more during the Ice Age.

Gravel

Accumulation of more or less rounded and polished rock fragments comprising pebbles and drift. Not to be confused with the gravel used in the building industry which is broken angular rock material.

Windkanter [2]

Angular relics of rock, polished by fine grained sand in desert regions.

Current oriented river gravel showing imbrication, Isar/Upper Bavaria/Germany

1 Pebble (silicified limestone), Abenrade/Denmark
2 Windkanter (limestone), Saudi Arabia
3 Fragment (dolomite rock), Italy
4 Striated drift pebble (limestone), Upper Bavaria/Germany

1

2

3

4

Terminology of coarse clastic sediments

Individuals	In association	
	loose	consolidated
Fragment	Rubble	Breccia
Pebble, drift	Gravel	Conglomerate

Breccia [1]

Breccia (old High German "break-fracture") is a consolidated rock composed of angular debris, often brightly coloured. The deposited fragments are of similar or different rock types depending on the source area. Usually no grain size sorting, no orientation, no grain selection, no kind of layering, no fossils. Frequently angular cavities as a result of fragments falling out. Cementing agent can be clayey, calcareous or siliceous. Occurs on mountain sides. Originates as hillwash or landslide material. Used in the building industry depending on composition, packing density as well as on type and amount of cementing agent. The overall level of consolidation should be approximately uniform with the included fragments being firmly embedded. Compact limestone breccias are suitable for grinding and polishing and for use for internal decoration. Types with calcareous cement used externally are very susceptible to carbonic acid and sulphur compounds in the air. There are many trade types on the market frequently designated as MARBLE. LOCALITIES: S Tyrol, Tuscany, Sicily/Italy, Western Alps, Pyrenees/France, Portugal, Turkey, Mendips and Vale of Eden/England, Beekmantown/Pennsylvania and Rocky Mountains/USA.

Tectonic breccia [2] In addition to sedimentary breccias there are also pyroclastic and tectonic breccias. The latter develop in situations where the parent rock is first of all broken up as a result of orogenic and seismic processes but is not completely disrupted as a rock formation. The fractured surfaces are soon cemented together again by mineral solutions.

Terrazzo Artificial stone with splinters or cubes of natural stone in a breccia-like fabric.

Tillite

Consolidated moraine with a great deal of loamy clay matrix and not many boulders. No kind of layering, no fossils. The drift is sometimes oriented in the direction of ice movement. Some authors designate only pre-Quaternary moraines as tillite.

Fanglomerate

Fanglomerates (English-Latin "fan accumulation") represent an intermediate stage between breccia and conglomerates consisting of unsorted angular and rounded rock debris. Feebly layered, rare selectivity of grain size, much coarse material, a little fine grained matrix, Formed as a fan-shaped debris stream in arid areas in the geological past. Rockflow-like floods spread out the debris, which has accumulated during a long dry period, into a cone shape.

1 Rough fractured breccia, Pyrenees/Spain   2 Cut limestone breccia, Western Alps/France

Conglomerate, so-called puddingstone. Vosges/France

Conglomerate [1,2]

Conglomerate (Latin "rolled together") is a consolidated gravel. Rounded rock debris is cemented together with a clayey, calcareous, siliceous bonding agent. The ratio of coarse to fine materials is variable. The proportion of coarse material must be more than 50% if the name conglomerate is to be applied. Only very occasionally are these rolled fragments up to head size. Not well sorted, usually no layering, largish pebbles sometimes oriented. Composition depends on source. Where the rock types of the region of origin are uniform the resulting conglomerate is correspondingly homogeneous. In general, however, several rock types are present and the conglomerate consequently has a brightly coloured flecked appearance. Grey, bluish and yellowish colours predominate, they are reddish where the cementing agent is strongly iron-rich.

The pebble content is more uniform where the transport has been over long distances. The destruction of the softer components of the gravel brings about a selection in favour of the more resistant rocks such as quartzite, amphibolite, diabase, granite and siliceous limestone. Good grain sorting in beach conglomerates.

Occurs in old gravel fields, alluvial cones and fans as well as in valley depressions usually in the foreland regions of rising mountain chains. LOCALITIES: Inn Valley/Upper Bavaria/Germany, Lower Austria, Wallis/Switzerland, Dalmatia/Yugoslavia, Sicily/Italy, Midland Valley and Torridon/Scotland, Connemara/Ireland, Appalachians/USA, Devon/England.

Solid types are used as building stone and for monuments. Siliceous cement is particularly advantageous but calcareous cement is easily dissolved by carbonic acid and sulphur compounds. Only usable as dimension stone if the individual pebbles are firmly embedded and the strength of the aggregate is approximately uniform. It can be distinguished from similar artificial stones by numerous round and empty holes. Even in types which can be ground there is never a close, compact surface. Less consolidated conglomerates are used for gravels and chippings.

Nagelfluh Local term (Swiss-nagelfels, "nail rock") for conglomerates in the Alpine region.

Puddingstone Term originally used only in English and French-speaking areas for very coarse grained conglomerates. Nowadays generally synonymous with conglomerate.

1 Rough fractured conglomerate, Isar Valley/Upper Bavaria/Germany
2 Cut conglomerate, Inn Valley/Upper Bavaria/Germany

Diamond placer deposit, Oranjemund/Namibia

PSAMMITE FAMILY

Sand

Sand is the term for a loose mixture of minerals and rock fragments in which at least 50% have grain sizes from 0.02 to 2mm diameter. Quartz and feldspars as well as mica and heavy minerals are predominant. There are also sands which contain no quartz at all. For example, in the White Sands desert in New Mexico/USA, 75000 hectares in extent, the extensive sand areas and the high migrating dunes consist only of small gypsum crystals.

Sands usually have a very wide range of grain size distribution. They include the coarser psephites as well as pelites, the very fine grained clays. The further the sands are transported before being deposited the richer they are in quartz. This is because quartz on account of its chemical resistance, lack of cleavage, and high Mohs' hardness is more resistant to destruction than other minerals.

Sands are differentiated according to the mineral content. There is no uniform nomenclature. Quartz sand should have at least 85% content of quartz.

Sand has many different uses in the building industry; quartz sands are also used for the production of glass, for sand blasting and as raw material for grinding.

Placers Heavy minerals concentrate in sands through the separating out of materials. If economically exploitable they are known as placer deposits (cf p.97).

Sandstone [1 and Nos 1-4, p.275]

Sands which have been lithified by clay, calcareous or siliceous cement. Sandstones are always layered. As a result of the joint system which usually runs perpendicular to the bedding planes, sandstone rock faces usually breakdown gradually during weathering into rectangular blocks (photo p.274).

1 Sandstone, Linda vista, California/USA
2 Sedimentary quartzite, Rhineland/Germany
3 Greywacke, Sauerland/Westphalia/Germany
4 Arkose, Vosges/France

1

2

3

4

Yellow and brown shades caused by limonite are most common. Reddish colours are caused by hematite, blue and black shades by bitumen and carbonaceous material. Green sandstones derive their colour from glauconite mica.

Sandstones are named according to mineral content, texture, matrix or cementing agent; to colour or type of diagenesis; to use, distribution or time of origin. To these can be added the outstanding qualities of the rock. There is no uniform nomenclature.

Occurs over large areas in the foothills of the Alps, in the Keuper districts of Franconia and Thuringia, the Bunter sandstone regions on either side of the Upper Rhine; wide areas in South Wales and the Midlands of England; Midland Valley and the Northwest of Scotland. Used as building stone in earlier times for cathedrals, castles and prestige buildings. Calcite-cemented sandstones are subject to decay because of carbonic acid and sulphur compounds in the air. Measures can be taken to combat rock decay but a real "magic formula" does not exist. Where possible, replacement with weather resistant rocks e.g from the basalt family is to be recommended.

Bituminous sandstones, also termed tar-sands and oil-sands, are increasingly being mined in order to extract oil from them. Exploited on a very large scale in Alberta/Canada.

Sedimentary quartzite [No. 2 p.273] (Tertiary quartzite, cemented quartzite, quartzite) Quartz-rich sandstone with siliceous cement and at least 85% quartz or quartzitic rock fragments. Not to be confused with meta quartzite (p.318). Develops only in a warm wet climate so that the widely distributed feldspars of the sands weather away and the quartz grains are left behind. Used as crushed rock for railway and road aggregates.

Arkose [No. 4, p.273] Feldspar-rich usually reddish sandstone. Generally coarse grained, difficult to classify on grain size, many angular rock fragments. Develops predominantly in a dry climate otherwise the feldspars would be weathered.

Greywacke [No. 3, p.273] Grey to grey green sandstone with at least 25% feldspar content and rich in psammitic rock fragments but also with a clayey matrix. Overall difficult to distinguish on grain size. A very compact, solid rock as a result of crystallization of siliceous cementing materials. Frequently refers only to Palaeozoic sandstones. LOCALITIES: Rheinischers Schiefergebirge, Harz/Germany, Massif Central/France, Wales, S. Uplands/Scotland, West Virginia/USA. Used locally as aggregates and chippings for building roads.

Calcareous sandstone Sandstone with high carbonate content either as cement or as small pieces of carbonate. There are artificial stones using the same name.

Rectangular block formation caused by weathering in sandstone, Externsteine/Teutoburger Wald/Germany

1 Main sandstone, visible surface cut
2 Glauconitic sandstone, visible surface embossed
3 Molasse sandstone, visible surface tooled
4 Bunter sandstone, visible surface fine axed

PELITE FAMILY

Loose and lithified clay rocks belong to the pelites; they include the clay grain sizes as well as the coarser silt.

Clay and claystone (tonstein) [4]

The rock flour which is transported in suspension down rivers is called fluviatile suspended material or float. Once it has been deposited it is called mud or ooze providing it is saturated with water. Partially de-watered, plastic, finely clastic rocks are called clay, dried out and de-watered sometimes claystone.

Constituents of clays and claystones are quartz, feldspars and micas, remains of calcareous organisms and organic substances as well as very fine grained clay minerals which can only be identified by x-rays. These clay minerals are predominantly neoformational; they only develop during sedimentation. Clay rocks thus represent a link between clastic and chemical-biogenic sedimentary rocks.

Clay rocks are always stratified. Their strength is the result of overburden pressure (compaction) and of carbonate-rich cement.

Secondary constituents cause the colour; limonite yellow to brown, hematite reddish, carbonaceous substances bitumen and sulphides grey, bluish to black.

Clay and claystone are the most widely distributed of all sedimentary rocks. They occur on alluvial plains, former lake basins and in river valleys.

Water is trapped in the clay by the large number of extremely fine pores. As a result clay is impermeable to other water and serves as a barrier to groundwater.
Fat and lean clays Clays, with a high proportion of clay minerals, which appear particularly plastic are termed fat, others are termed lean.
Bentonite Grey-white variety of argillaceous rock which develops from the alteration of volcanic ash. High swelling capacity, ionic exchange and absorption capacity as a result of the high montmorillonite content. Used as drilling mud in drilling for oil, in the slit screen process, as a filter, as a fulling (degreasing) agent.
Lean clay (lette) Clay rock without any particular definition.

Loam and loam rock

Loose or lithified variety of clay. Contains very little or no lime but, on the other hand, a great deal of sand. Characteristically coloured yellow by iron hydroxides. Extremely important raw material for the brick and tile industry.
Boulder clay Decalcified clay full of boulders.
Loess loam Decalcified loess, heavy loam soil.

Banded clay with dark winter and pale summer layers. The annual double layer (about 2-10mm) is called varve. Uppsala/Sweden

1 Kaolin mixed with some calcareous material, Oberpfalz/Bavaria/Germany
2 Loess, Dadschai/China
3 Loess doll, Remagen/Rhineland/Germany
4 Claystone, Uppsala/Sweden
5 Marlstone, South Dakota/USA

1

2

3

4

5

Marl and marlstone [No. 5, p.277]

Loose or lithified clay/claystone variety containing a great deal of carbonate either as calcite or dolomite. Raw material for the production of cement.

Clay ironstone Marlstone with high carbonate content in the form of siderite.

Marly boulder clay A marl containing many boulders. Originates as a glacial deposit especially as ground moraine.

Loess [No. 2, p.277]

Lithified yellowish dust sediment. Usually unstratified, porous, forms vertical faces, permeable to water and air. Quartz content up to 50% with feldspars, mica, clay minerals in addition; plenty of lime. Formed by ablation from dry zones into areas of steppe where plants trap the dust and consolidate it into a calcareous hair-like capillary texture. Occurs in all continents especially at the margins of the Pleistocene ice sheets.

Loess doll [No. 3, p.277] Calcareous concretion with a doll-like shape. Develops as a result of the concentrated precipitation of lime from previously dissolved limy materials.

Kaolin [No. 1, p.277]

Kaolin (named after a mountain in China) is an argillaceous rock which contains predominantly kaolinite together with quartz and mica. A residual rock formed by the weathering of rocks rich in feldspars (granite, rhyolite, arkose). The reworking of raw kaolin results in a natural washing to form kaolinite clay with kaolinite and quartz constituents. Colour varies from snow white to grey yellowish. LOCALITIES: Oberpfalz/Bavaria/Germany, Saxony/Germany, Cornwall/England, China, Virginia and Georgia/USA.

Kaolin is the raw material in the production of porcelain and as a filler for paper.

Shale [1]

Argillaceous rock consolidated by diagenesis. A slate-like parallel fabric (but not cleavage) results from the deposition of the platy clay minerals with the same orientation. No clear definition of the term.

Sedimentary clay slate [2] Argillaceous rock which has been altered by strong diagenesis or weak metamorphism; should be ascribed to shale as a sedimentary rock. True clay slate (p.314) is more strongly metamorphosed; it is a metamorphic rock.

Oil shale [4] Umbrella term for dark shales containing bitumen. Used to some extent in the production of oil.

Kupferschiefer (Copper slate) Marly shale containing bitumen and with strong enrichment in sulphides, particularly copper minerals and pyrite.

Septaria, a marl concretion with characteristic radial contraction cracks which are partially infilled with new crystal formations.

1 Shale, Siebengebirge/Rhineland/Germany
2 Shale, called clay slate, Harz/Germany
3 Halyseriten schiefer, shale with plant remains, Eifel/Rhineland/Germany
4 Posidonia shale, shale with ammonites, Holzmaden/Württemberg/Germany

1

2

3

4

CHEMICAL-BIOGENIC SEDIMENTARY ROCKS

Sedimentary rocks which owe their formation to some kind of chemical processes or which were formed through the agency of organisms belong to this group.

ORIGIN

All chemical-biogenic sedimentary rocks are neoformations preceded by chemical weathering processes. Hence in this rock group, in contrast to the clastic sedimentary rocks, nothing of the original material can any longer be recognized optically.

Chemical weathering is rock decomposition. Its basis is that minerals and rocks react chemically with water, atmospheric gases or other substances. In this process individual minerals have a different level of resistance. Whilst a part of the chemically produced material is transported away in solution, a further undissolvable remainder is left behind. The waters of land and sea receive the chemically dissolved products and distribute them, mix them up or sort them out. The deposition of the dissolved substances takes place through physico-chemical precipitation and/or the agency of organisms.

CLASSIFICATION

A grouping can be made on the basis of chemico-mineralogical principles (calcareous, siliceous, saline, phosphatic, ferriferous rocks), of manner of deposition (precipitated rocks or precipitates, evaporated rocks or evaporates), of environments of sedimentation or on the organogenic content.
Biogenic rocks (Biolites) Sedimentary rocks which have formed through the life processes or the death assemblages of organisms (calcareous, siliceous, carbonaceous rocks).

CALCAREOUS ROCK FAMILY

Calcareous rocks are those sedimentary rocks which have a predominantly calcareous composition regardless of the way in which they originate. To this group belong the limestones which have formed in the sea and the dolomitic rocks which have developed from them, formations of terrestrial origin such as spring deposits, calc sinter, and those formed in lakes, lacustrine limestones.

Limestone [photos pp.281, 283, 285]
In this section only limestones of marine origin are discussed. Limestone is a monomineralic rock consisting essentially of the single mineral calcite which can make up to 95% of the rock. Medium constituents are dolomite, siderite, quartz, feldspars, mica and clay minerals; colour is caused by accessory constituents. Almost pure limestones are snow white [No. 1, p.281]. Limonite and siderite cause yellow brown shades, hematite reddish, glauconite and chlorite greenish, bitumen grey to black colours.

---

1 Chalk, Champagne/France
2 Crinoidal limestone,
   Crailsheim/Württemberg/Germany

3 Solenhofen platy limestone, Franconian
   Alps/Germany
4 Plattenkalk, Walchensee/Upper
   Bavaria/Germany

1
2
3
4

Limestone mountains with sheer faces and crenellated ridges, Calcareous Alps.

Origin Only in the sea from fragments of the hard parts of animals and plants, from physical precipitation of calcareous mud and from calcareous precipitation by organisms. The main sources of calcareous substances are organisms, including calcareous algae, corals, calcareous sponges, foraminiferids, bryozoa, brachiopods, echinoderms, molluscs, crustacea and pteropods. They build up their support structures from calcium carbonate which has been dissolved in the water and these structures accumulate after death on the sea floor either as complete units, as broken skeletal remains or finely broken up as calcareous mud. In many limestones hard parts of former organisms can be clearly recognised [No. 2, p.281]. In others the shell remains are completely fragmented or even obliterated during the consolidation by diagenesis, as a result of recrystallization or through cementation.

With the exception of reef formations limestones are always stratified. The texture is compact or porous, fine- or coarse-grained. Depending on the admixture of foreign material there are all kinds of transitions to rock types which are genetically or mineralogically related, particularly to dolomite rock and to clastic rocks but also to siliceous rocks.

The essential recognition characteristics of limestone are the low hardness (Mohs' hardness 3, like calcite) and the hydrochloric acid test. If dilute hydrochloric acid is dripped onto limestone it effervesces very strongly as a result of the formation of carbon dioxide.

Topographically, mountains show characteristic weathering structures, steep faces and crenellated ridges. Karst forms develop when the limestone is dissolved.

Nomenclature There is no general classification scheme for the very different types of limestone. Grouping can be on the basis of mineral content, texture or mode of origin. As a consequence no uniform nomenclature exists. The names refer to organisms involved, to distribution, texture, additional constituents, bedding or to geological epochs.

In composite terms the suffix "stone" is usually omitted, e.g. chalk instead of chalkstone.

---

1 Limestone SOLOTHURN, Jura/Switzerland
2 Limestone UNTERSBERG, Salzburg/Austria
3 Limestone VILLON, Jura/France

4 Limestone GERMAN RED, Bavaria/Upper Franconia/Germany
5 Limestone BELGIAN GRANITE, Belgium
6 Limestone VERONA RED, Verona/Italy

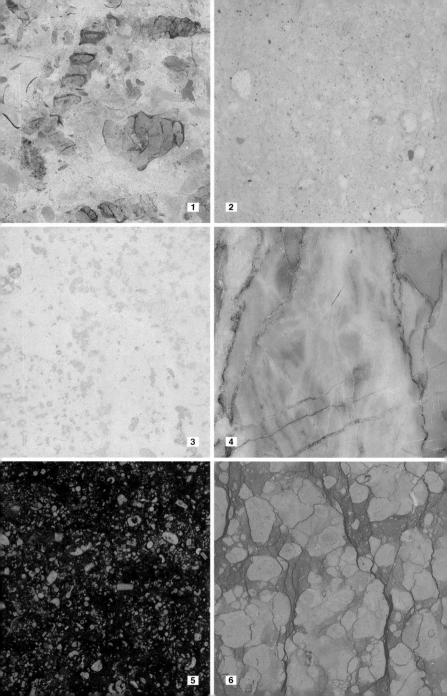

Uses Limestones are widespread. They form whole mountain ranges: N and S Calcareous Alps; Swiss, Swabian and Franconian Jura. Used in the building industry as aggregates and chippings, for cement production and as building stone, in the manufacture of sugar, for the manufacture of glass and paints, as additive in the smelting of iron-ore, as fertilizer.

Compact, indurated kinds of limestone which can be polished are used as decorative stone. In the building trade they are known as MARBLE. This is purely a trade name and must not be confused with genuine metamorphic marble (p.324). Distinction between the two is sometimes difficult, for the transition from limestone to true marble is not well defined.

Limestones are very susceptible to smoke fumes. Rainwater which is saturated with carbonic acid has a rapid solution effect on limestone on the weather side of buildings. On the lee side sulphur compounds effect a transformation to gypsum which causes a volume increase and thus a flaking off of the limestone.

Chalk [No. 1, p.281] (Writing chalk). Light coloured limestone. Usually snow-white, occasionally light grey or yellowish, not very indurated, porous. Forms from the hard parts of micro-organisms especially algae and foraminiferids. Almost pure calcite-aggregate. LOCALITIES: Rügen/Germany, Dover/England, Mon/Denmark. Used to be used as writing chalk but nowadays replaced by gypsum.

Plattenkalk (platy limestone) [Nos 3 & 4, p.281] Thinly bedded limestone which can be split into plate-like slabs. Always very compact and fine grained. Wrongly called slate. Plattenkalk is stratified not cleaved.
Solnhofen Plattenkalk [No. 3, p.281] (Solnhofen slate) Yellowish very compact, fine grained limestone. It became known through Alois Senefelder, who used the platy limestone for stone- printing, developed by him in 1793, and it is hence also called lithographic stone. The Solnhofen stone became even more famous because of its rich fossil content especially through the discovery in it in 1861 of the first primitive bird, Archaeopteryx. The moss-like forms on the bedding and fracture surfaces of the plattenkalk are precipitates of iron and manganese, so called dendrites. They are not plant impressions. LOCALITIES: Mittelfranken/Bavaria/Germany. Used for floor and wall slabs.

Fossiliferous limestone [No. 2, p.281; No. 1, p.283] Limestone in which recognisable fossil remains constitute at least 50% of the mass. The names are derived from the organism e.g. crinoidal limestone.
Bioclastic limestone (Schill limestone) Fossiliferous limestone consisting of broken up fossil fragments.

Oolitic Limestone [4] Limestone composed of small spheres (ooids) built up in shell-like (concentric) layers. If similar to fish-roes, sometimes called roe-stone. It develops where there is supersaturation of lime in shallow water. LOCALITIES: Harz/Germany, Thuringia/Germany, Swiss Jura, Cotswolds/England, Texas/USA.

Reef Limestone [2,3] Limestone which has formed through the continuous deposition of lime by reef-forming organisms (algae, corals, bryozoa, calcareous sponges). Occurs in unstratified, stock-like, rock bodies. LOCALITIES: Franconian Jura/Bavaria/Germany, Harz/Germany, Thüringia/Germany, New Mexico/USA, Yorkshire/England.

Massive Limestone Limestone of massive appearance without recognisable bedding.

1 Muschelkalk, Unterfranken/Bavaria/Germany
2 Reef Limestone, Oahu/Hawaii/USA
3 Coral Limestone, Tegernseer Berge/Upper

Bavaria/Germany
4 Oolitic Limestone (Roe-stone) Harz/Lower
Saxony/Germany

Calcareous sinter

The nomenclature of terrestrial limestone formations has no uniformity whatsoever and is, in part, confusing. In the following section calcareous sinter is taken to be all limy precipitates from springs and the similarly-formed dripstones.

Calcareous tufa [1,2] (Tufa) Highly porous, not very well indurated, calcitic limestone. The cause of the precipitation of the lime is the loss of carbon dioxide which had previously been combined with lime. The warming up of the spring water is the primary reason for the release of the carbon dioxide but plants have also contributed by extracting the carbon dioxide from the water to take it into their system. Stems, small branches and leaves are frequently enclosed in calcareous tufa.

Used as light-weight building stone for arches, for filling-in half-timbered walls and, on account of its purity, for burning for lime. In many areas the deposits, which in general are only small, have been exhausted.

Some authors use calcareous tufa as a synonym for calcareous sinter and travertine.

Calcareous tufa, or tufa for short, must not be confused with volcanic tuff (p.232)

Travertine [3,4] Porous, but overall well-consolidated limy precipitate from springs. In some types a diagenetically altered calcareous tufa seems to be present in which many pores have been filled in by a calcareous cement. Generally banded. Colour whitish, yellow to brown. LOCALITIES: Cannstatt/Württemberg and Ehringsdorf/Thüringia/Germany, Sabine Mts/Central Italy. Used as slabs for floors and cladding. Easy to polish. Some authors use travertine as a synonym for calcareous tufa.
Roman Travertine [3] The best known travertine with its light colours and delicate banding. Named after the Italian city.

Dripstones Columnar or curtain-like formation of calcareous sinter in caves (photo p.288). Inorganically formed by lime being deposited drop by drop because the carbon dioxide present in solution is expelled either as a result of evaporation or through increased temperature. Dripstones usually consist of calcite; only in the Dolomites do they consist of dolomite. Aragonite can very occasionally be interstratified. Lime deposition occurs at projecting corners, along ridges or at other points which are suitable for the development of water droplets. Depending on the direction of growth we distinguish between dripstones which hang down from the ceiling of a cave, stalactites, and those which grow upwards towards them from the floor, stalagmites. All sorts of fantastic dripstone formations develop because of the unequal deposition of the lime as small forms coalesce or because of changes in the supply of water.

Onyx-Marble (Marble-Onyx) Trade term for white, yellow, brown or greenish translucent calcareous sinter. Always banded. Develops as a dripstone formation or as a precipitate from warm springs. Consists of calcite or aragonite. LOCALITIES: Yugoslavia, Turkey, Iran, Argentina, Mexico, USA. Used for *objets d'art* or costume jewellery – not to be confused with chalcedonic onyx (p.180). The term onyx used on its own for this calcareous rock is misleading. Sometimes passed off as alabaster.

---

1 Calcareous tufa with plant remains, California/USA
2 Calcareous tufa with desert varnish, Saudi Arabia
3 Polished travertine, Sabine Mts/Central Italy
4 Polished travertine, Slovakia/Czechoslovakia

1

2

3

4

Sprudelstein [1] A carbonate calcareous sinter deposited at hot springs and containing the mineral aragonite. Usually has a wavy banding and is coloured yellowish, brown or reddish because of the presence of iron. LOCALITIES: Carlsbad/Czechoslovakia, Argentina, Mexico. Used for *objets d'art*.

Pisolite [2] (Peastone) Accumulation of little calcareous spheres (ooids) made of the mineral aragonite. Develops at hot springs as the result of shell-like deposition around floating foreign bodies. As a result of the gradual increase in weight the ooids finally sink to the bottom and form small sedimentary aggregates. LOCALITIES: Carlsbad/Czechoslovakia, Lower Austria, Switzerland, France.

Lacustrine limestone

Limnic limestone. Precipitated as a result of oversaturation because of water inflow or with the help of plants which extract carbon dioxide from the water for absorption into their system.

Lake Chalk [3] Fine grained lacustrine limestone of whitish grey colour. Pure forms used in the manufacture of glass and in the chemical industry.

Alm (Lake Marl) Highly porous lacustrine limestone deposited from bog water. Some authors would prefer to restrict the term alm to inorganic precipitates.

Freshwater limestone [4] Fine-grained lacustrine limestone full of rather large fossil remains. The term freshwater limestone is also used as a synonym for lacustrine limestone and even for all terrestrial limestone formations in wet climates.

Dripstone Caves, Carlsbad Caverns/New Mexico/USA

1 Sprudelstein, Carlsbad/Czechoslovakia	Germany
2 Pisolite, Carlsbad/Czechoslovakia	4 Freshwater limestone, Steinheim/Württemburg/
3 Lacustrine limestone, Roseheim/Bavaria/	Germany

Dolomite Rock [1-3] Dolomite

Dolomite rock (usually abbreviated to dolomite, like the mineral) is a monomineralic rock. It consists of at least 50% of the mineral dolomite. Where there are also lime or clay constituents there is every transition to limestone or marl.

The texture is saccharoidal because the individual minerals have a well developed shape. Dolomite feels rough; all shades of colour are found.

Occurs almost exclusively as a marine sedimentary rock associated with limestone. Where it is deposited in alternation with limestone, dolomite stands out in rib-like forms because it is less susceptible to weathering. LOCALITIES: Swabian and Franconian Jura, Rheinisches Schiefergebirge/Germany, Dachstein/Austria, Dolomites/ Italy, Central England, Arkansas, Iowa/USA. Much less used than limestone in the building trade. Used as hard core for roads, occasionally as ornamental stone. Of importance in the production of blast-furnace linings, as a flux in the smelting of iron, as a magnesium-lime fertilizer, and, more recently, for the extraction of the light metal magnesium. Widespread as a reservoir rock for oil because of its high porosity.

Dolomitization To this day there is no absolutely clear explanation of how dolomite is formed; it probably develops mainly from limestone or lime bearing rocks. This diagenetic process is called dolomitization. There is a distinction between so-called early and late diagenesis. In early diagenesis the transformation of calcite to magnesium-bearing dolomite is brought about by the action of seawater on the yet unconsolidated calcareous sediment. The characteristic features of limestones, such as stratification and fossils, are to a large extent preserved. The dolomite crystals scarcely reach a diameter of 0.02mm. Diagenetic alteration takes place as a result of magnesium concentration which is obviously enhanced by evaporation of saline solutions. Dolomites frequently occur as alternations with saline rocks.

Late diagenesis takes place in consolidated limestone away from the marine environment because of magnesium-bearing waters which flow through the pores of the rock. In this subsequent effect on the limestone the calcite crystals are metasomatically replaced by dolomite and by this process the original textural characteristics of the limestone are obscured or completely obliterated. As a consequence fine stratification and fossils are absent from such dolomites. Massive and coarse grained texture is characteristic. Size of the dolomite crystals usually greater than 0.02mm. High porosity. The more intensive the dolomitization the greater the volume of the pores.

Distinction from limestone Dolomite and limestone are very similar and often cannot be distinguished optically. Dilute hydrochloric acid is an essential aid to determination. If dilute hydrochloric acid is dripped onto limestone it effervesces violently but dolomite effervesces only when it is first powdered. The hydrochloric acid test is not totally reliable with impure carbonate rocks or where limestone and dolomite occur in alternate layers. In such cases the expert uses staining methods. Mohs' hardness and specific gravity ($3\frac{1}{2}$-4 and 2.85-2.95) for dolomite are noticeably higher than for calcite (3 and 2.6-2.8).

Rauhwacke [4] Crystallized dolomite. Cavernous to cellular dolomite. The cavities have developed because embedded pieces or gypsum or calcite breccia have been dissolved away.

1 Calcitic dolomite, S Tyrol/Italy
2 Marly dolomite, California/USA
3 Cut dolomite, Franconian Jura/Germany
4 Rauhwacke, Oahu/Hawaii/USA

FAMILY OF SILICEOUS ROCKS

All non-clastic sedimentary rocks with a silica content of at least 50% belong to the siliceous rocks. Their formation, although open to question in certain details, takes place as the result of the accumulation of siliceous organic remains, as siliceous precipitation from springs or as inorganic siliceous precipitation. Nomenclature according to the organism involved, origin or external appearance.

Diatomite

Collective term for diatomaceous rocks: diatomaceous ooze in the sea, kieselguhr, tripolite. Diatoms are unicellular, free-floating algae with siliceous shells: fractions of a millimetre in size, they live in the sea and in freshwater lakes.

Kieselguhr [1] (Diatomaceous earth) Siliceous rock composed of diatom skeletons mainly of an opaline substance. High porosity. Density less than $1 g/cm^3$, kieselguhr floats on water. Pure forms are white. Because of secondary constituents usually yellowish and brown, greenish grey to almost black. Occurs only as a freshwater sediment. LOCALITIES: Lüneburger Heide/Lower Saxony/Germany, Halle/Germany, Central Italy, California/USA. Because of its high absorption capacity, its resistance to chemicals and its high porosity it is used for insulation, as a filler for paper and explosives (dynamite), as filter material and as a polishing medium.

Tripolite [2] (Polishing earth, Klebschiefer) More strongly consolidated variety of diatomite. Sticks to the tongue because of its high porosity. Used as a polishing medium and as filler material. Named after Tripoli in Libya.

Radiolarite [3]

Siliceous rock made up of radiolarian skeletons. Radiolaria are free floating, unicellular animals which live exclusively in the sea. Usually fractions of a millimetre in size, very occasionally up to 3mm diameter. Radiolarites have a dense texture and break with a sharp edge and a conchoidal fracture. Grey, brownish, also green and reddish in colour. LOCALITIES: Bohemia/Czechoslovakia, Hohe Tauern/Austria, Corsica/France, E Australia, Rocky Mountains/USA.

Chert [4]

Layered (not schistose) siliceous rock with no essential fossil content. Opinions differ as regards mode of origin; flocculation of silica in the sea, precipitation from submarine hot springs or diagenetically altered radiolarian deposits. Texture very compact, hard and brittle, often strongly jointed. Colour reddish brown or greenish. LOCALITIES: Frankenwald/Bavaria, Harz, Rheinisches Schiefergebirge/Germany, Bohemia/Czechoslovakia, Thüringia/Germany, Scotland, Northern England, Illinois, California, Minnesota/USA. Occasionally the term chert is used with reference only to Palaeozoic siliceous rocks.

Lydite [5] Siliceous rock variety coloured black by carbonaceous substance. Some authors use lydite as a synonym for chert, others use it as a synonym for radiolarian rock which has been strongly altered diagenetically and, moreover, one which is usually Palaeozoic.

1 Kieselguhr, Luneburger Heide/Germany
2 Tripolite, Massif Central/France
3 Radiolarite, river pebble, Isar/Bavaria/Germany

4 Chert, Mittelharz/Germany
5 Lydite, chert variety, Frankenwald/Bavaria/Germany

Siliceous sinter

Siliceous rock which develops by precipitation at or near hot springs, sometimes through the activity of algae. Deposited either in porous form or as a solid crust, microcrystalline or as opal. White in colour, also various tints because of impurities. LOCALITIES: Iceland, New Zealand, Wyoming/USA.

Geyserite Variety of siliceous sinter deposited by geysers.

Chert [1]

In the more general sense of the term, chert embraces all dense, siliceous rocks of a horn-like appearance; in a more restricted sense only the nodular, irregularly shaped siliceous forms. Rounded, nodular aggregates are called flints. The origin of chert nodules has not been completely explained. What probably happens is that circulating, silica-bearing solutions bring about replacement of carbonates in concretion like accumulations. The nodules can be several decimetres across. The colour is grey, yellow, brown to reddish. Accumulates in individual limestone beds. LOCALITIES: Calcareous Alps/Switzerland, Franconian Jura, Bavaria/ Germany, Mendips and Yorkshire/England, British Columbia/ Canada, Illinois/USA.

Flint [2]

Roundish, chalcedonic form of silica, rarely more than 10cm in diameter. Light grey to almost black, very occasionally also brownish or greenish. Dark colour tones result from organic impurities. As a result of water loss a white patina or skin forms. Texture very dense, conchoidal fracture. Frequently remains of siliceous sponges are embedded inside. For origin see chert.

Occurs in some quantity in horizons in the Chalk, in particular in the Upper Chalk. LOCALITIES: Rugen/Germany, Mon/Denmark, Dover/England. In the Stone Age used as raw material for weapons, tools and implements. Used in the 17th Century for the firing spark in flint-lock weapons (flints).

PHOSPHATE ROCK FAMILY

Phosphate rocks are bearers of phosphoric acid. Main representatives; bird-lime guano, bone accumulations in bone-beds and the grey, brownish, earthy or dense phosphorite [3]. Important raw material for fertilizer and the chemical industry. Deposits in Morocco, Algeria, Tunisia.

FAMILY OF IRON-BEARING ROCKS

By the term ferriferous rock is meant sedimentary iron ores which have an iron content of at least 15%.

Minette [4] Finely-oolitic iron-ore. Siliceous or carbonate ground mass. The more ooids, the richer in iron is the rock.

For origin see p.98.

Banded ores (taconite, itabirite) Iron-rich layers alternating with siliceous layers. Massive iron ore deposits, formed in the Precambrian.

Residual ore Iron rich pebble-ore with calcareous cement and approximately 30% iron content. Localities: Salzgitter and Peine-Revier/Lower Saxony/Germany.

---

1 Chert, Abenrade/Denmark	3 Phosphorite, Upper Austria
2 Flint, Rugen/Germany	4 Minette (iron oolite), Luxembourg

SALINE ROCK FAMILY

Saline rocks (also known as evaporates or evaporites) are formed by precipitation from water when evaporation exceeds inflow, thus in warm-arid climatic regions. Most salt beds, and the most important economically, have been formed under marine conditions. Of the continental deposits only the saltpetre beds in Chile are of regional significance.

Sedimentation takes place in lagoons or in other parts which are only partly cut-off from the sea. Thick saline deposits are found when oceanic water flows into these partly cut-off bays and if the saline solutions, which become ever more strongly enriched in salts as a result of high evaporation in the dry climate, are not able to flow back into the ocean.

The precipitation of the salts from the enriched sea-water takes place in order of increasing solubility. First of all limestone and dolomite are deposited followed by gypsum and anhydrite then rock salt (halite) and finally potassium and magnesium salts. Since the last two mentioned are very quickly dissolved they are missing in most salt deposits. Dilution by freshwater or by the flow of the saline solutions back into the sea often prevents the full development of the complete salt series.

Nomenclature Saline rocks are sometimes named by adding the suffix -ite to the name of the dominant mineral e.g. sylvite and sylvitite. The exceptions to this are the old terms anhydrite and gypsum which as consolidated rocks should always be identified by adding the suffix rock, thus anhydrite rock and gypsum rock.

Rocksalt [1]

Rocksalt (more correct to say salt stone) is a monomineralic sedimentary rock with halite as the major constituent. Medium constituents are anhydrite, carnallite, kieserite, polyhalite with frequent clay impurities.

The original colourless or white rock salt can be bluish, brown or red as a result of contamination by iron, bitumen and clays. A characteristic banding results from the rhythmic alternation of rock salt layer with clay and sulphate layers.

Rock salt has been worked by miners for 3000 years. Nowadays it is only mined from very pure salt beds. Salts which have many impurities are dissolved below ground in water which is then evaporated or boiled off at the surface.

In dry areas or regions which have a very hot summer rock salt is also extracted by the natural evaporation of sea water in so called salt farms. For uses and localities see p.64 under halite.

Haselgebirge (Austrian miner's term) Breccia-like mixture of rock salt, gypsum and anhydrite as well as clayey substances.

Gypsum [3,4] Gypsum rock

Gypsum rock is a monomineralic sedimentary rock with the mineral gypsum as the main constituent. Frequently mixed with anhydrite, rock salt, limestone and dolomite. Originates by precipitation as sea water is evaporated or by the hydration of anhydrite.

Texture saccharoidal to compact, finely layered or banded in alternation with impurities. Colour white but often grey, yellowish, reddish or even black because of impurities. Occurs with other saline rocks.

1 Rocksalt, Grasleben/Lower Saxony/Germany
2 Alabaster, Tuscany/Italy
3 Gypsum, Osterode/Harz/Germany
4 Fibrous gypsum (satin spar) Perm/Russia

Harz, Thüringia, Bavaria/Germany, Salzburg, Kärnten/Austria, Nottinghamshire, Durham/England, Utah, New Mexico, Texas, Florida/USA. Used as a binding and setting material, for stucco and plaster. If used for these purposes some of the crystalline water is driven off from the gypsum by heating; a volume increase results when water is added again later. Also used as a cement additive and for lightweight building materials in the interior of houses.

Tripestone (Snake gypsum) Strongly folded gypsum rock. Originates by the hydration of anhydrite (and the consequent volume increase).

Fibrous gypsum (Satin spar) [No. 4, p.297] Fibrous gypsum. Develops as the infilling of small veins. The length of the fibres is limited since they are at right angles to the vein walls.

Gypsum cap Gypsum rock on saline intrusions. Develops as residual rock when the uppermost salt series are dissolved away by the groundwaters.

Alabaster [No. 2, p.297] Collective term for compact and fine grained, white or pretty coloured, rocks especially gypsum or calcareous sinter (so called onyx marble p.286), sometimes also fine grained marble.

Anhydrite [2]

Anhydrite rock (Greek "without water") is a monomineralic rock made of anhydrite. Medium constituents are gypsum, calcite, dolomite, clay minerals and bitumen. Originates by precipitation from seawater or diagenetically from gypsum as a result of high temperature and thick overburden in mountain ranges. Texture finely layered or homogeneous; compact or granular. Colour whitish, grey, bluish, red. Occurs with other saline rocks. LOCALITIES: Lower Saxony, Upper Bavaria/ Germany, Wallis/Switzerland, Kärnten/Austria, Yorkshire, Cumbria/England, Great Lakes, Utah, New Mexico, Florida/USA. Raw material for fertilizer and the production of sulphuric acid; materials for the building industry.

Bittern salts Abraum or "rubbish" salts.

Collective term for the potassium and magnesium salts which are the final precipitates when seawater is evaporated: sylvite, carnallite, kainite rocks. Formerly skimmed off as worthless (rubbish salts) but today valuable as raw material for fertilizers (Edelsalze – precious or rare salts). Since they dissolve very easily they are present in very few salt deposits. Localities: Stassfurt/Germany, Canada, New Mexico/USA, Yorkshire/England.

Sylvite rock [1] Saline rock with sylvite and halite the major constituents; anhydrite, kieserite and clays are present in addition. Usually well layered because of alternations in deposition. Usually red. Most important of the bitterns (precious salts).

Carnallite rock [3] Saline rock with carnallite and halite as the major constituents; anhydrite, kieserite, sylvite and clay substances also present. Minerals deposited in alternate layers. Colour predominantly reddish, more rarely white or green.

Kainite rock [4] Saline rock with kainite and halite. Texture phacoidal (like muscle fibres) thickly bedded or massive. Colour usually orange to reddish, yellow, rarely white, not lustrous.

Hartsalz (hard salt) Saline rock with sylvite and halite as the major constituents, together with anhydrite, kieserite, polyhalite and clays. Phacoidal texture, rarely well layered. Colour usually red. Name is an old miners' term; this saline rock was considered to be particularly hard.

---

1 Sylvite rock, Philippstal/Hessen/Germany   3 Carnallite rock, Philippstal/Hessen/Germany
2 Anhydrite rock, Tettenborn/S Harz/Germany   4 Kainite rock, Philippstal/Hessen/Germany

FAMILY OF RESIDUAL ROCKS

Residual rocks are classified as sedimentary rocks even though no material transport has taken place in their formation. They develop from the residues of rocks which have been chemically weathered at the place where the original rock is broken down. This rock group is quantitively unimportant but has an important role economically. The essential facts about the individual rock types have been presented elsewhere: kaolin p.278, bauxite p.148, bentonite p.276.

CARBONACEOUS ROCK FAMILY

Carbonaceous rocks (also caustobioliths) are residual rocks but they are regarded as a separate group because of their organic origin.

Coalification

Carbonaceous rocks develop from an accumulation of plant material which cannot decompose because it is cut-off from oxygen by water and is coalified instead. Coalification means a relative increase of carbon as a result of oxygen impoverishment. Mountain building and volcanic processes bring about diagenesis and metamorphism, in part through pressure and high temperature. Older carbonaceous rocks are normally more strongly coalified than younger formations.

Coalification series	%C	%H	%O	%N
Wood (dry)	50	6	43	1
Peat	60	6	33	1
Brown coal (lignite)	73	6	19	1
Bituminous coal	83	5	10	1
Anthracite	94	3	2	1
Graphite	100	–	–	–

Peat [1] Plant remains can clearly be recognized. Colour brown, dull; specific gravity 1.0.
Brown coal (lignite) [2] Plant remains can now only be recognized in part. Colour brown, black, dull lustre; specific gravity 1.2, streak brown. Easily distintegrates.
Xylite [3] Little altered wood remains embedded in brown coal.
Glance coal Young formation which is none the less strongly coalified by tectonic processes; almost like bituminous coal. Pitch-like lustre. Also called pitch coal.
Bituminous coal [4] Plant remains only very occasionally recognized. Colour black, greasy lustre; specific gravity 1.3. Streak black, often striped.
Cannel coal [5] Type of bituminous coal consisting predominantly of plant spores and pollen. Mostly dull, high lustre when polished. Occasionally used for small decorative pieces. Similar to jet, a bituminous type of coal.
Anthracite Plant remains cannot be recognized, similar to bituminous coal. High metallic lustre; specific gravity 1.5, conchoidal fracture. Difficult to ignite.
Graphite Formed by high grade metamorphism, crystalline, not combustible (see p.88).

1 Small leaved sphagnum peat, Upland peat, Stiftsmoor/L Saxony/Germany
2 Brown coal, Ville/Rhineland/Germany
3 Xylite, Ville/Rhineland/Germany
4 Bituminous coal, Essen/Ruhr area/Germany
5 Cannel coal, Duisburg/Ruhr area/Germany

Technical properties of sedimentary rocks

	Bulk density Density	Grain density Specific gravity	True porosity Total porosity	Water absorption	Apparent porosity
	g/cm³	g/cm3	Volume %	Weight %	Volume %
Quartzite, greywacke	2.60–2.65	2.64–2.68	0.4 – 2.0	0.2 –0.5	0.4– 1.3
Quartzitic sandstone	2.60–2.65	2.64–2.68	0.04– 2.0	0.2 –0.5	0.4– 1.3
Quartz sandstone	2.00–2.65	2.64–2.72	0.5 –25.0	0.2 –9.0	0.5–24.0
Limestone dolomite (dense, consolidated)	2.65–2.85	2.70–2.90	0.5 – 2.0	0.02–0.6	0.4– 1.8
Limestone (not very consolidated)	1.70–2.60	2.70–2.74	0.2–10.0	0.5–25.0	
Travertine	2.40–2.50	2.69–2.72	5 –12	2.0–5.0	4 –10
Sandstone	1.95–2.70	2.60–2.72	0.5–35.0	0.2–13.0	
Greywacke, arkose	2.58–2.73	2.62–2.77	0.4– 6.6	0.1–2.3	
Dolomite	2.05–2.84	2.62–2.77	0.4–27.5	0.1–10.0	
Limestone	1.75–2.75	2.64–2.80	0.6–31.0	0.2–12.0	
Travertine, calcareous, tufa	2.18–2.56	2.69–2.73	5.0–19.0	2.0–5.0	
Gypsum	2.05–2.28	2.28–2.32	1.0– 8.0	0.4–3.6	

	Dry compressive strength kg/cm^2	Tensile strength in bending kg/cm2	Impact strength – number of blows to destruction	Abrasion resistance – loss in cm^3 from 50cm^2
Quartzite, greywacke	1500–3000	130–250	10–15	7– 8
Quartzitic sandstone	1200–2000	120–200	8–10	7– 8
Quartz sandstone	300–1800	30–150	5–10	10–14
Limestone, dolomite (dense, consolidated)	800–1800	60–150	8–10	15–40
Limestone (not very consolidated)	200– 900	50– 80		
Travertine	200– 600	40–100		

METAMORPHIC ROCKS

ORIGIN

Metamorphic rocks develop by the transformation (metamorphism) of all sorts of rocks – igneous, sedimentary and older metamorphic rocks. This transformation takes place under the influence of high pressure and high temperature, and thus goes beyond the point at which diagenesis is effective. The boundary between diagenesis and metamorphism lies at about 200-300˚C.

In all metamorphic transformations the rock mass remains, to all intents and purposes, in the solid state. Only in high grade metamorphic reactions when the temperature reaches 650-700˚C plus is the point of partial melting (called anatexis) reached. Complete melting (palingenesis) takes place above 800˚C. The distinction between contact and regional metamorphism is made on the areal extent of the metamorphism.

Contact metamorphism When magmatic material (either plutonic or as lava) forces its way into parts of the Earth's crust the adjacent rocks are altered by the high temperatures, very occasionally also by gases but less so by pressure. The alteration of the rocks is most intense in the immediate contact zone. The contact aureole, that is the area of metamorphic transformation, only extends for 2-3km. Fruchtschiefer, garnet rock, hornfels and marble are rocks typical of contact metamorphism.

Regional metamorphism If, as a result of the thickness of the geological succession or of tectonic down-sinking, parts of the Earth's crust are taken down into areas of great pressure and high temperature, a metamorphic transformation takes place across wide rock complexes; under some circumstances across hundreds of square kilometres.   The extent of the metamorphism depends on the level of the temperature and the magnitude of the pressure, both of which increase with depth into the Earth's interior. As a result of this discovery it was believed that it was possible to relate the intensity of the regional metamorphism to the depth to which the rock complexes had sunk. The result was a subdivision into epi- , meso- and kata- zone.

Outdated concept of depth categories of regional metamorphism

Depth stage	Depth in km	Temperature in ˚C	Pressure in kbar
Epizone	8-10	300-400	3
Mesozone	18-20	500-600	5
Katazone	30-35	700-800	9

This division of intensity according to depth stages, as shown in the table above, has now been superseded in petrology; however, it does indicate to the non-specialist, in very simplified form, how the processes of regional metamorphism can be envisaged.

The actual processes in rock transformations are much more complex. Metamorphism is, of course, not only dependent on high temperature and pressure but also on the relation of both factors to one another as well as to the rate at which the rock complexes sink. This is illustrated in simplified form on the diagram on p.306.

Metamorphic process The means by which metamorphism is effected is revealed by changes in texture, recrystallization and by the introduction and removal of mineral substances. Fossils are generally destroyed during the process. When there is unilateral pressure (stress) a parallel texture, the so called schistosity (or foliation) is formed by the preferred orientation of minerals (such as mica and chlorite) with a platy or columnar habit. This is a characteristic feature of most metamorphic rocks (see also photos on pp.308 and 314). There is no schistosity in contact metamorphism. Another kind of textural change takes place by recrystallization forming larger minerals. This is especially so in monomineralic rocks (such as quartzite and marble) in which the smaller constituents are absorbed in the process and the rock acquires a coarse-grained appearance while the mineral types remain the same. Often in metamorphism new minerals appear either by transformation of pre-existing crystals or by the introduction of substances from outside the rock.

Characteristic foliation in crystalline clay-slate, Wallis\Switzerland

SYNONYMS

The following terms are used as synonyms for metamorphic rocks: metamorphite, transformed or changed rock, crystalline schist. This latter term should be avoided since it is not unambiguous because not all metamorphic rocks are schistose; furthermore, the term is occasionally used only for metamorphic rocks which are indeed schistose.

CLASSIFICATION AND NOMENCLATURE

In no rock group is it so difficult to gain an overview as it is with metamorphic rocks. There is no generally valid classification and in consequence a unified terminology is lacking.

The number of metamorphic rocks is considerable since for every igneous rock and every sedimentary rock there is one or more metamorphic rocks. It is possible to group metamorphic rocks according to appearance (texture, mineral content) or according to origin (parent rock, kind and intensity ofmetamorphism). Metamorphic rocks are named according to texture, significant minerals or parent rock. Occasionally "meta-" is used as a prefix to the parent rock.

Ortho- and para-rock The term "ortho-" is used to designate metamorphic rocks of igneous parentage; para-rocks have been derived from sedimentary parents. It is often not possible to distinguish these in hand specimens since the same end-products can develop through different kinds of metamorphism.

New scientific classification. Attempts to classify metamorphic rocks are tending more and more in the direction of a genetic scheme. It has been shown that certain mineral assemblages (known as parageneses) can be used as an indicator of all the factors which lead to metamorphism. Depending on the parent material metamorphic rocks develop from these parageneses which may be completely different but which are nonetheless genetically related to one another.

Such a group of metamorphic rocks which is characterized by a mineral assemblage as a result of pressure/temperature conditions is called a metamorphic facies. In modern petrology metamorphic rocks are subdivided according to these facies.

Simple classification for practical use The scientific grouping of metamorphic rocks is not acceptable for anyone doing field work or working practically with rocks or for the broad field of the sciences allied to geology since it presupposes a great deal of expert knowledge which is not in fact available.

For this reason the classification in this book uses a division of metamorphic rocks according to external, clearly discernible, textural characteristics: into gneisses, schists and felses.

Classification of metamorphic rocks according to external characters

	Gneiss family	Schist family	Fels family
Mineral form	medium to coarse grained	platy	fine to coarse grained
Schistosity	weak to evident	very evident	none
Cleavage plates	medium to thick	thin	none
Type minerals	feldspars, quartz	mica, clay minerals	numerous

Schematic pressure/temperature diagram of metamorphic types (after several authors)

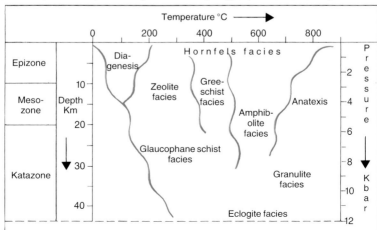

Well known metamorphic rocks (selection, C = contact metamorphic)

Metamorphic facies	Parent rock		Metamorphic rock
	Igneous	Sedimentary	
Hornfels		Claystone	Knotenschiefer C
		Claystone	Hornfels C
		Limestone, Dolomite rock	Calc silicate hornfels C
		Limestone	Marble C
		Sandstone	Quartzite C
Zeolite		Greywacke	Meta greywacke
	Pyroclastite		Meta-pyroclastite
	Peridotite, Picrite	Dolomite rock	Serpentinite
		Limestone	Marble
Greenschist	Basic rock	Marl	Green schist
		Shale	Clay slate
	Rhyolite tuff	Pelite	Phyllite
	Pyroclastite	Shale	Mica schist
	Peridotite, Pyroxenite	Marl	Talc schist
	Pyroclastite		Chlorite schist
		Siliceous limestone	Calc silicate schist
	Peridotite, Pyroxenite	Dolomite rock	Serpentinite
		Limestone	Marble
		Sandstone, Radiolarite	Quartzite
Amphibolite		Pelite	Mica schist
		Siliceous limestone	Calc silicate rock
	Basic rock	Marl	Amphibolite
		Limestone	Marble
	Granite		Orthogneiss
		Sandstone, Radiolarite	Quartzite
Granulite		Sandstone, Radiolarite	Quartzite
	Granite		Orthogneiss
	Basic rock		Granulite
		Limestone	Marble
Glaucophane schist	Pyroclastite		Chlorite schist
	Diabase		Glaucophance schist
	Peridotite, Picrite		Serpentinite
Eclogite	Basic rock	Marl	Eclogite

Diagnostic features of metamorphic rocks

1 Completely crystalline, the whole mass crystallized
2 Mostly large crystals, recognizable with the naked eye
3 Frequently with a silky lustre
4 Parallel texture, schistose
5 Very compact, no cavities
6 Generally unfossiliferous
7 No smooth cleavage surfaces
8 Topography smooth and rolling

GNEISS FAMILY

The common characteristics of gneisses are a coarse grained texture, weak to distinct foliation and a feldspar content of more than 20%.
The name gneiss is from the language of German miners in the Erzgebirge.

Texture The foliation is caused by the biotite which, as a result of unilateral pressure (stress) is oriented with its basal plane perpendicular to the stress. The gneiss can be split into thick plates (of centimetre to decimetre thickness) parallel to the foliation surfaces. Thinner plates are very occasionally possible when there is a high proportion of mica. Granular minerals predominate.

Mineral content Mineral components have a wide variation. Major constituents are feldspars and quartz with feldspars clearly predominant. Medium constituents are biotite, muscovite, hornblende, cordierite, garnet, sillimanite. High silica content. Light colours, grey, greenish, brownish, reddish.

Occurrence Parent rocks, both igneous and sedimentary, such as granite, acid volcanic rocks, greywacke, arkose, sandstone and also pure mudrocks. The gneisses derived from igneous rocks are called orthogneiss, those from sedimentary rocks are paragneiss. It is scarcely possible to distinguish between ortho- and paragneiss in hand specimens but it is possible to do so in the field if transitions to the parent rock or to typical sedimentary formations can still be discerned over a wider area. The mineral content of orthogneiss is only very little different from the parent rock. LOCALITIES: Central Alps, Bayerischer Wald, Erzgebirge/Germany, Vosges, Massif Central and Brittany/France, Scandinavia, NW Scotland, Appalachians/USA, Canadian Shield.

Uses Used as building stone, aggregates, chippings, thin splitting types for cladding, earlier used as roofing tiles. Gneisses with continuous layers of mica are less easy to work mechanically and are susceptible to frost.

Nomenclature According to parent rock (granite-gneiss, syenite- gneiss, pebble-gneiss), to characteristic constituents (biotite- , muscovite-, augite-, garnet-gneiss), to texture (augen-, flaser-, platy-, banded-gneiss), to type of metamorphism (epigneiss), to colour (grey-, red-gneiss).

Direction of pressure

Foliation: as a result of unilaterally directed pressure lamellar minerals are oriented to form a parallel texture.

1 Granite-gneiss, Ukraine
2 Riebeckite granulite, Lower Austria

3 Augen-gneiss, Graubünden/Sweden
4 Migmatite, Fichtelgebirge/Bavaria/Germany

1

2

3

4

Augen gneiss [No. 3, p.309] Variety of gneiss with phacoidal texture defined by feldspars which have a lens shaped, eyed form.

Foliated gneiss (gneissose micaschist) Variety of gneiss transitional to phyllite. Contains at least 50% of lamellar minerals, particularly mica, which are arranged in continuous layers and hence make it possible to be split into thin plates.

Leptite gneiss (leptite) Fine grained, light coloured variety of gneiss of Precambrian age from Scandinavia and Finland.

Halleflinta Mica-poor, fine grained to dense variety of gneiss from Sweden and Finland. High strength, flinty fracture.

Kinzigite Local term for cordierite-bearing garnet gneiss, Black Forest.

False trade names In the trade the term gneiss is very little used and is usually replaced by GRANITE and QUARTZITE.

Granulite [No. 2, p.309]

In general granulite can be regarded as a mica free gneiss. Major constituents are feldspars and coarsely developed plate-like quartz. Medium constituents are mainly pyroxene, garnet, kyanite and sillimanite. Texture usually thickly schistose to almost massive, frequently banded, fine to medium grained. Colour light, sometimes almost white. LOCALITIES: Black Forest/Germany, Lower Austria, Saxony/Germany, Czechoslovakia, Finland, NW Scotland. Used as aggregate, very resistant to pressure and the weather.

Charnockite Is considered to be a variety of granulite because of its assumed origin but as an igneous rock on account of its texture. Unlike granulite it never contains garnets. The quartz too lacks the platy form typical of granulites. Characteristic constituent is hypersthene. Colour yellow green to dark green. LOCALITIES: Sweden, India, Brazil.

Migmatite [No. 4, p.309]

Migmatite (mixed rock) consists of two different clearly recognizable rock types which are interdigitated with sharp boundaries. The host rock is a gneiss-like metamorphic rock, the "intruder" or injected rock is a granitic igneous rock. The host rock is, by nature, always older; the "intruder" is always lighter than the host. The origin is variously interpreted: either through partial melting (anatexis) and crystallizing out of granite or through a kind of injection of molten material into the metamorphic complex; perhaps also through metasomatic exchange of mineral substances. Occurs in zones of very strong metamorphism. LOCALITIES: Black Forest, Bayerisher Wald/Germany, Central Alps, Auvergne/France, Scandinavia, Sutherland/Scotland, Adirondacks, New Jersey, Washington/USA. Used as aggregates, for decorative slabs and monuments.

Some authors classify migmatites neither as metamorphic rocks nor as igneous rocks but regard them rather as a fourth rock group in their own right and place them alongside igneous, sedimentary and metamorphic rocks.

Anatexite

Term for rocks whose origin is connected in some way or another with high grade melting processes. There is no generally agreed definition.

---

1 Chlorite gneiss VERDE SPRIANA, polished, Italy
2 Paragneiss VERDE VERZASCA, Switzerland
3 Orthogneiss NYSTAD GREY, polished, Finland
4 Orthogneiss VANGA, polished, Sweden

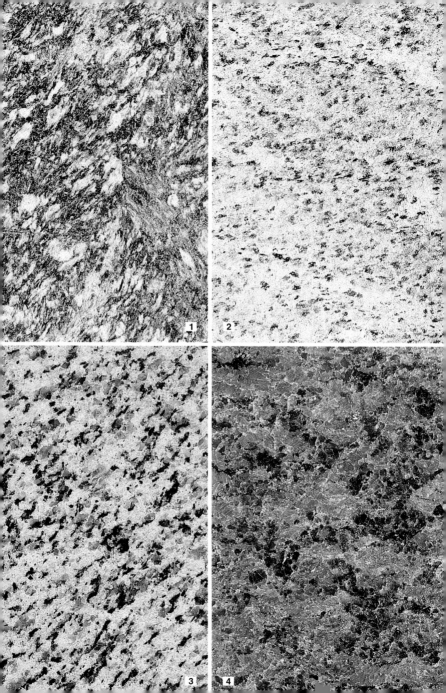

SCHIST FAMILY

The factors common to schists are a fine to medium grained texture, very distinct schistosity and a feldspar content of less than 20%.

Schistosity

The essential characteristic of this rock family is the distinct parallel texture which is reminiscent of sedimentary bedding. However, whereas in bedding continuous layer boundaries can be recognized and the bedding planes are always smooth, in schistose rocks there are never any even cleavage surfaces because the platy "schist minerals" lie not behind one another but in juxtaposition (cf photos pp.314 and 308).

Thinly laminated sedimentary rocks are frequently designated as schistose. The term schist ought to be reserved for metamorphic rocks as it is one of their most characteristic features.

Nomenclature There are a great many types of schist. The rocks are designated according to outstanding properties, notable minerals or colour.

Phyllite [1,2]

Phyllite (Greek "leaf") is a finely laminated schist with a distinct silky lustre on the foliation surfaces. Major constituents are sericite (a variety of muscovite with a maximum diameter of 0.2mm) and quartz. Medium constituents are biotite, feldspars, chlorite, pyrophyllite, graphite, epidote. Can be split into sheets down to 0.1mm thick. Individual crystals (so-called porphyroblasts) are noticeably larger than the minerals in the groundmass. As a result of this the little mica plates are arranged in a bow-shape so that the phyllite shows a wavy texture in cross section. Colour usually silver grey and greenish. LOCALITIES: Bayerischer Wald, Fichtelgebirge, Erzgebirge, Harz/Germany, Central Alps, Vosges/France, Cornwall/England, Scandinavia, Connecticut, New York/USA.
Used locally for roofing tiles, sensitive to frost.
Quartz phyllite Quartz predominates as one of the major constituents compared with micas and other lamellar minerals.
Sericite phyllite (sericite schist) Variety of phyllite consisting predominantly of sericite and quartz with no essential medium constituents. Occasionally also understood as a general synonym for phyllite.

Mica schist [3.4]

Mica schist is the epitome of schistose rocks. It has a coarser texture than phyllite, with the mica flakes being larger than 0.2mm and hence visible to the naked eye. Usually cleaves into millimetre to centimetre thick slabs with almost plane surfaces when there is a high mica content.

Major constituents are quartz and muscovite, medium constituents are biotite, kyanite, chlorite, graphite, garnet, staurolite and sillimanite; frequently porphyroblastic. Colour normally light and slightly greenish.

LOCALITIES: Fichtelgebirge, Schwarzwald, Erzgebirge/Germany, Central Alps, Scandinavia, Scotland, Connemara/Ireland, Appalachians, Dutchess County/New York/New Hampshire/USA, Quebec/Canada. Used as platy building stone. More weather resistant than phyllite. The abbreviated form schist is often used instead of micaschist when varieties are described.

1 Phyllite, Tyrol/Austria
2 Sericite phyllite, Erzgebirge/Germany
3 Garnet mica schist, Ticino/Switzerland
4 Mica schist, E Tyrol/Austria

1

2

3

4

Clayslate [1] Killas

Genetically clayslate is intermediate between shale and phyllite. Some authors consider it to be a sedimentary rock but the true clayslate has undoubtedly been subject to a metamorphic imprint. Clearly recognizable by both foliation and bedding which usually lie at an angle to one another (as is shown in the extreme form by pencil slates). The boundary between pelitic sedimentary and metamorphic rocks is placed where the ability to absorb water ceases. Shales swell but metamorphic clayslates do not. The latter are also harder, have either no fossils or strongly deformed ones, and unlike shales do not give off an earthy smell in damp conditions.

Texture fine grained to dense, excellent foliation with flat planes of splitting. Even-splitting is also possible along the bedding planes.

Major constituents are quartz and micas especially muscovite, newly formed from the pre-existing clay minerals. Grey and black colours are caused by bitumen graphite admixtures, brown by limonite, red by hematite and green by chlorite. There are also multicoloured types, both striped and spotted. LOCALITIES: Fichtelgebirge, Thüringia/Germany, Ardennes/France, Cornwall/England, Wales. Used as roofing and wall tiles, for insulating slabs and switchblocks, very occasionally for school blackboards.

Contact slate [2,3]

Clayslate formed by contact metamorphism. Granular or columnar minerals. Major constituents are mica, quartz, andalusite and cordierite.

Spotted slate   Spots caused by bitumen or carbonaceous material.

Knotenschiefer   (knotted or spotted slate) Knot-like mica patches as a result of increase in grain size.

Fruchtschiefer   ("ears of corn" slate) [3] The new minerals andalusite and cordierite look similar to grains of corn.

Garbenschiefer   (chiastolite slate) [2] The newly formed mineral chiastolite, a variety of andalusite, appears in tufted form in the clay slate.

Hornblende schist [4]

Major constituents are hornblende, quartz and biotite; medium constituents are pyroxene, muscovite, garnet, plagioclase feldspars. LOCALITIES: Tyrol/Austria, S Tyrol/Italy, St Gotthard Massif/Switzerland, Scotland, Connemara/Ireland, Mitchell County/North Carolina/USA, Quebec/Canada.

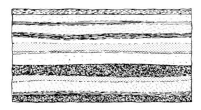

Bedding: continuous layer boundary (bedding plane) with smooth surface when split

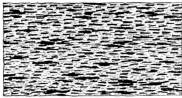

Schistosity (foliation): oriented minerals, split surface not smooth

---

1 Clay slate, Thüringia/Germany
2 Garbenschiefer,
   Fichtelgebirge/Bavaria/Germany

3 Fruchtschiefer, Saxony/Germany
4 Hornblende schist, S Tyrol/Italy

1

2

3

4

Greenschist

Collective term for finegrained schists of a greenish appearance. Major constituents are chlorite, epidote, actinolite, talc, glaucophane and albite feldspar. Muscovite and quartz are lacking or present in only very small quantites. Name derives from the predominantly greenish minerals. The most important representative of the true greenschists are amphibole-, chlorite- and epidote-schists as well as prasinite. Talc- and glaucophane-schists are only included in the wider grouping of the greenschists because of their somewhat different origin.

Actinolite schist [4] Variety of amphibole schist with the major constituent being actinolite. LOCALITIES: Erzgebirge and Bohemia/Czechoslovakia and Saxony, Harz, Fichtelgebirge/Germany, Hohe Tauern/Austria, Western Alps, Vermont, New Hampshire/USA.

Chlorite schist [3] Greenschist with chlorite the major constituent. Nicely coloured varieties used as decorative stone for flooring slabs and cladding. LOCALITIES: L Tauern/Austria, S Tyrol, Lombardy, Piemont/Italy, Argyll/Scotland, Sierra Nevada/California/USA.

Prasinite Fine-grained greenschist. Banded, hardly schistose appearance because of the zone-like enrichment of the different major constituents (chlorite, actinolite, albite and epidote). Used locally as road-building material, nicely coloured types as decorative stone. LOCALITIES: Zillertal/Austria, Ticino/Switzerland, N Italy, Brittany/France. The name prasinite is occasionally also used as a general synonym for greenschist.

Talc schist [1] A soft greenschist with very good cleavage and with talc as its major constituent. Medium constituents are magnesite, magnetite, calcite, dolomite, quartz. Colour white grey, speckled green. Feels greasy. LOCALITIES: Karnten, Zillertal/Austria, Graubunden/Switzerland, Transvaal/South Africa, New York/USA. Pure sorts are used for the industrial extraction of talc. *Steatite* [2] (Potstone, Soapstone) Compact variety of talc schist with few impurities. Light grey and quite soft. Used for centuries for jewellery, carved figures and various kinds of vessels. Since it is also heat and acid resistant it has many uses in technology and industry, in particular for containers for chemicals and for fire-resistant ceramics. Steatite becomes very hard when heated. In technology only heated talc is designated as steatite. LOCALITIES: Fichtelgebirge/Germany, India, Virginia/USA. The names listed as synonyms are occasionally also used with a somewhat different meaning.

Glaucophane schist (blue schist) Greenish schist with bluish or light violet tint, mostly coarsely schistose. The only major constituent is glaucophane, a blue amphibole. Medium constituents are epidote, calcite, quartz, garnet, albite, talc, zoisite, jadeite. Relatively rare. LOCALITIES: Calabria, Tuscany, Val d'Aosta/Italy, Spitzbergen, Channel Islands and Anglesey/Great Britain, Western Alps, California/USA. Significant in prospecting for ores since it may be associated with copper and nickel deposits.

Glaucophanite Either a synonym for glaucophane schist or a term for massive, non-schistose glaucophane rock.

---

1 Talc schist, Upper Franconia/Bavaria/Germany   3 Chlorite schist, Tyrol/Austria
2 Steatite, Fichtelgebirge/Bavaria/Germany   4 Actinolite schist, Ticino/Switzerland

FELS FAMILY

No directional structures are to be seen in rocks of the fels family. The suffix "fels" is often used in their names.

Metaquartzite [1,2] Quartzite

In petrology the term quartzite is used for a sedimentary rock (p.274) as well as for a metamorphic quartzite. The distinction could be indicated in the name if the terms sedimentary quartzite and metaquartzite were used.

Metaquartzite is usually massive, non foliated and often forms thick beds. Where a disproportionately large amount of muscovite is present a slight schistosity results which on cleavage surfaces gives the false impression that there is far too high a proportion of mica; this is because the quartzite breaks along the planes of micas.

The major constituent is quartz which makes up at least 80% of the total. All other rock-forming minerals can occur as medium constituents especially feldspars, mica, chlorite, magnetite, hematite, garnets and graphite.

The quartz grains are usually interlocked with one another because of the way the cement has crystallized out during the metamorphism. On the other hand in sedimentary quartzites the cement has not recrystallized. Colour white, but also grey, brown, reddish if impurities are present. LOCALITIES: Taunus, Harz/ Germany, Steiermark/Austria, Wallis/Switzerland, S Tyrol, Norway, Sweden, Islay and the Highlands/Scotland, Anglesey/Wales, North and South Carolina/USA. Because of its strength and weather-resistance it is used as aggregates; types which can be easily split (especially micaceous quartzite) are used as decorative stone, for floors and cladding. Pure quartzites are used as raw materials for glass and as fire-resistant stones, ore-bearing quartzite for the extraction of ores.

Varieties Varieties are named according to their accessory constituents (eg micaeous quartzite) or to the most important economic mineral (eg magnetite quartzite). Many trade names for decorative stones.

Calcsilicate hornfels [3]

Metamorphic rock made up of calcsilicate minerals, massive structure, compact to coarse grained. Sometimes zoned because of the way the minerals associate together in groups. Colour light green, brownish.

Very varied in composition. Major constituents can be calcite, vesuvianite, wollastonite, diopside, grossular and andradite varieties of garnet. All minerals which otherwise appear in metamorphic rocks are possible as medium constituents. Frequently large individual crystals. LOCALITIES: Fichtelgebirge/ Germany, Ticino/Switzerland, Bohemia/Czechoslovakia, Triente/Italy, Sierra Nevada/California/USA. Quite rare. Nicely coloured types used in the building industry under the name MARBLE as decorative slabs for floors and wall decor.

Skarn [4] A mineralized calcsilcate rock. Name derived from Swedish miners' expression. Used for the extraction of iron and non- ferrous metals. LOCALITIES: Central Sweden, Elba/Italy, Trepca/Yugoslavia, Banat/Rumania, Arkansas, Crestmore/California/USA, Dartmoor/England.

---

1 Quartzite, Morocco
2 Sericite quartzite, Wallis/Switzerland

3 Calcsilicate hornfels, Fichtelgebirge/Bavaria/ Germany
4 Skarn, Gällivara/Sweden

Amphibolite [1,3]

Fine-to-coarse grained metamorphic rock, usually with a massive structure. The rare schistose varieties are transitional to related rocks such as gneiss, granulite, eclogite and greenschist. Major constituents are the amphibole variety hornblende and plagioclase. Medium constituents are biotite, chlorite, garnets, epidote, zoisite and others. Colour grey, greygreen to dark green and greenblack. LOCALITIES: Fichtelgebirge, Spessart, Schwarzwald, Bohemian-Saxonian Erzgebirg, Thüringer Wald/Germany, Hohe Tauern/Austria, St Gothard Massif/Switzerland, Connemara, Donegal/Ireland, Grampian Highlands/Scotland, Adirondacks, Arizona, California/USA, Quebec/Canada. Amphibolites possess great strength and are weather-resistant so they provide high quality aggregates for building. Types which can be split are used for slabs.

There is a large number of varieties because of the high variation in the amounts of major and medium constituents. Named according to the predominant medium constituent (eg epidote- amphibolite, quartz amphibolite).

Eclogite [4]

Eclogite (Greek – "selection") is a metamorphic rock with major constituents garnet (red pyrope and almandine) and pyroxene (usually light green omphacite). Medium constituents are kyanite, rutile, hornblende, zoisite, plagioclase and quartz. The specific gravity of 3.2-3.6 is the highest of all silicate rocks. Massive structure, sometimes thickly foliated. Large roundish red garnets lie in a fine to coarse grained green groundmass. Rare occurrence and only in small masses. Lens shaped masses embedded in migmatitic gneisses or pegmatitic granites. LOCALITIES: Fichtelgebirge, Schwarzwald/Germany, Hohe Tauern/Austria, Norway, Glenelg/Scotland, California/USA. Although very strong and weather-resistant eclogite is rarely used because it is not very widely distributed. Locally used as aggregates and decorative slabs.

Hornfels [2]

Collective name for massive, hard, compact to fine grained metamorphic rock with a typical conchoidal fracture. The term hornfels should only be used for rocks which have been formed by contact metamorphism. Not to be confused with sedimentary hornstone (p.294). Occasionally feebly porphyroblastic. Under the microscope a characteristic mosaic texture can be recognized; at thin edges has a horn-like translucence.

The mineralogy varies considerably depending on the parent rock; common representatives are andalusite, biotite, cordierite, garnets, hypersthene, sillimanite. Although usually composed of light minerals the colour of hornfels, because of impurities, is often dark, grey to black, greenish, only very occasionally tending to white. LOCALITIES: Fichtelgebirge/Harz/Eifel/Germany, Elba/Italy, Vosges/France, South Norway, Skiddaw/Cumbria and Dartmoor/Cornwall/England, Comrie/Scotland, Sierra Nevada/California, Nova Scotia/USA. Very solid and weather-resistant, used only locally as aggregate because not very widespread. Numerous varieties named after the parent rock (eg pelitic hornfels [2] or according to the mineralogy (e.g. andalusite hornfels).

Adinole Hornfels variety in the vicinity of dolerite; rich in albite.

---

1 Garnet amphibolite, Tauern/Austria
2 Pelitic hornfels, England

3 Amphibolite, Kinzigtal/Baden/Germany
4 Eclogite, Fichtelgebirge/Bavaria/Germany

Serpentinite [2-4]

More or less green metamorphic rock consisting predominantly of serpentine minerals. The name (Latin for snake) refers to the flecked appearance or it may be derived from its alleged antidotal effect against snake poison. Major constituents chrysotile or antigorite. Large number of medium constituents possible, among others being olivine, pyroxene, garnets, amphibole, chromite and magnetite. Calcite is almost always present. Texture compact, sometimes fibrous or lamellar, almost always massive, occasionally thickly-bedded. A slight schistosity is evident very occasionally. As a result of the varying proportions and different distribution of the minerals the coloration is usually irregular (flecked, striped, wavy, veined). Colour varies from light grey green through to green black. Bluish, brown and reddish tones also sometimes occur. Originates during regional metamorphism from ultra-basic igneous rocks (peridotite, pyroxenite, picrite) through the alteration (serpentinization) of olivine or more rarely of pyroxenes, amphibole or chlorite. The iron compounds released in this process can give rise to ore deposits. Very occasionally serpentinites can also form from dolomite rocks. LOCALITIES: Fichtelgebirge, Schwarzwald/Germany, Erzgebirge/Germany, Tyrol, Kärnten, Waldviertel/Austria, Graubünden/Switzerland, Pyrenees, Vosges/France, Liguria/ Italy, Lizard/Cornwall/England, Shetland Isles/Scotland, Montana, Oregon, California, Maine/USA, Quebec/Canada. Used since ancient times for jewellery and *objets d'art* because of its low hardness, good polishability and decorative appearance. In the trade and the stone industry serpentinite is usually just called serpentine like the mineral.

Many serpentinites contain ores which are worth mining or are very closely associated with deposits – among others with iron-, chromium-, magnesite- talc- and asbestos-occurrences.

The varieties are designated according to their most significant medium constituent (bronzite- or garnet-serpentinite) or to the rock from which they are derived (harzburgite serpentinite). The green colour of serpentinite is frequently mentioned in the names of the types used in the trade. Often also classified as a MARBLE.

Cipollino [1]

A metamorphic rock which is a transition between serpentinite, marble and ophicalcite. Mica, feldspars, clay minerals, chlorites or serpentine in a groundmass of calcite have a stripy folded pattern like an onion. Frequently a noticeable quartz content. The name meaning onion (Italian "cipolla") is derived from the patterning. Matrix white or yellowish, veins usually greenish. LOCALITIES: Tuscany, Piemont/Italy, Euboea/Greece. A popular decorative stone termed MARBLE in the trade.

Ophiolite

Group name for genetically related, green coloured, basic and ultrabasic rock such as serpentinite, peridotite, gabbro, basalt.

---

1 Cipollino VERSILIA, Tuscany/Italy
2 Serpentinite VERDE VARZEA, Alentejo/Portugal
3 Serpentinite VERDE GIADA, Val d'Aosta/Italy
4 Serpentinite breccia VERDE ANTICO, Larissa/Greece

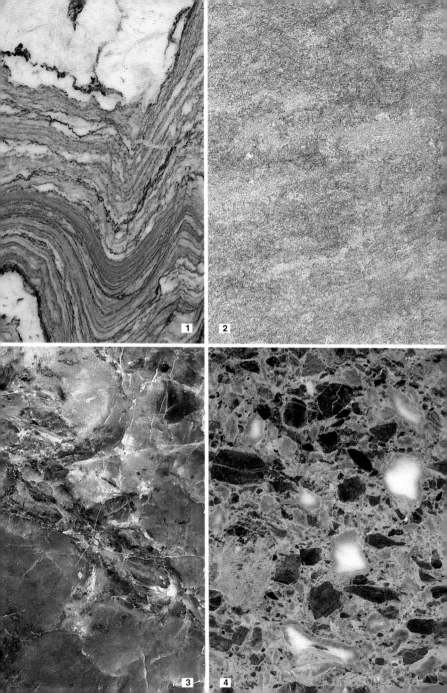

1   2

3   4

Marble [1 and 4, also Nos 1-3, p.327] Calcite marble

The term marble (Greek "shimmering block of stone") is defined in different ways. In scientific petrology it is defined as a calcitic metamorphic rock; this is the true, crystalline marble. Occasionally, however, the term marble is used as an umbrella term for calcite marble and dolomite marble, so marble can be referred to in the wider or the narrower sense of the term.

In the building industry, in the trade and in the vernacular any solid limestone which will take a polish is called marble. To some extent even non-calcareous rocks like serpentinite are also called marble. One feature is common to all the groups: the marbled quality, a particular patterning of the surface.

Texture True marble is developed from limestone by contact or regional metamorphism. It is massive, medium to coarsely crystalline and, like limestone, is monomineralic (with up to 99% calcite). The crystals were made coarser by the metamorphism at the expense of other crystals and so, being equigranular, they are visible to the naked eye.

Many minerals may be present as medium constituents. Among others there are amphibole, chlorite, epidote, mica, garnets, graphite, hematite, limonite, plagioclase, pyrite, pyroxene, quartz, serpentine, vesuvianite, wollastonite. Marble is extremely compact because of its granular texture. The pore volume is below 1%. It is translucent in slabs up to 30cm thick. The deep penetration of light into the marble is rare. Usually because of the parent material or because of foreign constituents which have been incorporated during the metamorphism it has a wavy, flecked, grained, veined or striped appearance. All shades and nuances of colour are possible.

Distinction from limestone The boundary between crystalline marble and marmorized limestone is ill-defined. A few characteristics make it possible to distinguish marble from limestone which frequently appears similar to it.

Crystalline marble	Limestone
Coarse grained. Crystals visible with the naked eye.	Fine grained. Crystals cannot be discerned with the naked eye
Sparry fracture	Fine grained dull fracture
Translucent at edges	Not translucent at edges
No cavities	Occasional cavities
No fossils	Frequent fossils

Localities Marble is found in many places. However most beds are so fractured by tectonism that it is not worth mining or quarrying them. LOCALITIES: Fichtelgebirge/Germany, Tyrol, Kärnten/Austria, Ticino, Wallis/Switzerland, Tuscany, S Tyrol/Italy, France, Spain, Greece, Devon/England, Connemara/Ireland, Talladega County/Alabama and Vermont, Georgia, Harford County/Maryland/USA.

Uses Cladding, interior architecture, table tops, ornaments, control panels. Takes a polish well but very quickly becomes dull in the air.

---

1 Marble, Fichtelgebirge/Bavaria/Germany
2 Dolomite marble, Steiermark/Austria

3 Ophicalcite, Wallis/Switzerland
4 Marble, Alentejo/Portugal

1

2

3

4

Trade types   Whereas in petrology marbles are named according to their characteristic constituents, in the trade nomenclature is determined by colour, patterning, texture or locality. There are also pure "fantasy" terms.

Carrara Marble   [1] Collective term for the marbles which are quarried near the town of Carrara in Tuscany/Italy. The extraction sites lie in the Apuane Apennines in a mountain range 60km long by 20-25km wide. Four main valleys lead from Carrara to the numerous quarries. The snow-white marble is to be found right to the top of the mountain peaks.

In the vicinity of Carrara are the most significant occurrences of white crystalline marble in the whole world, both qualitatively and quantitatively. The deposits were already being exploited in Roman times but later they fell into disuse. In the High Middle Ages and at the time of the Renaissance the quarries were reopened. The beds seem to be inexhaustible.

Besides a number of highly coloured types of marble the common type is that of Bianco chiaro (Blanc clair). The basic colour is milky white to a slightly bluish white. Sculptors prefer the pure white types. Michelangelo found this material for his sculptures on the Monte Altissimo. Such marbles consist of up to 98% pure calcium carbonate.

The Bianco marbles are usually lightly clouded and delicately veined. There are different trade names according to patterning.

Onyx marble   Trade name for calcareous sinter (see p.286).

Dolomite marble [No. 2, p.325]
A marble which has been formed by the metamorphism of dolomite rock. Dolomite is the predominant constituent besides calcite.
Texture generally more fine grained than calcite marble; on fracture surfaces it has a saccharoidal appearance. Otherwise it is scarcely distinguishable optically from calcite marble. However, it is easily identifiable using the hydrochloric acid test (cf p.290). LOCALITIES: Fichtelgebirge/Germany, Steiermark/Austria, S Tyrol/ Italy, Norway, Sweden, Karelia/Russia, Utah/USA, Glen Tilt/Scotland. Dolomite marble is not as common as calcite marble. Used in the same way as the latter.

When the term marble is used on its own then calcite marble is meant; the prefix "dolomite" should always be added if dolomite marble is meant.

Ophicalcite [4 and No. 3, p.325] Silicate marble
A metamorphic rock which contains, as its major constituents, calcite and up to 20% silicate minerals especially forsterite and talc, together with amphibole, mica, feldspars, pyroxene and quartz. The name ophicalcite, which means much the same thing as serpentine calcite, expresses the close relationship with both marble and serpentinite. Structure massive, without orientation, grainy-crystalline Occurrence as for marble. LOCALITIES: Fichtelgebirge/Germany, Wallis/ Switzerland, W Alps/France, Piemont/Italy, Estremadur/Portugal, Spain, Connemara/Ireland, Sutherland/Scotland.

Urkalk (German, "primeval limestone")
Urkalk is an older German term for crystalline marble because it was considered to be the oldest limestone formation. Nowadays we know that marble can develop in any geological epoch. The term urkalk is therefore outdated.

---

1 Marble CARRARA, Tuscany/Italy
2 Marble CALACATTA D'ORO, Tuscany/Italy
326   3 Marble PASCHA, W Turkey

4 Ophicalcite CONNEMARA, County Galway/ Ireland

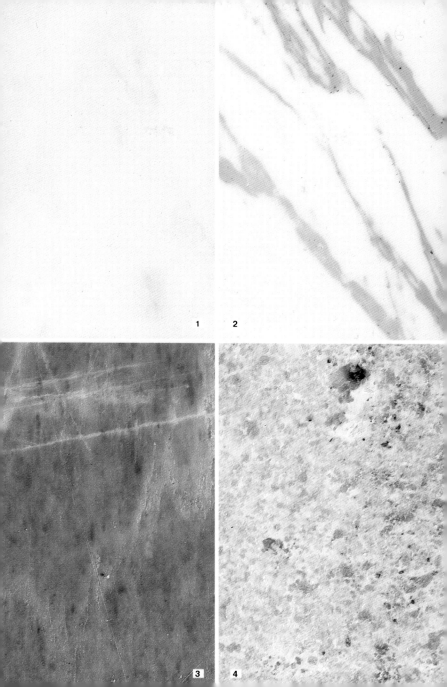

1

2

3

4

Technical properties of metamorphic rocks

	Bulk density Density	Grain density Specific gravity	True porosity Total porosity	Water absorption	Apparent porosity
	g/cm^3	g/cm3	Volume %	Weight %	Volume %
Gneiss, granulite	2.65–3.00	2.67–3.05	0.4– 2.0	0.1–0.6	0.3–1.8
Amphibolite	2.70–3.10	2.75–3.15	0.4– 2.0	0.1–0.4	0.3–1.2
Serpentinite	2.60–2.75	2.62–2.78	0.3– 2.0	0.1–0.7	0.3–1.8
Roofing slate	2.70–2.80	2.82–2.90	1.6– 2.5	0.5–0.6	1.4–1.8
Marble	2.65–2.85	2.70–2.90	0.5– 2.0	0.2–0.6	0.4–1.8
Clay slate	2.60–2.80	2.71–2.86	0.4– 4.5	0.1–1.7	
Gneiss, micaschist	2.60–2.97	2.64–3.05	0.4– 5.5	0.1–1.9	
Granulite	2.64–3.12	2.67–3.20	0.4– 7.8	0.1–1.4	
Quartzite	2.60–2.65	2.64–2.70	0.4– 3.9	0.1–1.4	
Marble, ophicalcite	2.60–2.76	2.70–2.78	0.4– 4.0	0.1–1.5	
Serpentinite	2.41–2.95	2.63–3.00	0.3–10.5	0.1–3.8	

	Dry compressive strength kg/cm^2	Tensile strength in bending kg/cm2	Impact strength – number of blows to destruction	Abrasion resistance – loss in cm^3 from 50cm^2
Gneiss, granulite	1600–2800		6–12	4–10
Amphibolite	1700–2800		10–16	6–12
Serpentinite	1400–2500		6–15	8–18
Roofing slate		500–800		
Marble	800–1800	60–150	8–10	15–40

METEORITES

STONES FROM OUTER SPACE

Meteorites (Greek "heavenly apparition"), also known as meteor stones or aerolites, are solid fragments which have come down to Earth from outer space. They can be defined as extra-terrestrial rocks. Many glow red-hot as they enter the atmosphere, producing the well known phenomenon of the shooting star. Most meteorites are small black spheres, fractions of a millimetre in size, which are constantly falling to Earth. The annual accretion of such cosmic dust amounts to thousands of tonnes.

Large meteorites are rare. The largest meteorite found to date fell in prehistoric times close tothe Hoba Farm near Grootfontein in Namibia. It has a volume of $9m^3$ and weighs over 50 tonnes (photo p.334).

Very heavy meteorites cannot make a soft landing on Earth. The atmosphere exerts scarcely any braking effect on them, so they hit the Earth at a cosmic velocity of 20-70km per second, disintegrate, and vaporize completely. This results in melting within the crater rocks and the formation of the high-pressure minerals coesite and stishovite.

Classification of meteorites

Iron meteorites	Hexahedrites Octahedrites Ataxites	Stony-iron meteorites	Siderophyres Pallasites Mesosiderites	Stony meteorites	Chondrites Achondrites

METEORITE CRATERS

Large meteorites excavate round-shaped craters when they collide with the Earth. Approximately 50 quite large meteorite craters have been proven or suggested to be present on Earth. In addition many hundreds of small impact points have been caused by swarms of meteorites.

Arizona Crater (Barringer Crater, Canyon Diablo) The best known and best researched crater is near Winslow in Arizona/USA. It has a diameter of 1220m and a depth of 175m. Its ring wall rises 35m above the surrounding flat terrain. It was formed 30,000 years ago. A main body of the meteorite has never been found but more than 20 tonnes of meteoritic iron was collected as debris.

Nordlinger Ries One of the largest meteorite craters, a basin 25km wide, originally 500m deep but now only 200m, situated between the Swabian and Franconian Jura, Germany. Formed 15 million years ago. The meteorite vaporized completely on impact and no piece of it has ever been found.

IMPACTITES

When large meteorites strike, the rocks of the Earth's surface can melt and even vaporize to form clouds of red-hot material similar to that in volcanic eruptions. When these melt products solidify they form glass-like rock debris, a few tens of centimetres in diameter, called impactites, which occasionally accumulate to form breccias, an example of which is the suevite of the Nördlinger Ries.

Large meteorites crash to Earth with a striking fiery tail (photomontage).

Iron-meteorite [1,2,5] Siderite

Iron-meteorites are crystalline alloys of native iron with 4-40% nickel and a small amount of cobalt and copper. This composition of ore does not occur in the Earth's crust.

Hexahedrite Iron-meteorite with 6-7% nickel content and cubic crystals which can be cleaved along the faces of the cube (hexahedron). When the surfaces are polished and etched with nitric acid a fine, parallel oriented or intersecting striation, called Neumann lines, is formed.

Octahedrite [1] Iron-meteorite with up to 40% nickel, crystallizing with octahedral form. Surfaces polished and etched with nitric acid reveal a system of lamellae which is called Widmanstatten (or Widmanstetten) structure. So far it has not proved possible to produce such a system of lamellae experimentally. Three components of the fabric can be distinguished: kamacite, taenite and plessite.

Kamacite (beam-iron) Dark grey nickel-iron alloy with 6-7% nickel in the form of thick plates.

Taenite (ribbon-iron) Nickel-iron alloy, containing about 30% nickel, with silvery lustre bordering the kamacite.

Plessite ("filling" iron) Grey black mixture of extremely small crystals of kamacite and taenite which fill in the spaces in the system of lamellae.

Ataxite Finely crystalline, nickel-rich iron meteorite without a clearly defined structure. Probably derived from octahedrite because of the effects of heating.

Stony-meteorite [3,4] aerolite, meteor stone

Stony meteorites are similar to terrestrial rocks. Their mineral content corresponds approximately to peridotites or gabbros. Small amounts of nickel-iron are also present. They are more abundant than iron meteorites.

Chondrite [3] Stony-meteorites with individual, small, up to pea- sized spheres (chondrules) made of silicate minerals (such as bronzite, diopside, olivine, and plagioclase), very occasionally of chromite, graphite, magnetite, spinel or of rock-glass. The groundmass consists of the same minerals or of glass. Colour usually light to dark grey, sometimes black.

Achondrite [4] Stony-meteorite without chondrules usually possessing a gleaming black fused skin. Rarer than chondrites.

Stony-iron meteorite

In composition transitional between stony and iron meteorites and consisting of about equal proportions of silicate minerals and nickel iron. They account for less than 10% of all meteorites which have fallen on the Earth.

Siderophyre Variety of meteorite with a high nickel-iron content as well as a high proportion of bronzite in a net-like fabric. Tridymite is also present.

Pallasite Variety of meteorite with large olivine crystals in an octahedrite, nickel-iron groundmass.

Mesosiderite Variety of meteorite with irregularly distributed nickel-iron in a silicate groundmass of bronzite, olivine and plagioclase.

---

1 Iron meteorite (octahedrite) with Widmanstätten structure, fell 40,000 years ago in Toluka/Mexico

2 Iron-meteorite, fell 30,000 years ago, Arizona Crater/USA

3 Stony meteorite with chondrules fell on 8 February 1969, Allende/Mexico

4 Stony-meteorite, fell on 8 February 1969, Allende/Mexico

5 Iron-meteorite, fell 30,000 years ago, Arizona Crater/USA

The largest meteorite ever found, on the Hoba farm in Namibia.

Tektite [1-4]

There is considerable dispute about the origin of tektites (Greek "to melt"). It was formerly thought that they were non-crystalline meteorites and hence they were called glassy meteorites.

Nowadays tektites are considered to be terrestrial products which developed in connection with meteorite impacts. They condensed from the vaporized materials which were formed as a result of the high velocity with which huge meteorites collided with the Earth and they developed drip-like forms with a glassy amorphous texture. Accordingly tektites are found in the "strewn fields" of meteorite craters.

Tektites are green to black, rarely yellowish, and have a more or less scarred surface. They are usually about 4cm in diameter but very occasionally can reach apple-size. They have no fused skin. Named after the locality in which they are found eg australite, georgiaite (USA), thailandite.

Moldavite [1] (bouteillenstein (bottle stone) water chrysolite). Dark green to black green tektite from Moldavia (Czechoslovakia) with a surface which is ragged and partly rounded.

Transparent types of a bottle green colour were formerly polished as gemstones. Their origin can be traced back to the meteorite impact which excavated the Ries basin (p.331).

Fulgurite Lightning pipes

Fulgurites (Latin "lightning") have some relationship to meteorites in that they are of extraterrestrial origin. Their pipe-like shapes are the result of melting of rocks which have been struck by lightning. They are a few centimetres wide and sometimes a few metres long.

1 Moldavites Bohemia/Czechoslovakia
2 Pitted tektites, Thailand
3 Tektite (australite), Central Australia
4 Tektite (thailandite), Thailand

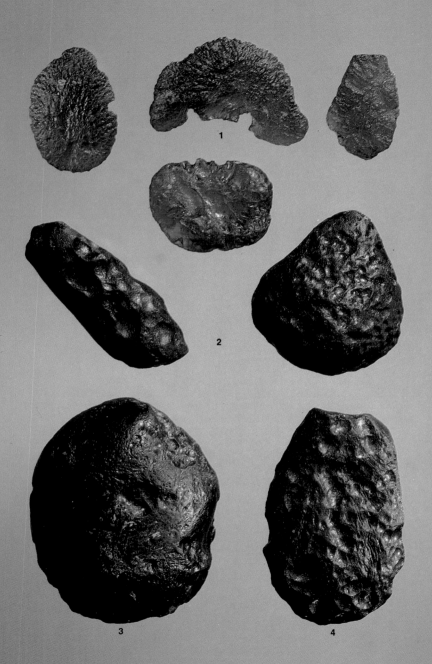

APPENDIX

HINTS FOR COLLECTORS

A few hints which the rock collector should observe for his own safety and that of others, to achieve greater success and more lasting pleasure in his collection.

Equipment for field and determinative work   Good footwear is always necessary; rubber boots are not suitable on rubbly slopes and in quarries since they offer too little protection. Wear gloves with a good grip made of rubberised fabric when trimming the specimen. Heavy leather gloves are needed when working with a chisel; they dampen the shock and give protection if the hammer slips off the chisel. When working with chemicals use acid-resistant gloves which retain a good grip even in wet conditions.

In all hammering and chiselling work, when trimming specimens and when using acids, it is essential to use glasses with splinter-proof lenses and eye protection at the sides. For people who wear spectacles there are protective shields or clear-lensed goggles which can be pushed over the corrective spectacles. Wear a protective helmet everywhere where there is a threat of falling rock. The danger of rock falls is increased after blasting, after a period of winter frost and after sunrise.

Do's and don'ts   In many countries collecting minerals and rocks in the field is subject to greater or lesser restrictions. All amateur rock-hounds must inform themselves about the relevant regulations before beginning collecting activities. If regulations are broken punishment under some circumstances can be very harsh. There is the threat that the collected material and the equipment, including the car, may be impounded; there may also be fines and even imprisonment. It is self-evident that one may not take anything away from private property without permission. Entry to private property requires prior permission. The fact that a warning sign is not there in no way implies that rock collecting is allowed.

In Germany, in Austria and in Switzerland there is no general regulation about searching for and collecting rocks and minerals. However, individual restrictions are in force in many places. Numerous communities have issued their own decrees. Frequently permission to prospect is only granted on payment of a fee.

In the United Kingdom the Geologists' Association issues a pamphlet "A code for geological fieldwork" (1973) and the Institution of Geologists has published "A code of practice for geological visits to quarries, mines and caves" (1986).

Conservation of collected specimens   In the conservation of specimens particular attention must be paid to those which are at risk and those which are dangerous. Some minerals can absorb moisture from the air and then dissolve, others give off water and disintegrate. Iron meteorites rust, light sensitive minerals bleach. In the specialist literature for collectors tips are given as to how specimens at risk can be protected.

Do not store radioactive minerals and rocks in living rooms, bedrooms or studies, and never let them get into the hands of children. Only collect small specimens, in order to avoid radiation damage.

TABLE OF CHEMICAL ELEMENTS

Symbol	Name	Atomic Number	Symbol	Name	Atomic Number
Ac	Actinium	89	Mn	Manganese	25
Ag	Silver	47	Mo	Molybdenum	42
Al	Aluminium	13	Mv	Mendelevium	101
Am	Americium	95	N	Nitrogen	7
Ar	Argon	18	Na	Sodium	11
As	Arsenic	33	Nb	Niobium	41
At	Astatine	85	Nd	Neodymium	60
Au	Gold	79	Ne	Neon	10
B	Boron	5	Ni	Nickel	28
Ba	Barium	56	No	Nobelium	102
Be	Beryllium	4	Np	Neptunium	93
Bi	Bismuth	83	O	Oxygen	8
Bk	Berkelium	97	Os	Osmium	76
Br	Bromine	35	P	Phosphorus	15
C	Carbon	6	Pa	Protactinium	91
Ca	Calcium	20	Pb	Lead	82
Cd	Cadmium	48	Pd	Palladium	46
Ce	Cerium	58	Pm	Promethium	61
Cf	Californium	98	Po	Polonium	84
Cl	Chlorine	17	Pr	Praseodymium	59
Cm	Curium	96	Pt	Platinum	78
Co	Cobalt	27	Pu	Plutonium	94
Cr	Chromium	24	Ra	Radium	88
Cs	Caesium	55	Rb	Rubidium	37
Cu	Copper	29	Re	Rhenium	75
Dy	Dysprosium	66	Rh	Rhodium	45
Er	Erbium	68	Rn	Radon	86
Es	Einsteinium	99	Ru	Ruthenium	44
Eu	Europium	63	S	Sulphur	16
F	Fluorine	9	Sb	Antimony	51
Fe	Iron	26	Sc	Scandium	21
Fm	Fermium	100	Se	Selenium	34
Fr	Francium	87	Si	Silicon	14
Ga	Gallium	31	Sm	Samarium	62
Gd	Gadolinium	64	Sn	Tin	50
Ge	Germanium	32	Sr	Strontium	38
H	Hydrogen	1	Ta	Tantalum	73
He	Helium	2	Tb	Terbium	65
Hf	Hafnium	72	Tc	Technetium	43
Hg	Mercury	80	Te	Tellurium	52
Ho	Holmium	67	Th	Thorium	90
In	Indium	49	Ti	Titanium	22
Ir	Iridium	77	Tl	Thallium	81
I	Iodine	53	Tm	Thulium	69
K	Potassium	19	U	Uranium	92
Kr	Krypton	36	V	Vanadium	23
La	Lanthanum	57	W	Tungsten	74
Li	Lithium	3	Xe	Xenon	54
Lu	Lutetium	71	Y	Yttrium	39
Lw	Lawrencium	103	Yb	Ytterbium	70
Mg	Magnesium	12	Zn	Zinc	30
			Zr	Zirconium	40

SELECTION OF BRITISH STANDARD AND ASTM REGULATIONS ON NATURAL STONE

BSI - BRITISH STANDARDS INSTITUTION

BS 63   Road aggregates
BS 680   Specification for roofing slates
BS 812   Testing aggregates
BS 882   Specification for aggregates from natural sources for concrete
BS 5390   Code of practice for stone masonry
CP 298   Natural stone cladding (non-loadbearing)
—   Standards catalogue (published annually)

ASTM - AMERICAN SOCIETY FOR TESTING AND MATERIALS

C92(12)   Tests for Absorption and Bulk SG of Natural Building Stone
C119(12)   Definition of terms relating to Natural Building Stone
C503(12)   Specification for Exterior Marble
C568(12)   Specification for Dimension Limestone
C615(12)   Specification for Structural Granite
C616(12)   Specification for Building Sandstone
C629(12)   Specification for Structural Slate

Annual Book of ASTM Standards

DIN - DEUTSCHES INSTITUT FÜR NORMUNG E.V.

DIN 52104 Testing of natural stone - freeze thaw cyclic test
DIN 52110 Testing of natural stone - determination of bulk density of stone gradings

English translation of German Standards Catalogue

Subdivisions of Earth History - the Geological Column

Aeon	Era	System	Series	Millions of years before present
P H A N E R O Z O I C	C E N O Z O I C	Quaternary	Holocene Pleistocene	1.6
		Neogene	Pliocene Miocene	23
		Palaeogene	Oligocene Eocene Palaeocene	65
	M E S O Z O I C	Cretaceous	Upper Lower	135
		Jurassic	Upper Middle Lower	205
		Triassic	Upper Middle Lower	250
	P A L A E O Z O I C	Permian	Upper Lower	290
		Carboniferous	Stephanian Westphalian Namurian Visean Tournaisian	355
		Devonian	Upper Middle Lower	410
		Silurian	Pridoli Ludlow Wenlock Llandovery	438
		Ordovician	Ashgill Caradoc Llandeilo-Llanvirn Arenig Tremadoc	510
		Cambrian	Upper Middle Lower	570
P R E C A M B R I A N	Proterozoic	Late		900
		Middle		1600
		Early		2500
	Archaean	Late		3000
		Middle		3400
		Early		4600

BIBLIOGRAPHY

ADAMS, A.E., MACKENZIE, W.S. & GUILFORD, C. *Atlas of sedimentary rocks under the microscope*. Longman, London. Halsted, New York. 1984

ANDERSON, B.W. *Gem Testing* (9th Ed.) Butterworth, London. 1980

BATTEY, M.H. *Mineralogy for Students* (2nd Ed.) Longman, London and New York. 1981

BAUER, M. *Precious Stones* (2 vols.) Dover, New York. 1968

BEST, M.G. *Igneous and Metamorphic Petrology*. Freeman, San Francisco. 1982

BLATT, H., MIDDLETON, G. & MURRAY, R. *Origin of Sedimentary Rocks* (2nd Ed.) Prentice-Hall, New Jersey. 1980

BRUTON, E. *Diamonds* (2nd Ed.) Northwood, London. 1977

CIPRIANI, C. *The Macdonald Encyclopedia of Precious Stones*. Macdonald, London. 1986

CORRENS, C.W. *Introduction to Mineralogy, Crystallography and Petrology*. Allen & Unwin, London. Springer Verlag, Berlin. 1969

COX, K.G., BELL, J.D. & PANKHURST, R.J. *The Interpretation of Igneous Rocks*. Allen & Unwin, London. 1979

COX, K.G., PRICE, N.B. & HARTE, B. *(An Introduction To) The Practical Study of Crystals, Minerals and Rocks*. McGraw-Hill, London. 1988

DANA, E.S. (revised by HURLBUT, C.S.) *Minerals and how to study them*. John Wiley & Sons, New York. 1963

DEER, W.A., HOWIE, R.A. & ZUSSMAN, J. *An Introduction to the Rock-Forming Minerals*. Longmans, London & New York. 1966

DESAUTELS, P.E. *The Mineral Kingdom*. Madison Square Press, New York. 1968

ELWELL, D. *Man-made Gemstones*. John Wiley & Sons, New York. 1979

EMBREY, P.G. & SYMES, R.F. *Minerals of Cornwall and Devon*. British Museum (Natural History), London. Mineralogical Record, Tucson, Arizona. 1987

EVANS, A.M. *An Introduction to Ore Geology* (2nd Ed.) Blackwell, Oxford & London. 1989

EVANS, R.C. *An Introduction to Crystal Chemistry* (2nd Ed.) Cambridge University Press, 1966

FIRSOFF, V.A. *Gemstones of the British Isles*. Oliver and Boyd, Edinburgh. 1971

FORD, W.E. *Dana's Textbook of Mineralogy* (4th Ed.) John Wiley and Sons, New York. 1955

FRY, N. *The Field Description of Metamorphic Rocks*. Open University, Milton Keynes. Halsted, New York & Toronto. 1984

GILLEN, C. *Metamorphic Geology*. Allen & Unwin, London. 1982

GREENSMITH, J.T. *Petrology of the Sedimentary Rocks* (6th Ed.) Allen & Unwin, London. 1978

GREG, R.P. & LETTSOM, W.G. *Manual of the Mineralogy of Great Britain and Ireland*. John Van Voorst, London. 1858. Facsimile Reprint 1977 Broadstairs.

GRIBBLE, C. *Rutley's Elements of Mineralogy*. Murby, London. 1990

GRIM, R.E. *Applied Clay Mineralogy* (2nd Ed.) McGraw-Hill, New York. 1962

GÜBELIN, E. *The Internal World of Gemstones*. Butterworths, London. 1974

HAMBLIN, W.K. *The Earth's Dynamic Systems* (5th Ed.) Macmillan, London. 1989

HAMILTON, W.R., WOLLEY, A.R. & BISHOP, A.C. *Minerals, Rocks and Fossils*. Hamlyn, London & New York. 1976

HARKER, A. *Metamorphism*. Methuen, London. 1950

HATCH, F.H., WELLS, A.K. & WELLS, M.K. *Petrology of the Igneous Rocks* (12th Ed.) Murby, London. 1961

HEDDLE, M.F. (J.G. Goodchild Ed.) *The Mineralogy of Scotland* (Vols 1 & 2) David Douglas, Edinburgh. 1901

HOLMES, A. *Principles of Physical Geology* (2nd Ed.) Nelson, London. 1965

HURLBUT, C.S. *Minerals and Man*. Thames & Hudson, London. 1969

KIRSCH, H. *Applied Mineralogy (for engineers, technologists and students)*. Chapman & Hall, London. 1968

KUKAL, Z. *Man and Stone*. Geological Survey, Prague. 1989

MACKENZIE, W.S., DONALDSON, C.H. & GUILFORD, C. *Atlas of igneous rocks and their textures.* Longman, London. Halsted, New York. 1982

MACKENZIE, W.S. & GUILFORD, C. *Atlas of rock-forming minerals in thin section.* Longman, London. Halsted, New York. 1980

MASON, B. *Meteorites.* Wiley, New York & London. 1962

MASON, B. & BERRY, L.G. *Elements of Mineralogy.* Freeman, San Francisco. 1968

MIDDLEMOST, E.A.K. *Magmas and Magmatic Rocks.* Longman, London & New York. 1985

MOTTANA, A., CRESPI, R. & LIBORIO, G. *The Macdonald Encyclopedia of Rocks and Minerals.* Macdonald Orbis, London & Sydney. 1983

NASSAU, K. *Gems made by Man.* Chilton Book Company, Radnor, Pennsylvania. 1980

NOCKOLDS, S.R., KNOX, R.W.O'B. & CHINNER, G.A. *Petrology for Students.* Cambridge University Press, Cambridge. 1978

PARK, C.F. & MACDIARMID, R.A. *Ore Deposits.* Freeman, San Francisco. 1975

PHILLIPS, F.C. *An Introduction to Crystallography* (4th Ed.) Longman, London. 1971

POUGH, F.H. *A Field Guide to Rocks and Minerals.* Constable, London. 1970

PRESS, F. & SIEVER, R. *Earth* (4th Ed.) Freeman, San Francisco. 1986

ROBERTS, W.L., RAPP, G.R. & WEBER, J. *Encyclopedia of Minerals.* New York. 1974

RODGERS, P.R. *Rock and Mineral Collecting in Britain.* Faber & Faber, London. 1979

ROGERS, C. *A Collector's Guide to Minerals, Rocks and Gemstones in Cornwall and Devon.* Bradford Barton, Truro. 1968

ROGERS, C. (Ed.) *Finding Britain's Gems.* Lapidary Publications, London.

SCHUMANN, W. *Gemstones of the World.* NAG Press, London. Sterling Publishing, New York. 1977

SINKANKAS, J. *Gemstones of North America.* Van Nostrand, Princeton, New Jersey. 1959

SINKANKAS, J. *Mineralogy - A First Course.* Van Nostrand. 1966

SKINNER, B.J. & PORTER, S.C. *Physical Geology.* Wiley, New York. 1987

SMITH, G.F.H. (rev. by PHILLIPS, F.C.) *Gemstones* (14th ed.) Methuen, London. 1972

SORRELL, C.A. *Minerals of the World.* Golden Press, New York. 1973

STANTON, R.L. *Ore Petrology.* McGraw-Hill, New York. 1972

THORPE, R.S. & BROWN, G.C. *The Field Description of Igneous Rocks.* Open University Press, Milton Keynes. 1985

TOMKEIEFF, S.I. (E.K. WALTON et al Eds.) *Dictionary of Petrology.* John Wiley & Sons, New York. 1983

TUCKER, M.E. *The field description of sedimentary rocks.* Open University Press, Milton Keynes. 1982

TUCKER, M.E. *Sedimentary Petrology.* 1991

WEBSTER, R. *Gems.* Newnes Butterworth, London. 1975

WILLIAMS, H., TURNER, F.J. & GILBERT, C.M. *Petrography* (2nd Ed.) Freeman, San Francisco. 1982

YARDLEY, B.W.D. *An Introduction to Metamorphic Petrology.* Longman. 1989

JOURNALS

Canadian Rockhound, Vancouver
Australian Gemmologist, Sydney
Australian Lapidary Magazine, Croydon, New South Wales
Gems and Gemology, Los Angeles
Rock and Gem, Encino, California
Rocks and Minerals, Peekshill, New York
Mineralogical Record, Maryland, New York
Lapidary Journal, San Diego, California
Journal of Gemmology, London
Gems and Minerals, Mentone, California
Geology Today, Oxford
The American Mineralogist, Washington
The Canadian Mineralogist, Ottawa
Mineralogical Magazine, London
Journal of Petrology
Journal of Metamorphic Petrology
Sedimentology

Mohs' hardness	Vitreous ⎱ lustre Resinous ⎰	Silky ⎱ lustre Pearly ⎰	Adamantine lustre
1	Carnallite 1.60 Pyrophyllite 2.66-2.90	Pyrophyllite 2.66-2.90 Talc 2.7-2.8	Calomel 6.4-6.5
1½	Carnallite 1.60 Halotrichite 1.73-1.79 Sylvite 1.99 Gypsum 2.2-2.4 Vivianite 2.6-2.7 Pyrophyllite 2.66-2.90	Halotrichite 1.73-1.79 Gypsum 2.2-2.4 Vivianite 2.6-2.7 Pyrophyllite 2.66-2.90	Chlorargyrite 5.5-5.6 Calomel 6.4-6.5
2	Amber 1.05-1.30 Carnallite 1.60 Epsomite 1.68 Borax 1.7-1.8 Ulexite 1.96 Sylvite 1.99 Sulphur 2.0-2.1 Chrysocolla 2.0-2.2 Halite 2.1-2.2 Gypsum 2.2-2.4 Pharmacolite 2.6 Vivianite 2.6-2.7 Muscovite 2.78-2.88 Lepidolite 2.80-2.90 Zinnwaldite 2.90-3.20 Annabergite 3.0-3.1	Ulexite 1.96 Gypsum 2.2-2.4 Vivianite 2.6-2.7 Phlogopite 2.75-2.97 Muscovite 2.78-2.88 Lepidolite 2.80-2.90 Fuchsite 2.85 Zinnwaldite 2.90-3.20 Annabergite 3.0-3.1 Hydrozincite 3.5-3.8	Sulphur 2.0-2.1 Senarmontite 5.50 Chlorargyrite 5.5-5.6 Phosgenite 6.0-6.3 Calomel 6.4-6.5
2½	Epsomite 1.68 Borax 1.7-1.8 Kernite 1.91 Gaylussite 1.99 Chrysocolla 2.0-2.2 Serpentine 2.0-2.6 Schoenite 2.03 Kainite 2.1-2.2 Gibbsite 2.3-2.4 Penninite 2.5-2.6 Pharmacolite 2.6 Thenardite 2.66-2.67 Biotite 2.70-3.30 Muscovite 2.78-2.88 Lepidolite 2.80-2.90 Zinnwaldite 2.90-3.20 Cryolite 2.95 Stolzite 7.9-8.2	Serpentine 2.0-2.6 Gibbsite 2.3-2.4 Penninite 2.5-2.6 Biotite 2.70-3.30 Phlogopite 2.75-2.97 Muscovite 2.78-2.88 Lepidolite 2.80-2.90 Fuchsite 2.85 Zinnwaldite 2.90-3.20 Cryolite 2.95 Hydrozincite 3.5-3.8 Valentinite 5.6-5.8 Leadhillite 6.45-6.55	Valentinite 5.6-5.8 Phosgenite 6.0-6.3

Mohs' hardness	Greasy } lustre Waxy }	Metallic lustre	No lustre Dull
	Carnallite 1.60 Talc 2.7-2.8	Carnallite 1.60	
1½	Carnallite 1.60 Sylvite 1.99 Chlorargyrite 5.5-5.6	Carnallite 1.60 Vivianite 2.6-2.7	Chlorargyrite 5.5-5.6
	Amber 1.05-1.30 Carnallite 1.60 Borax 1.7-1.8 Sylvite 1.99 Sulphur 2.0-2.1 Chrysocolla 2.0-2.2 Senarmontite 5.50 Chlorargyrite 5.5-5.6 Phosgenite 6.0-6.3	Carnallite 1.60 Vivianite 2.6-2.7 Phlogopite 2.75-2.97 Muscovite 2.78-2.88 Fuchsite 2.85 Zinnwaldite 2.90-3.20	Sepiolite 2.0 Hydrozincite 3.5-3.8 Chlorargyrite 5.5-5.6
2½	Borax 1.7-1.8 Chrysocolla 2.0-2.2 Serpentine 2.0-2.6 Phosgenite 6.0-6.3 Leadhillite 6.45-6.56 Stolzite 7.9-8.2	Biotite 2.70-3.30 Phlogopite 2.75-2.97 Muscovite 2.78-2.88 Fuchsite 2.85 Zinnwaldite 2.90-3.20 Silver 9.6-12.0	Sepiolite 2.0 Serpentine 2.0-2.6 Hydrozincite 3.5-3.8

Mohs' hardness	Vitreous ⎱ lustre Resinous ⎰	Silky ⎱ lustre Pearly ⎰	Adamantine lustre
3	Amber 1.05-1.30	Kurnakovite 1.86	Valentinite 5.6-5.8
	Kurnakovite 1.86	Serpentine 2.0-2.6	Phosgenite 6.0-6.3
	Chrysocolla 2.0-2.2	Laumontite 2.25-2.35	Anglesite 6.3-6.4
	Serpentine 2.0-2.6	Cacoxenite 2.3	Cerussite 6.4-6.6
	Kainite 2.1-2.2	Gibbsite 2.3-2.4	Wulfenite 6.7-6.9
	Laumontite 2.25-2.35	Pearl 2.60-2.78	
	Cacoxenite 2.3	Biotite 2.70-3.30	
	Gibbsite 2.3-2.4	Muscovite 2.78-2.88	
	Hanksite 2.56	Lepidolite 2.80-2.90	
	Coral 2.6-2.7	Zinnwaldite 2.90-3.20	
	Calcite 2.6-2.8	Cryolite 2.95	
	Thenardite 2.66-2.67	Celestite 3.9-4.0	
	Biotite 2.70-3.30	Barite 4.48	
	Polyhalite 2.77-2.78	Valentinite 5.6-5.8	
	Muscovite 2.78-2.88		
	Lepidolite 2.80-2.90		
	Strengite 2.87		
	Zinnwaldite 2.90-3.20		
	Cryolite 2.95		
	Celestite 3.9-4.0		
	Witherite 4.28		
	Barite 4.48		
	Cerussite 6.4-6.6		
	Wulfenite 6.7-6.0		
	Stolzite 7.9-8.2		
3½	Chrysocolla 2.0-2.2	Serpentine 2.0-2.6	Sphalerite 3.9-4.2
	Serpentine 2.0-2.6	Stilbite 2.09-2.20	Anglesite 6.3-6.4
	Stilbite 2.09-2.20	Heulandite 2.18-2.22	Cerussite 6.4-6.6
	Heulandite 2.18-2.22	Laumontite 2.25-2.35	Pyromorphite 6.7-7.1
	Laumontite 2.25-2.35	Gibbsite 2.3-2.4	Mimetesite 7.1
	Gibbsite 2.3-2.4	Pearl 2.60-2.78	
	Wavellite 2.3-2.4	Anhydrite 2.9-3.0	
	Hanksite 2.56	Ankerite 2.9-3.8	
	Kieserite 2.57	Celestite 3.9-4.0	
	Coral 2.6-2.7	Barite 4.48	
	Polyhalite 2.77-2.78		
	Dolomite 2.85-2.95		
	Strengite 2.87		
	Anhydrite 2.9-3.0		
	Ankerite 2.9-3.8		
	Aragonite 2.95		
	Rhodochrosite 3.3-3.6		
	Strontianite 3.76		
	Celestite 3.9-4.0		
	Witherite 4.28		
	Adamite 4.3-4.5		
	Barite 4.48		
	Cerussite 6.4-6.6		

Mohs' hardness	Greasy ⎱ lustre Waxy ⎰	Metallic lustre	No lustre Dull
3		Serpentine 2.0-2.6	
	Amber 1.05-1.30	Biotite 2.70-3.30	Laumontite 2.25-2.35
	Chrysocolla 2.0-2.2	Muscovite 2.78-2.88	Hanksite 2.56
	Serpentine 2.0-2.6	Zinnwaldite 2.90-3.20	Coral 2.6-2.7
	Coral 2.6-2.7	Silver 9.6-12.0	Witherite 4.28
	Polyhalite 2.77-2.78		
	Celestite 3.9-4.0		
	Witherite 4.28		
	Phosgenite 6.0-6.4		
	Anglesite 6.3-6.4		
	Cerussite 6.4-6.6		
	Stolzite 7.9-8.2		
3½	Chrysocolla 2.0-2.2		Serpentine 2.0-2.6
	Serpentine 2.0-2.6		Laumontite 2.25-2.35
	Coral 2.6-2.7		Hanksite 2.56
	Polyhalite 2.77-2.78		Coral 2.6-2.7
	Ankerite 2.9-3.8		Witherite 4.28
	Aragonite 2.95		
	Strontianite 3.76		
	Celestite 3.9-4.0		
	Sphalerite 3.9-4.2		
	Witherite 4.28		
	Anglesite 6.3-6.4		
	Cerussite 6.4-6.6		
	Pyromorphite 6.7-7.1		
	Mimetesite 7.1		

Mohs' hardness	Vitreous } lustre Resinous }	Silky } lustre Pearly }	Adamantine lustre
4	Chrysocolla 2.0-2.2	Serpentine 2.0-2.6	Colemanite 2.44
	Serpentine 2.0-2.6	Stilbite 2.09-2.20	Sphalerite 3.9-4.2
	Chabazite 2.08-2.16	Heulandite 2.18-2.22	Pyromorphite 6.7-7.1
	Stilbite 2.09-2.20	Pearl 2.60-2.78	Mimetesite 7.1
	Heulandite 2.18-2.22	Ankerite 2.9-3.8	
	Phillipsite 2.2	Margarite 2.99-3.08	
	Wavellite 2.3-2.4	Kyanite 3.53-3.65	
	Colemanite 2.44	Siderite 3.7-3.9	
	Variscite 2.52		
	Coral 2.6-2.7		
	Dolomite 2.85-2.95		
	Magnesite 2.9-3.1		
	Ankerite 2.9-3.8		
	Aragonite 2.95		
	Fluorite 3.18		
	Rhodochrosite 3.3-3.6		
	Kyanite 3.53-3.65		
	Siderite 3.7-3.9		
4½	Chabazite 2.08-2.16	Apophyllite 2.3-2.4	Colemanite 2.44
	Phillipsite 2.22	Wollastonite 2.78-2.91	Scheelite 5.9-6.1
	Colemanite 2.44	Margarite 2.99-3.08	
	Harmotome 2.44-2.50	Kyanite 3.53-3.65	
	Variscite 2.52	Siderite 3.7-3.9	
	Wollastonite 2.78-2.91		
	Magnesite 2.9-3.1		
	Kyanite 3.53-3.65		
	Siderite 3.7-3.9		
5	Chabazite 2.08-2.16	Natrolite 2.20-2.36	Sphene 3.4-3.6
	Sodalite 2.13-2.29	Mesolite 2.2-2.4	Scheelite 5.9-6.1
	Natrolite 2.20-2.26	Scolecite 2.26-2.40	
	Mesolite 2.2-2.4	Okenite 2.28-2.33	
	Analcite 2.24-2.31	Apophyllite 2.3-2.4	
	Apophyllite 2.3-2.4	Thomsonite 2.3-2.4	
	Variscite 2.52	Wollastonite 2.78-2.91	
	Scapolite 2.54-2.77	Pectolite 2.8	
	Turquoise 2.6-2.8	Bronzite 3.25-3.35	
	Wollastonite 2.78-2.91	Smithsonite 4.3-4.5	
	Wardite 2.81		
	Datolite 2.9-3.0		
	Melilite 2.95-3.05		
	Apatite 3.16-3.22		
	Augite 3.2-3.6		
	Bronzite 3.25-3.35		
	Diopside 3.27-3.31		
	Hemimorphite 3.3-3.5		
	Hypersthene 3.35-3.84		
	Smithsonite 4.3-4.5		
	Monazite 4.6-5.7		

Mohs' hardness	Greasy ⎫ lustre Waxy ⎭	Metallic lustre	No lustre Dull
	Chrysocolla 2.0-2.2 Serpentine 2.0-2.6 Variscite 2.52 Coral 2.6-2.7 Ankerite 2.9-3.8 Aragonite 2.95 Sphalerite 3.9-4.2 Pyromorphite 6.7-7.1 Mimetesite 7.1	Platinum 14-19	Serpentine 2.0-2.6 Coral 2.6-2.7
4½	Variscite 2.52 Scheelite 5.9-6.1	Platinum 14-19	
	Sodalite 2.13-2.29 Variscite 2.52 Scapolite 2.54-2.77 Turquoise 2.6-2.8 Datolite 2.9-3.0 Melilite 2.95-3.05 Apatite 3.16-3.22 Sphene 3.4-3.6 Scheelite 5.9-6.1		

Mohs' hardness	Vitreous ⎱ lustre Resinous ⎰	Silky ⎱ lustre Pearly ⎰	Adamantine lustre
5½	Opal 1.98-2.50	Natrolite 2.20-2.26	Sphene 3.4-3.6
	Sodalite 2.13-2.29	Mesolite 2.2-2.4	Anatase 3.8-3.9
	Natrolite 2.20-2.26	Hauyne 2.44-2.50	Brookite 4.1
	Mesolite 2.2-2.4	Tremolite 2.9-3.1	
	Analcite 2.24-2.31	Actinolite 2.9-3.3	
	Nosean 2.28-2.40	Bronzite 3.25-3.35	
	Hauyne 2.44-2.50	Rhodonite 3.40-3.73	
	Leucite 2.45-2.50		
	Scapolite 2.54-2.77		
	Nepheline 2.60-2.65		
	Turquoise 2.6-2.80		
	Datolite 2.9-3.0		
	Tremolite 2.9-3.1		
	Actinolite 2.9-3.3		
	Melilite 2.95-3.05		
	Lazulite 3.1-3.2		
	Augite 3.2-3.6		
	Bronzite 3.25-3.35		
	Enstatite 3.26-3.28		
	Diopside 3.27-3.31		
	Hypersthene 3.35-3.84		
	Rhodonite 3.40-3.73		
	Arfvedsonite 3.44-3.46		
	Willemite 4.0		
	Monazite 4.6-5.7		
6	Opal 1.98-2.50	Opal 1.98-2.50	Anatase 3.8-3.9
	Sodalite 2.13-2.29	Kaliophilite 2.49-2.67	Fayalite 4.0-4.35
	Leucite 2.45-2.50	Microcline 2.53-2.56	Brookite 4.1
	Kaliophilite 2.49-2.67	Plagioclase 2.61-2.77	
	Microcline 2.53-2.56	Prehnite 2.8-3.0	
	Orthoclase 2.53-2.56	Tremolite 2.9-3.1	
	Scapolite 2.54-2.77	Actinolite 2.9-3.3	
	Nepheline 2.60-2.65	Amblygonite 3.0-3.1	
	Turquoise 2.6-2.8	Zoisite 3.15-3.36	
	Plagioclase 2.61-2.77	Spodumene 3.16-3.20	
	Prehnite 2.8-2.77	Sillimanite 3.22-3.25	
	Tremolite 2.9-3.1	Bronzite 3.25-3.35	
	Actinolite 2.9-3.3	Rhodonite 3.40-3.73	
	Fassaite 2.96-3.34	Kyenite 3.53-3.65	
	Lazulite 3.1-3.2		
	Zoisite 3.15-3.36		
	Spodumene 3.16-3.20		
	Augite 3.2-3.6		
	Sillimanite 3.22-3.25		
	Bronzite 3.25-3.35		
	Diopside 3.27-3.31		
	Hypersthene 3.35-3.84		
	Rhodonite 3.40-3.73		
	Arfvedsonite 3.44-3.46		
	Kyanite 3.53-3.65		

Mohs' hardness	Greasy ⎱ lustre Waxy ⎰	Metallic lustre	No lustre Dull
½	Opal 1.98-2.50 Sodalite 2.13-2.29 Nosean 2.28-2.40 Hauyne 2.44-2.50 Leucite 2.45-2.50 Scapolite 2.54-2.77 Nepheline 2.60-2.65 Turquoise 2.6-2.8 Datolite 2.9-3.0 Melilite 2.95-3.05 Lazulite 3.1-3.2 Sphene 3.4-3.6 Willemite 4.0 Perovskite 4.0-4.8	Bronzite 3.25-3.35 Hypersthene 3.35-3.84 Anatase 3.8-3.9 Perovskite 4.0-4.8	Leucite 2.45-2.50
	Opal 1.98-2.50 Sodalite 2.13-2.29 Leucite 2.45-2.50 Scapolite 2.54-2.77 Nepheline 2.60-2.65 Turquoise 2.6-2.8 Lazulite 3.1-3.2 Sillimanite 3.22-3.25	Bronzite 3.25-3.35 Hypersthene 3.25-2.84 Anatase 3.8-3.9	Leucite 2.45-2.50

Mohs' hardness	Vitreous ⎱ lustre Resinous ⎰	Silky ⎱ lustre Pearly ⎰	Adamantine lustre
6½	Opal 1.98-2.50	Plagioclase 2.61-2.77	Zircon 3.9-4.8
	Cristobalite 2.20	Prehnite 2.8-3.0	Fayalite 4.0-4.35
	Tridymite 2.27	Zoisite 3.15-3.36	
	Scapolite 2.54-2.77	Spodumene 3.16-3.20	
	Plagioclase 2.61-2.77	Sillimanite 3.22-3.25	
	Prehnite 2.8-3.0	Diaspore 3.3-3.5	
	Zoisite 3.15-3.36	Rhodonite 3.40-3.73	
	Spodumene 3.16-3.20	Kyanite 3.53-3.65	
	Forsterite 3.22		
	Sillimanite 3.22-3.25		
	Axinite 3.26-3.36		
	Vesuvianite 3.27-3.45		
	Olivine 3.27-4.20		
	Jadeite 3.30-3.36		
	Diaspore 3.3-3.5		
	Rhodonite 3.40-3.73		
	Garnet 3.4-4.6		
	Kyanite 3.53-3.65		
	Benitoite 3.7		
7	Tridymite 2.27	Spodumene 3.16-3.20	Boracite 2.9-3.0
	Cordierite 2.50-2.75	Sillimanite 3.22-3.25	Zircon 3.9-4.8
	Quartz 2.65	Diaspore 3.3-3.5	Cassiterite 6.8-7.1
	Boracite 2.9-3.0	Kyanite 3.53-3.65	
	Tourmaline 3.02-3.26		
	Spodumene 3.16-3.20		
	Sillimanite 3.22-3.25		
	Axinite 3.26-3.36		
	Olivine 3.27-4.20		
	Jadeite 3.30-3.36		
	Diaspore 3.3-3.5		
	Garnet 3.4-4.6		
	Kyanite 3.53-3.65		
	Staurolite 3.65-3.77		
7½	Cordierite 2.50-2.75		Boracite 2.9-3.0
	Beryl 2.63-2.91		Zircon 3.9-4.8
	Boracite 2.9-3.0		
	Euclase 3.0-3.1		
	Tourmaline 3.02-3.26		
	Andalusite 3.11-3.22		
	Garnet 3.4-4.6		
	Staurolite 3.65-3.77		
8	Beryl 2.63-2.91		
	Topaz 3.53-3.56		
	Spinel 3.58-3.61		
8½	Chrysoberyl 3.70-3.72		
9	Corundum 3.97-4.05		

Mohs' hardness	Greasy ⎫ lustre Waxy ⎭	Metallic lustre	No lustre Dull
½	Opal 1.98-2.50 Scapolite 2.54-2.77 Chalcedony 2.58-2.64 Jasper 2.58-2.91 Sillimanite 3.22-3.25 Vesuvianite 3.27-3.45 Olivine 3.27-4.20 Garnet 3.4-4.6 Zircon 3.9-4.8		Chalcedony 2.58-2.64 Jasper 2.58-2.91
	Cordierite 2.50-2.75 Chalcedony 2.58-2.64 Jasper 2.58-2.91 Quartz 2.65 Danburite 2.9-3.0 Sillimanite 3.22-3.25 Olivine 3.27-4.20 Garnet 3.4-4.6 Staurolite 3.65-3.77 Zircon 3.9-4.8 Cassiterite 6.8-7.1		Chalcedony 2.58-2.64 Jasper 2.58-2.91 Staurolite 3.65-3.77
½	Cordierite 2.50-2.75 Danburite 2.9-3.0 Garnet 3.4-4.6 Staurolite 3.65-3.77 Zircon 3.9-4.8		Andalusite 3.11-3.22 Staurolite 3.65-3.77
½	Chrysoberyl 3.70-3.72		

Mohs' hardness	Vitreous }lustre Resinous }	Silky } lustre Pearly }	Adamantine lustre
1			
1½			
2	Borax 1.7-1.8 Chlorite 2.6-3.4 Chamosite 3.0-3.4	Chlorite 2.6-3.4	
2½	Borax 1.7-1.8 Chlorite 2.6-3.4 Chamosite 3.0-3.4 Bismuth ochre 6.7-7.4	Chlorite 2.6-3.4 Thuringite 3.2 Jamesonite 5.63	
3	Chlorite 2.6-3.4 Chamosite 3.0-3.4 Tenorite 6.0 Bismuth ochre 6.7-7.4	Chlorite 2.6-3.4	

Mohs' hardness	Greasy ⎫ lustre Waxy ⎭	Metallic lustre	No lustre Dull
		Graphite 2.1-2.3 Molybdenite 4.7-4.8	Graphite 2.1-2.3 Patronite 2.81
½	Covellite 4.68	Covellite 4.68 Molybdenite 4.7-4.8 Polybasite 6.0-6.2 Sylvanite 8.0-8.3	Patronite 2.81 Covellite 4.68
	Borax 1.7-1.8 Covellite 4.68	Pyrolusite 4.5-5.0 Berthierite 4.6 Antimonite 4.6-4.7 Covellite 4.68 Polybasite 6.0-6.2 Stephanite 6.2-6.4 Bismuthinite 6.8-7.2 Argentite 7.2-7.4 Sylvanite 8.0-8.3 Bismuth 9.7-9.8	Chlorite 2.6-3.4 Patronite 2.81 Chamosite 3.0-3.4 Pyrolusite 4.5-5.0 Antimonite 4.6-4.7 Covellite 4.68 Stephanite 6.2-6.4 Argentite 7.2-7.4
½	Borax 1.7-1.8	Pyrolusite 4.5-5.0 Berthierite 4.6 Chalcocite 5.5-5.8 Jamesonite 5.63 Bournonite 5.7-5.9 Boulangerite 5.8-6.2 Stephanite 6.2-6.4 Schapbachite 6.9-7.2 Argentite 7.2-7.4 Galena 7.2-7.6 Petzite 8.7-9.2 Bismuth 9.7-9.8	Chlorite 2.6-3.4 Chamosite 3.0-3.4 Pyrolusite 4.5-5.0 Chalcocite 5.5-5.8 Bournonite 5.7-5.9 Stephanite 6.2-6.4 Argentite 7.2-7.4 Galena 7.2-7.6
		Pyrolusite 4.5-5.0 Berthierite 4.6 Tennantite 4.6-4.8 Tetrahedrite 4.6-5.2 Bornite 4.9-5.3 Schwazite 5.1 Arsenic 5.4-5.9 Chalcocite 5.5-5.8 Bournonite 5.7-5.9 Boulangerite 5.8-6.2 Tenorite 6.0 Antimony 6.7 Galena 7.2-7.6 Petzite 8.7-9.2	Chlorite 2.6-3.4 Chamosite 3.0-3.4 Pyrolusite 4.5-5.0 Tennantite 4.6-4.8 Tetrahedrite 4.6-5.2 Schwazite 5.1 Arsenic 5.4-5.9 Chalcocite 5.5-5.8 Bournonite 5.7-5.9 Tenorite 6.0 Galena 7.2-7.6

Mohs' hardness	Vitreous Resinous } lustre	Silky Pearly } lustre	Adamantine lustre
3½	Dolomite 2.85-2.95 Ankerite 2.9-3.8 Tenorite 6.0 Bismuth ochre 6.7-7.4	Ankerite 2.9-3.8	
4	Dolomite 2.85-2.95 Ankerite 2.9-3.8 Siderite 3.7-3.9 Tenorite 6.0	Ankerite 2.9-3.8 Siderite 3.7-3.9	
4½	Siderite 3.7-3.9	Siderite 3.7-3.9	
5	Melilite 2.95-3.05 Riebeckite 3.0-3.4 Hornblende 3.02-3.27 Augite 3.2-3.6	Riebeckite 3.0-3.4 Hornblende 3.02-3.27	

ohs' rdness	Greasy ⎱ lustre Waxy ⎰	Metallic lustre	No lustre Dull
½	Ankerite 2.9-3.8	Cubanite 4.10 Chalcopyrite 4.1-4.3 Enargite 4.4 Freibergite 4.5-5.0 Pyrolusite 4.5-5.0 Tennantite 4.6-4.8 Pentlandite 4.6-5.0 Tetrahedrite 4.6-5.2 Schwazite 5.1 Millerite 5.3 Arsenic 5.4-5.9 Tenorite 6.0 Antimony 6.7	Pyrolusite 4.5-5.0 Tennantite 4.6-4.8 Tetrahedrite 4.6-5.2 Schwazite 5.1 Arsenic 5.4-5.9 Tenorite 6.0
	Ankerite 2.9-3.8 Pitchblende 9.1-10.6	Cubanite 4.10 Chalcopyrite 4.1-4.3 Manganite 4.3-4.4 Stannite 4.3-4.5 Freibergite 4.5-5.0 Pyrolusite 4.5-5.0 Pyrrhotite 4.6 Tennantite 4.6-4.8 Pentlandite 4.6-5.0 Tetrahedrite 4.6-5.2 Psilomelane 4.7 Hollandite 4.95 Schwazite 5.1 Arsenic 5.4-5.9 Tenorite 6.0 Platinum 14-19	Pyrolusite 4.5-5.0 Tennantite 4.6-4.8 Tetrahedrite 4.6-5.2 Psilomelane 4.7 Schwazite 5.1 Arsenic 5.4-5.9 Tenorite 6.0 Pitchblende 9.1-10.6
½	Pitchblende 9.1-10.6	Freibergite 4.5-5.0 Pyrolusite 4.5-5.0 Tennantite 4.6-4.8 Psilomelane 4.7 Linnaeite 4.8-5.8 Safflorite 6.9-7.3 Stibiopalladinite 9.5 Platinum 14-19	Pyrolusite 4.5-5.0 Tennantite 4.6-4.8 Psilomelane 4.7 Pitchblende 9.1-10.6
	Melilite 2.95-3.05 Wolframite 7.12-7.60 Pitchblende 9.1-10.6	Ilmenite 4.5-5.0 Pyrolusite 4.5-5.0 Psilomelane 4.7 Linnaeite 4.8-5.8 Gersdorffite 5.6-6.2 Safflorite 6.9-7.3 Löllingite 7.1-7.5 Wolframite 7.12-7.60 Niccolite 7.5-7.8	Cryptomelane 4.3 Ilmenite 4.5-5.0 Pyrolusite 4.5-5.0 Psilomelane 4.7 Gersdorffite 5.6-6.2 Niccolite 7.5-7.8 Pitchblende 9.1-10.6

Mohs' hardness	Vitreous } lustre Resinous }	Silky } lustre Pearly }	Adamantine lustre
5½	Anthophyllite 2.9-3.2 Melilite 2.95-3.05 Riebeckite 3.0-3.4 Hornblende 3.02-3.27 Augite 3.2-3.6 Arfvedsonite 3.44-3.46 Hedenbergite 3.5-3.6	Anthophyllite 2.9-3.2 Riebeckite 3.0-3.4 Hornblende 3.02-3.27	
6	Riebeckite 3.0-3.4 Hornblende 3.02-3.27 Augite 3.2-3.6 Epidote 3.35-3.38 Arfvedsonite 3.44-3.46 Hedenbergite 3.5-3.6	Riebeckite 3.0-3.4 Hornblende 3.02-3.27	
6½	Epidote 3.35-3.38		
7	Boracite 2.9-3.0 Epidote 3.35-3.38		Boracite 2.9-3.0
7½	Boracite 2.9-3.0 Gahnite 4.3-4.9		Boracite 2.9-3.0
8	Gahnite 4.3-4.9		

ohs' ardness	Greasy ⎱ lustre Waxy ⎰	Metallic lustre	No lustre Dull
½	Melilite 2.95-3.05 Wolframite 7.12-7.60 Pitchblende 9.1-10.6	Ilmenite 4.5-5.0 Pyrolusite 4.5-5.0 Psilomelane 4.7 Linnaeite 4.8-5.8 Magnetite 5.2 Arsenopyrite 5.9-6.2 Cobaltite 6.0-6.4 Chloanthite 6.4-6.6 Safflorite 6.9-7.3 Löllingite 7.1-7.5 Wolframite 7.12-7.60 Niccolite 7.5-7.8	Cryptomelane 4.3 Ilmenite 4.5-5.0 Pyrolusite 4.5-5.0 Psilomelane 4.7 Magnetite 5.2 Niccolite 7.5-7.8 Pitchblende 9.1-10.6
	Pitchblende 9.1-10.6	Ilmenite 4.5-5.0 Pyrolusite 4.5-5.0 Psilomelane 4.7 Marcasite 4.8-4.9 Pyrite 5.0-5.2 Columbite 5.2-8.1 Arsenopyrite 5.9-6.2 Skutterudite 6.8 Sperrylite 10.58	Cryptomelane 4.3 Ilmenite 4.5-5.0 Pyrolusite 4.5-5.0 Psilomelane 4.7 Pitchblende 9.1-10.6
½		Pyrolusite 4.5-5.0 Marcasite 4.8-4.9 Pyrite 5.0-5.2 Columbite 5.2-8.1 Coronadite 5.5 Sperrylite 10.58	Pyrolusite 4.5-5.0 Coronadite 5.5
		Coronadite 5.5 Sperrylite 10.58	Coronadite 5.5
½	Gahnite 4.3-4.9		
	Gahnite 4.3-4.9		

Mohs' hardness	Vitreous, Resinous lustre	Silky, Pearly lustre	Adamantine lustre
1½	Vivianite 2.6-2.7	Vivianite 2.6-2.7 Orpiment 3.48	Realgar 3.5-3.6
2	Vivianite 2.6-2.7 Chlorite 2.6-3.4 Autunite 3.2	Vivianite 2.6-2.7 Chlorite 2.6-3.4 Autunite 3.2 Orpiment 3.48 Molybdite 4.0-4.5	Realgar 3.5-3.6
2½	Chlorite 2.6-3.4 Autunite 3.2 Uranocircite 3.5 Uranophane 3.8-3.9	Chlorite 2.6-3.4 Autunite 3.2 Uranophane 3.8-3.9 Bismutite 6.7-7.6	Crocoite 5.9-6.1
3	Cacoxenite 2.3 Chlorite 2.6-3.4	Cacoxenite 2.3 Chlorite 2.6-3.4 Bismutite 6.7-7.6	Crocoite 5.9-6.1 Vanadinite 6.5-7.1
3½	Descloizite 5.5-6.2 Wurtzite 4.0	Bismutite 6.7-7.6	Sphalerite 3.9-4.2 Powellite 4.3 Descloizite 5.5-6.2
4	Siderite 3.7-3.9 Wurtzite 4.0	Siderite 3.7-3.9 Carnotite 4.5-4.6	Sphalerite 3.9-4.2
4½	Siderite 3.7-3.9 Thorite 4.4-4.8 Brannerite 6.35	Siderite 3.7-3.9 Bismite 8.64-9.22	Zincite 5.4-5.7 Bismite 8.64-9.22
5	Hornblende 3.02-3.27 Thorite 4.4-4.8 Brannerite 6.35	Hornblende 3.02-3.27 Goethite 3.8-4.3	Pyrochlore 3.5-4.6 Goethite 3.8-4.3 Lepidocrocite 4.0 Zincite 5.4-5.7
5½	Hornblende 3.02-3.27 Neptunite 3.23	Hornblende 3.02-3.27 Goethite 3.8-4.3	Pyrochlore 3.5-4.6 Goethite 3.8-4.3 Brookite 4.1
6	Hornblende 3.02-3.27 Aegirine 3.43-3.60	Hornblende 3.02-3.27	Brookite 4.1 Rutile 4.2-4.3
6½	Aegirine 3.43-3.60		Rutile 4.2-4.3
7			Cassiterite 6.8-7.1

Streak yellow + orange + brown

Mohs' hardness	Greasy / Waxy } lustre	Metallic lustre	No lustre / Dull
½	Orpiment 3.48 Realgar 3.5-3.6	Vivianite 2.6-2.7 Sylvanite 8.0-8.3	
	Orpiment 3.48 Realgar 3.5-3.6	Vivianite 2.6-2.7 Berthierite 4.6 Sylvanite 8.0-8.3	Chlorite 2.6-3.4 Ferrimolybdite 4.0-4.5 Molybdite 4.0-4.5
½	Crocoite 5.9-6.1	Berthierite 4.6 Gold 15.5-19.3	Chlorite 2.6-3.4
	Crocoite 5.9-6.1 Vanadinite 6.5-7.1	Berthierite 4.6 Tennantite 4.6-4.8 Tetrahedrite 4.6-5.2 Gold 15.5-19.3	Chlorite 2.6-3.4 Tennantite 4.6-4.8 Tetrahedrite 4.6-5.2
½	Sphalerite 3.9-4.2 Powellite 4.3	Tennantite 4.6-4.8 Tetrahedrite 4.6-5.2 Cuprite 5.8-6.2	Tennantite 4.6-4.8 Tetrahedrite 4.6-5.2 Cuprite 5.8-6.2
	Sphalerite 3.9-4.2 Pitchblende 9.1-10.6	Manganite 4.3-4.4 Tennantite 4.6-4.8 Tetrahedrite 4.6-5.2 Psilomelane 4.7 Cuprite 5.8-6.2	Carnotite 4.5-4.6 Tennantite 4.6-4.8 Tetrahedrite 4.6-5.2 Psilomelane 4.7 Cuprite 5.8-6.2
½	Zincite 5.4-5.7 Brannerite 6.35 Pitchblende 9.1-10.6	Tennantite 4.6-4.8 Psilomelane 4.7	Tennantite 4.6-4.8 Psilomelane 4.7 Pitchblende 9.1-10.6
	Pyrochlore 3.5-4.6 Zincite 5.4-5.7 Brannerite 6.35 Wolframite 7.12-7.60 Pitchblende 9.1-10.6	Ilmenite 4.5-5.0 Psilomelane 4.7 Wolframite 7.12-7.60 Niccolite 7.5-7.8	Goethite 3.8-4.3 Ilmenite 4.5-5.0 Psilomelane 4.7 Niccolite 7.5-7.8 Pitchblende 9.1-10.6
½	Pyrochlore 3.5-4.6 Chromite 4.5-4.8 Wolframite 7.12-7.60 Pitchblende 9.1-10.6	Chromite 4.5-4.8 Ilmenite 4.5-5.0 Hausmannite 4.7-4.8 Wolframite 7.12-7.60 Niccolite 7.5-7.8	Goethite 3.8-4.3 Ilmenite 4.5-5.0 Psilomelane 4.7 Niccolite 7.5-7.8 Pitchblende 9.1-10.6
	Pitchblende 9.1-10.6	Rutile 4.2-4.3 Ilmenite 4.5-5.0 Hematite 5.2-5.3 Columbite 5.2-8.1	Ilmenite 4.5-5.0 Psilomelane 4.7 Hematite 5.2-5.3 Pitchblende 9.1-10.6
½	Jasper 2.58-2.91	Rutile 4.2-4.3 Hematite 5.2-5.3 Columbite 5.2-8.1	Jasper 2.58-2.91 Hematite 5.2-5.3
	Cassiterite 6.8-7.1		

Mohs' hardness	Vitreous } Resinous } lustre	Silky } Pearly } lustre	Adamantine lustre
1			
1½		Orpiment 3.48	Realgar 3.5-3.6
2	Erythrite 3.07	Erythrite 3.07 Orpiment 3.48	Realgar 3.5-3.6 Cinnabar 8.0-8.2
2½			Proustite 5.57 Pyrargyrite 5.85 Crocoite 5.9-6.1 Cinnabar 8.0-8.2
3			Pyrargyrite 5.85 Crocoite 5.9-6.1
3½			
4			
4½			Zincite 5.4-5.7
5			Lepidocrocite 4.0 Zincite 5.4-5.7
5½			
6			
6½	Piemontite 3.4		
7			

Mohs' hardness	Greasy / Waxy } lustre	Metallic lustre	No lustre / Dull
1½	Orpiment 3.48 Realgar 3.5-3.6	Polybasite 6.0-6.2	
2	Orpiment 3.48 Realgar 3.5-3.6	Polybasite 6.0-6.2 Cinnabar 8.0-8.2	
2½	Crocoite 5.9-6.1	Cinnabar 8.0-8.2 Copper 8.3-8.7	
3	Crocoite 5.9-6.1	Tennantite 4.6-4.8 Copper 8.3-8.7	Tennantite 4.6-4.8
3½		Tennantite 4.6-4.8 Cuprite 5.8-6.2	Tennantite 4.6-4.8 Cuprite 5.8-6.2
4		Purpurite 3.2-3.4 Tennantite 4.6-4.8 Cuprite 5.8-6.2	Tennantite 4.6-4.8 Cuprite 5.8-6.2
4½	Zincite 5.4-5.7	Purpurite 3.2-3.4 Tennantite 4.6-4.8	Tennantite 4.6-4.8
5	Zincite 5.4-5.7		
5½		Hausmannite 4.7-4.8	
6		Franklinite 5.0-5.2 Hematite 5.2-5.3	Hematite 5.2-5.3
6½	Jasper 2.58-2.91	Franklinite 5.0-5.2 Hematite 5.2-5.3	Jasper 2.58-2.91 Hematite 5.2-5.3
7	Jasper 2.58-2.91		Jasper 2.58-2.91

Mohs' hardness	Vitreous ⎱ lustre Resinous ⎰	Silky ⎱ lustre Pearly ⎰	Adamantine lustre
1			
1½			
2	Chrysocolla 2.0-2.2 Chlorite 2.6-3.4 Ripidolite 2.75-2.90 Chamosite 3.0-3.4 Torbernite 3.3-3.7	Chlorite 2.6-3.4 Ripidolite 2.75-2.90 Daphnite 3.2 Torbernite 3.3-3.7 Aurichalcite 3.6-4.2	
2½	Chrysocolla 2.0-2.2 Penninite 2.5-2.6 Chlorite 2.6-3.4 Chamosite 3.0-3.4 Tobernite 3.3-3.7	Penninite 2.5-2.6 Delessite 2.6-2.9 Chlorite 2.6-3.4 Daphnite 3.2 Thuringite 3.2 Torbernite 3.3-3.7 Bismuthite 6.7-7.6	
3	Chrysocolla 2.0-2.2 Chlorite 2.6-3.4 Chamosite 3.0-3.4 Atacamite 3.76	Delessite 2.6-2.9 Chlorite 2.6-3.4 Daphnite 3.2 Bismutite 6.7-7.6	
3½	Chrysocolla 2.0-2.2 Malachite 3.75-3.95 Atacamite 3.76 Descloizite 5.5-6.2 Mottramite 5.7-6.2	Malachite 3.75-3.95 Brochantite 3.97 Bismutite 6.7-7.6	Powellite 4.3 Descloizite 5.5-6.2
4	Chrysocolla 2.0-2.2 Malachite 3.75-3.95	Malachite 3.75-3.95 Brochantite 3.97 Carnotite 4.5-4.6	
4½	Brannerite 6.35	Bismite 8.64-9.22	Bismite 8.64-9.22
5	Hornblende 3.02-3.27 Augite 3.2-3.6 Dioptase 3.28-3.35 Omphacite 3.29-3.37 Brannerite 6.35	Hornblende 3.02-3.27	
5½	Hornblende 3.02-3.07 Augite 3.2-3.6 Hedenbergite 3.5-3.6	Hornblende 3.02-3.27	
6	Hornblende 3.02-3.07 Augite 3.2-3.6 Aegirine 3.43-3.60 Hedenbergite 3.5-3.6	Hornblende 3.02-3.27	
6½	Aegirine 3.43-3.60		

Mohs' hardness	Greasy ⎫ lustre Waxy ⎭	Metallic lustre	No lustre Dull
		Molybdenite 4.7-4.8	Patronite 2.81
½		Molybdenite 4.7-4.8	Patronite 2.81
2	Chrysocolla 2.0-2.2 Garnierite 2.2-2.7		Glauconite 2.2-2.8 Chlorite 2.6-3.4 Patronite 2.81 Chamosite 3.0-3.4 Daphnite 3.2
½	Chrysocolla 2.0-2.2 Garnierite 2.2-2.7		Delessite 2.6-2.9 Chlorite 2.6-3.4 Chamosite 3.0-3.4 Daphnite 3.2
3	Chrysocolla 2.0-2.2 Garnierite 2.2-2.7		Delessite 2.6-2.9 Chlorite 2.6-3.4 Chamosite 3.0-3.4 Daphnite 3.2
½	Chrysocolla 2.0-2.2 Garnierite 2.2-2.7 Powellite 4.3	Chalcopyrite 4.1-4.3 Millerite 5.3	Malachite 3.75-3.95
4	Chrysocolla 2.0-2.2 Garnierite 2.2-2.7 Pitchblende 9.1-10.6	Chalcopyrite 4.1-4.3 Carnotite 4.5-4.6 Pitchblende 9.1-10.6	Malachite 3.75-3.95
½	Brannerite 6.35 Pitchblende 9.1-10.6		Pitchblende 9.1-10.6
5	Brannerite 6.35 Pitchblende 9.1-10.6		Pitchblende 9.1-10.6
½	Pitchblende 9.1-10.6		Pitchblende 9.1-10.6
6	Pitchblende 9.1-10.6	Marcasite 4.8-4.9 Pyrite 5.0-5.2	Pitchblende 9.1-10.6
½		Marcasite 4.8-4.9 Pyrite 5.0-5.2	

Mohs' hardness	Vitreous } lustre Resinous	Silky } lustre Pearly	Adamantine lustre	
1				
1½	Vivianite 2.6-2.7	Vivianite 2.6-2.7		
2	Vivianite 2.6-2.7	Vivianite 2.6-2.7 Aurichalcite 3.6-4.2		
2½	Chalcanthite 2.2-2.3 Linarite 5.3-5.5		Linarite 5.3-5.5	
3				
3½	Azurite 3.7-3.9			
4	Azurite 3.7-3.9			
4½				
5	Lapizlazuli 2.38-2.42 Riebeckite 3.0-3.4	Riebeckite 3.0-3.4		
5½	Lapislazuli 2.38-2.42 Riebeckite 3.0-3.4 Arfvedsonite 3.44-3.46	Riebeckite 3.0-3.4		
6	Lapislazuli 2.38-2.42 Riebeckite 3.0-3.4 Arfvedsonite 3.44-3.46	Riebeckite 3.0-3.4		
6½				
7		Dumortierite 3.26-3.41		

Mohs' hardness	Greasy } lustre Waxy }	Metallic lustre	No lustre Dull
$\frac{1}{2}$	Covellite 4.68	Vivianite 2.6-2.7 Covellite 4.68	Covellite 4.68
2	Covellite 4.68	Vivianite 2.6-2.7 Covellite 4.68	Covellite 4.68
$2\frac{1}{2}$			
3			
$3\frac{1}{2}$			
4			
$4\frac{1}{2}$			
5	Lapislazuli 2.38-2.42		
$5\frac{1}{2}$	Lapislazuli 2.38-2.42		
6	Lapislazuli 2.38-2.42		
$6\frac{1}{2}$			
7			

AIDS TO THE IDENTIFICATION OF ROCKS

In determining a rock, first attempt to allocate it to one of the main groups. Examine the textrue i.e. the arrangement of minerals in the unknown rock and ascertain whether an orientation can be seen in the texture and if possible what its direction is. In the following overview the four possible textural arrangements are sketched: texture without orientation (random), flow texture, bedding and schistocity. Then look for the illustration of texture in the boxes below which fits the unknown rock.

Examine as many specimens as possible from the same locality so as to eliminate any chance factors and to establish the typical characteristics. Large pieces of rock provide more details than small ones. Use a lens for finely bedded rocks.

Study the whole rock complex of the specimen either in a quarry or on a rock face; ascertain if the hand specimen is characteristic of the whole complex.

Random texture

Minerals randomly mixed up. No well-defined orientation

Flow texture

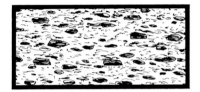

Individual minerals or pore spaces show a slight orientation effect as a result of flow of lava or magma

For further aid to identification see pp.368/369

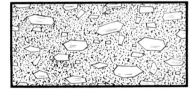

Some crystals show an orientation because of their position in the texture
volcanic rocks p.228
plutonic rocks p.195

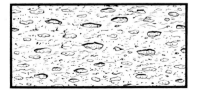

Elongated pores define an orientation in the texture
volcanic rocks p.228

Layering

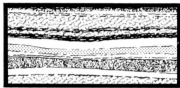

Continuous layer boundaries. Formed during sedimentation by a change in the conditions of deposition. On splitting they give smooth, even surfaces.

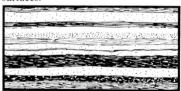

Continuous boundaries with uniform grain size within each layer.
sedimentary rocks p.260
schists p.312

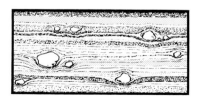

The bedding boundaries are indented or buckled by large individual fragments. Tuff p.234

Foliation

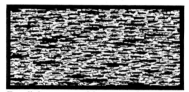

Parallel texture without continuous boundary planes. Formed by orientation of platy or elongated minerals. Cleavage surfaces are not smooth.

Parallel texture because of oriented crystals in an otherwise granular groundmass
gneiss p.308

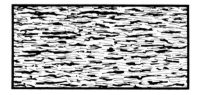

Well-marked parallel texture in fine to medium grained ground-mass.
schists p.312

367

ROCKS WITH NO RECOGNISABLE ORIENTATION IN THE TEXTURE

Rocks with large individual fragments

Angular individual fragments up to head-size in a variable groundmass
breccia p.268

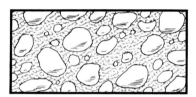

Rounded individual fragments up to apple-size in variable groundmass
conglomerate p.270

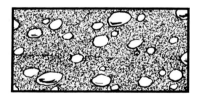

Rounded and angular individual fragments in a loamy groundmass
moraine p.261
tillite p.268

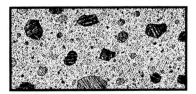

Many angular individual fragments up to nut-size in a fine grained highly porous groundmass. tuff p.234

Coarse grains in the texture

Holocrystalline mass, different sorts of minerals, approximately of similar size recognisable with the naked eye
plutonic rocks p.195

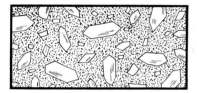

Individual fully-developed crystals in a fine grained or glassy ground-mass
volcanic rocks p.228

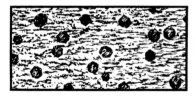

Single large crystals between recognisable smaller crystals
pegmatite p.258
fels p.318

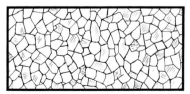

Only one mineral species; saccharoidal appearance easily scratched with metal
marble p.324
dolomite marble p.326

Fine grained texture

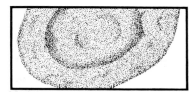

Nodular, up to apple-size aggregate, frequently banded
chert p.294
flint p.294

Equigranular fine grained texture, very hard
quartzolites p.198
felses p.318

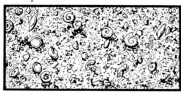

Fine grained mass, easily scratched with metal, usually fossiliferous
reef limestone p.284
dolomite rock p.290

Glassy texture

Homogeneous glass-like mass, conchoidal fracture
obsidian p.238

Highly porous, very light rock, usually light coloured
pumice p.236

All characteristics of the main groups at a glance on p.370

369

DIAGNOSTIC FEATURES OF THE MAIN ROCK GROUPS

Plutonic rocks p.195

1 Holocrystalline, the whole mass crystallized
2 Large crystals, recognisable with the naked eye
3 Orientation can usually not be recognised in hand specimen, minerals randomly distributed; rare flow texture
4 Very compact, virtually no cavities
5 Never fossiliferous
6 Joints at right angles to each other
7 Tor structure is the typical weathering form
8 Topography generally smooth and rolling

Volcanic rocks p.228

1 Only individual crystals well formed (porphyritic texture)
2 Groundmass dense (microcrystalline) or amorphous (formless, glassy)
3 Numerous small cavities
4 Often have flow texture
5 Frequently columnar jointed
6 Very rarely contain fossils

Sedimentary rocks p.260

1 Generally well-developed layering
2 Often fossiliferous
3 Topography in many cases rugged and bizarre
4 Moraines never bedded, not sorted
5 Reef limestones hardly ever bedded

Metamorphic rocks p.304

1 Completely crystalline, the whole mass crystallised
2 Mostly large crystals recognisable with the naked eye
3 Frequently with a silky lustre
4 Parallel texture, schistose
5 Very compact, no cavities
6 Generally unfossiliferous
7 No smooth cleavage surfaces
8 Topography smooth and rolling

INDEX

Page numbers in bold
  type indicate the main
  reference.

ILLUSTRATION CREDITS